ISLAM

PAUL LUNDE

DK PUBLISHING, INC.
LONDON · NEW YORK · MUNICH · MELBOURNE · DELHI
www.dk.com

LONDON, NEW YORK, MUNICH,
MELBOURNE, AND DELHI

ART EDITOR
Paul Jackson

SENIOR EDITOR
Ferdie McDonald

SENIOR DESIGNERS
Karen Gregory, Edward Kinsey

SENIOR CARTOGRAPHIC EDITOR
Simon Mumford

DESIGNERS
Peter Bailey, Victoria Clark,
Nicola Liddiard

EDITORS
Sam Atkinson, Debra Clapson,
Ailsa Heritage, Margaret Parrish

SYSTEMS COORDINATOR
Phil Rowles

DIGITAL MAPS - DK CARTOPIA
Rob Stokes

PRODUCTION
Michelle Thomas, Melanie Dowland

DK PICTURE LIBRARY
Fergus Muir, Hayley Smith

PICTURE RESEARCH
Anna Grapes, Carolyn Clerkin

DIGITAL SCANNING - DK
Dave Almond

EDITORIAL DIRECTION
Andrew Heritage

PROJECT MANAGER
David Roberts

First American Edition, 2002

02 03 04 05 10 9 8 7 6 5 4 3 2 1

Published in the United States by
DK Publishing, Inc.
375 Hudson Street
New York, NY 10014

Copyright © 2002 Dorling Kindersley Limited

A Cataloging-in-Publication record for this title is available from the Library of Congress
ISBN: 0-7894-8797-7

Reproduced by GRB, Italy
Printed and bound in Italy by L.E.G.O

see our complete product line at

www.dk.com

CONTENTS

PREFACE

THE EVENTS OF SEPTEMBER 11, 2001 have thrown into sharp relief the urgent necessity for Muslims and non-Muslims to confront and overcome the barriers that separate them.

Islam and the West share a common history, as the following pages make clear, and their destinies have been linked since the expansion of Islam in the 7th century. Medieval European civilization took shape in the shadow cast by powerful Islamic empires, and the Islamic world entered modernity in the shadow of European imperial powers.

Now we all inhabit the same global village, and it is of vital importance to learn from one another's failures and achievements. The ethical systems of the worlds religions are in remarkable agreement, and it is on this common ground that the future must be built. It is hoped that the following brief account of Islam will serve to correct misconceptions and contribute to this urgent necessity.

Paul Lunde, Seville, December 2001

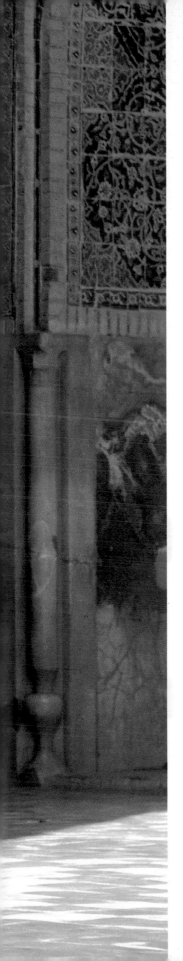

ISLAM IN CONTEXT

The imprint of Islamic culture on the modern geopolitical map is enormous. Confined for the most part to the Old World of Afro-Eurasia, the Islamic domain stretches from the Atlantic to the Pacific Rim, encompassing some of the richest countries in the world, and some of the poorest, some of the most fertile and densely populated, and some of the most harsh and desolate.

A Shi'ite Muslim *faces Mecca to pray at a mosque in Isfahan, Iran.*

ISLAM TODAY

THE POPULATION OF THE WORLD stands at about 5.7 billion. As many as 1.7 billion are Muslim, one-fifth of mankind. There are 44 countries with majority Muslim populations. They form a continuum from the Atlantic coast of Africa south of the Sahara to the shores of the Mediterranean, through the Middle East, Iran, and Afghanistan to Pakistan's border with India, then north to Kazakhstan, the northernmost Muslim country.

Beyond India, with its Muslim minority of some 120 million, is Bangladesh, with a population of 127 million Muslims. South, separating the Indian Ocean from the Pacific, is Indonesia, with some 200 million Muslims. There is a substantial Muslim minority in the Philippines.

Islam is currently spreading in Africa south of the Sahara, a process that began in the Middle Ages and accelerated in the 19th and 20th. Perhaps as many as one-fifth of the world's Muslims now inhabit sub-Saharan Africa. North Africa has been Muslim territory since the 8th century, and East Africa has had a steadily growing Muslim presence since about the same time.

There are large numbers of Muslims in China. Nobody knows exactly how many, but the figure of 40 million is probably closer to the truth than the 17 million of the official Chinese figure. There is a large mosque in Christchurch, New Zealand. There is a community of Muslims of Algerian decent in Fiji.

Between five and six million Muslims live in Europe, seven or eight million in the United States. Most large towns in England, France, and Germany, have mosques. English Muslims of Indian and Pakistani origins have made major economic and social contributions to postwar Britain. Turkish workers have contributed substantially to German postwar prosperity, some settling permanently in Germany, while retaining contacts with their homeland, others returning to Turkey to finance businesses and build homes. Most Muslim workers in France, predominantly from North Africa, maintain close ties with their countries of origin, returning to visit friends and relations whenever they can.

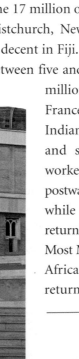

This modern mosque in Rome was finally built after much controversy. Its presence on the Gianicolo hill overlooking the Vatican makes it a symbol of the globalization of Islam.

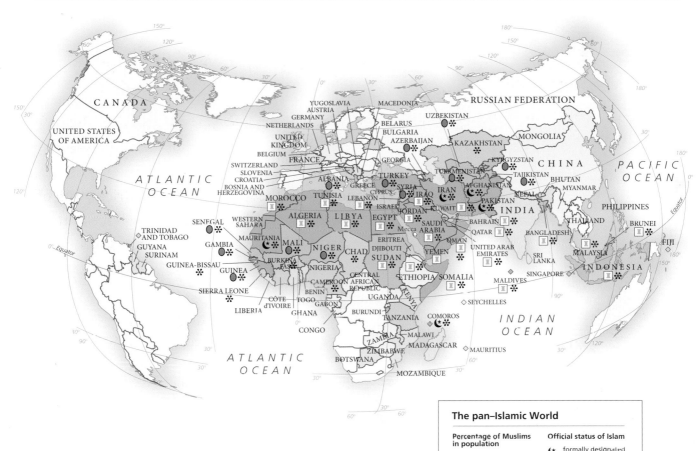

The pan–Islamic World

Percentage of Muslims in population

- 91–100%
- 51–90%
- 21–50%
- 6–20%
- 1–5%
- less than 1%

Official status of Islam

- ☪ formally designated Islamic republic
- ● secular state where population is more then 50% Muslim
- 🔲 established religion is Islam
- ✳ membership of Organization of the Islamic Conference (OIC)

MULTICULTURALISM IN THE WEST

Europe and the United States became multicultural in the years following World War II. Buddhist, Hindu, Sikh, and Muslim communities, the latter from a variety of different homelands, were established in most European countries as well as in the Americas. Food improved everywhere. New words entered our vocabularies. Academic historians began to devote themselves to non-Western cultures, global history flourished and even percolated into school curriculums, hundreds of new academic journals devoted to non-Western languages and cultures appeared. The classic academic reference work on Islam, the Encyclopedia of Islam, the first edition of which was completed in 1926, comprised four thick volumes; the second edition, still incomplete, so far fills 10 substantial volumes. The Encyclopedia Iranica, in the course of publication, will be even longer when completed.

Almost every major university in Europe has Muslim academics of the most varied origins, teaching and researching in every conceivable field. Male and female students from the Muslim world, many of them studying the sciences, are to be found in every major university in Europe and the United States. There are excellent universities in the Muslim world too, and almost everywhere education is considered a top government priority.

The globalization of Islam *is immediately apparent in this map of the modern world. All Muslims share the same essential beliefs, but Islam has many different cultural expressions.*

The intensive modernization of oil-producing countries such as Saudi Arabia and the Gulf States has taken place within a strongly traditional structure.

There are Muslim writers, scientists, doctors, engineers, IT specialists, academics, students, actors, pop stars, television hosts, journalists, firemen, filmmakers, taxi drivers, fashion designers, fruit pickers, steelworkers – you name it. Many of them are leaders in their chosen field. An Egyptian novelist, Naguib Mahfouz, won the Nobel Prize for Literature in 1988. The Nobel Prize for Physics went to a Muslim scientist, Abdus Salam, in 1979, and the Nobel Prize for Chemistry in 1999 was awarded to the Egyptian Ahmed Zewail. I even know of a young Saudi woman who is taking part in scientific research in Antarctica.

Anyone who has traveled in the Muslim world has met men and women from all walks of life with a perfect command of one or more European languages, mastered either in Europe or the US or in their own country. One does occasionally meet a European who speaks Arabic, Swahili, Hausa, Berber, Urdu, Uzbek, Pashtun, Persian, Tajik, Turkish, Malay, or Chechen, but it is rare, and regarded as an eccentricity of little utility, like collecting old flatirons.

Thousands of Americans and Europeans live and work in Islamic countries, particularly in Saudi Arabia and the oil-rich Gulf States. Americans connected with the petroleum industry have been working in Saudi Arabia since before World War II, and some working there now are the third generation of their families to do so. Yet it is easier to find an American or European who knows all about Zen Buddhism than it is to meet someone who knows anything at all about the basic beliefs, ethical principles and history of Islam.

TRADITIONAL LIFESTYLES

The nomadic pastoralists *of Arabia provided the manpower for the Islamic conquests, and Turkish and Mongol nomads were the state-builders of classical Islamic civilization. Although today nomadic pastoralists constitute an infinitesimal part of the world's population, many are still found in the North Africa, Arabia, and Central Asia.*

IMPRESSIONS OF ISLAM

Countries such as Morocco, Tunisia, Egypt, Jordan, and Turkey have long been major destinations for European tourists. Even tourists who visit these countries without any particular interest in their

Nomadic population

☐ Nomadic population area

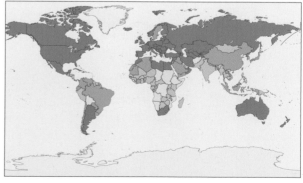

Daily calorie intake per capita

above 3,000   2,000–2,499   ☐ data not available
2,500–2,999   below 2,000

cultures learn something of local customs and get a feel for architecture, landscape, and cuisine. Bookshops in the West are filled with good books on Islamic art and architecture and it is now much easier than it once was to find authoritative books on Islamic history and culture. For those who have the time and inclination to learn one of the three classic languages of Islamic culture – Arabic, Persian, and Turkish – excellent grammar books and tapes are available.

Despite these reciprocal opportunities for learning about one another, more Muslims are familiar with European and American culture than Europeans and Americans are with Islamic culture.

The images of the Islamic world that appear in the European and American press are almost invariably negative and associated with violence. The fact that the vast majority of Muslims lead normal lives and follow an eminently rational faith notable for its emphasis on kindness, brotherhood, clemency, social justice, and peace has been obscured by the political events of recent years.

The picture most Muslims receive of the West is often similarly skewed. The West is consistently portrayed as bent on the exploitation of the rest of the world, a supporter of the enemies of Islam and an oppressor of the poor. The export image of Western society, derived from films and television, is lamentable, and needs no commentary. There is a generalized feeling among Muslims from all parts of the world of resentment and hostility toward the West. Its extreme manifestations in the form of internal and international terrorism are as lamented by Muslims as they are by non-Muslims, but Muslims comprehend the motivations of such actions in a way that non-Muslims seldom do.

Kurdish refugees *flee across the mountains from Iraq to Turkey in 1991 to escape persecution by the forces of Saddam Hussein. Sadly, the Western media turn their attention to the Islamic world only in such times of war or disaster.*

STANDARDS OF LIVING

The disparity *in calorie intake, life expectancy, and infant mortality between industrial and non-industrial nations is shown on the maps below. For the most part figures for Islamic countries lie somewhere in the middle range, but there are exceptions, notably among the oil-rich nations and poor war-torn regions, such as Afghanistan.*

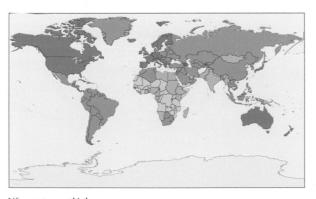

Life expectancy at birth

 above 75 years   55–64 years   below 44 years
65–74 years   45–54 years   data not available

World infant mortality rates (deaths per 1,000 live births)

above 125   35–74   below 15
75–124   15–43   data not available

Much of this resentment has to do with specific recent events – the bombing of Afghanistan, the violent means employed by the Israelis to crush the Palestinian intifada, American support for Israel, the presence of American troops in Saudi Arabia, the sanctions against Iraq and the continued bombing of that country. These are all cases where many non-Muslims share the outrage felt by Muslims.

At a deeper level, however, hostility derives from the impact of modernization on Islamic societies and the crisis of authority that arose from the actions of secularizing regimes based on Western models. The legitimacy of these regimes, frequently established by secularized military elites, is questioned by many devout Muslims and often opposed by militant revivalist movements. This has in turn led to the suppression of such movements despite their wide popular followings. Establishing an acceptable balance between the demands of a modern state and the Islamic concept of a just, consultative government is one of the challenges facing the Muslim world.

RELATIVE PROSPERITY

Disparities in wealth *between rich and poor nations have come into sharper focus as a result of globalization. This is particularly true of the Islamic world, where the oil-producing states enjoy per capita incomes undreamt of in poorer, more populous nations.*

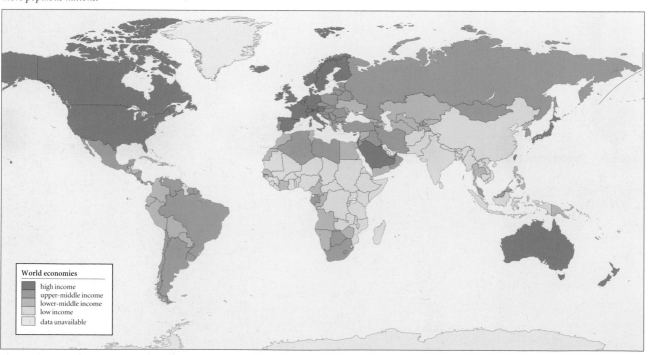

World economies
- high income
- upper-middle income
- lower-middle income
- low income
- data unavailable

THE ISLAMIC FAITH

Some 1.7 billion people in the world today are Muslim – about one-fifth of the world's population. The youngest of the three great monotheistic religions, Islam reveres the scriptures of its precursors, but regards the Holy Qur'an as the complete and final revelation of the One God to humanity.

The spiritual heart of the Muslim world *lies, as it has done since the 7th century, in the Haram, the sacred enclosure in Mecca, the birthplace of the Prophet. Hundreds of thousands of the faithful make the annual pilgrimage, the hajj, to Mecca each year.*

ORIGINS

The Islamic faith *encourages festivals and celebrations that involve the whole community. In this medieval illumination, a colorful procession celebrates the end of Ramadan, the month of fasting.*

I N THE EARLY 7TH CENTURY the Byzantine and the Persian empires dominated the heartlands of the Old World. The Byzantine empire was the Christian successor to the Roman empire, its territories reaching from Constantinople to the Atlantic. Since the reign of Constantine the Great, Christianity had been the official religion. Paganism was a thing of the past.

The religion of the other great empire, Sasanid Persia, was a form of Zoroastrianism, an ancient and complex religious system that had a profound influence on both Judaism and early Christianity. Both Byzantium and Sasanid Persia were theocracies with hierarchically organized priesthoods. Zoroastrian Persia and Christian Byzantium were bitter enemies and, during the lifetime of the Prophet Muhammad, engaged in a long war that exhausted the resources of both.

The last area in the region with a significant pagan presence was the Arabian Peninsula. Arabia was a vast land of desert and steppe, three times the size of France. Its interior was *terra incognita* to the ancient world. Indeed, it was not precisely mapped until the 1950s. It was inhabited by Arabic-speaking nomadic pastoralists who could survive in this hostile environment only by the presence of a few scattered oases and jealously protected wells. Without the camel, with its ability to travel long distances between waterings and to recycle desert shrubs and brackish water in the form of milk, these deserts would have been impassable.

Yemen, the Arabia Felix of the classical world, received the tail end of the monsoon rains and could therefore support agriculture. This mountainous land had been home to highly developed civilizations dating back to at least the early 2nd millenium BCE. These civilizations, speaking languages closely related to Arabic and with their own writing system, developed ingenious irrigation systems based on catchment dams that stored seasonal rainfall. The last of these civilizations, that of Himyar, came to an end shortly before the rise of Islam. Christianity had penetrated here, and at the time of the Prophet Muhammad there was a bishopric at Najran, not far south of Mecca. Across the Red Sea was another Christian kingdom,

Inscriptions in a Semitic language survive on the ruins of a dam at Ma'rib in Yemen. This alphabet was in use almost until the Islamic era and is the origin of the Ethiopian script.

Ethiopia, which, according to Arab tradition, invaded Yemen in 570 and then attempted to attack Mecca. Arabian tribes in the north, close to the Byzantine border, had been influenced by both Christianity and Judaism, and some pre-Islamic tribal poets, whose verses were later collected from the oral tradition, were avowedly Jewish or Christian. Central and western Arabia, however, were still pagan. Yet even here there were small islands of monotheism. One was Yathrib, later called Medina, which was inhabited by Jewish tribes, though what form of Judaism they professed is unknown.

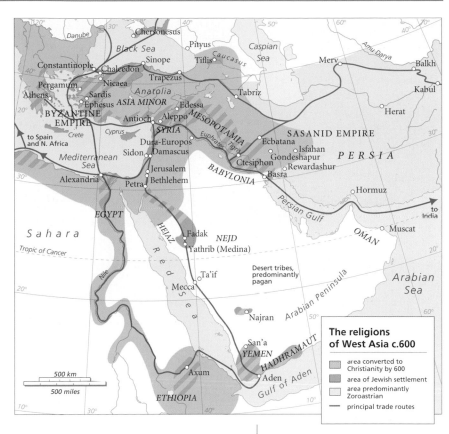

The religions
of West Asia c.600

- area converted to Christianity by 600
- area of Jewish settlement
- area predominantly Zoroastrian
- principal trade routes

Mecca

Mecca was a pagan cult center to which surrounding tribes made pilgrimages during stipulated months of the year in which a truce was observed, guaranteed by the ruling oligarchy, the tribe of Quraysh. The object of the pilgrimages was the Ka'ba, a square edifice built of black stone with an inner chamber containing images of pre-Islamic deities. It occupied the center of a taboo precinct, called the *haram*, in which it was forbidden to spill blood or even to pluck a blade of grass during the pilgrimage season. Near the Ka'ba were various sites associated with events in the life of Abraham *(Ibrahim)*. According to the Qur'an, Abraham originally built the Ka'ba to honor the One God, calling it the House of God, *bayt Allah*, and it was there that he offered to sacrifice his son in obedience to God's command. As time went on, polytheism once more took hold and idols were introduced into the Ka'ba.

Mecca lay just west of the ancient Incense Road from Yemen and south Arabia to Palestine and Syria. By the late 6th century the collapse of the irrigation system in Yemen and wars between Persia and Byzantium had probably reduced the trade in frankincense and myrrh to a trickle. They are scarcely mentioned in early Islamic tradition. Mecca nevertheless traded with the frontier cities of Byzantium and Persia, and this trade was significant enough to create a comparatively wealthy class in Mecca. This class was composed of members of the leading clans of the tribe of Quraysh.

Christianity, Judaism, and Zoroastrianism *were the three principal religions of West Asia at the time of Muhammad.*

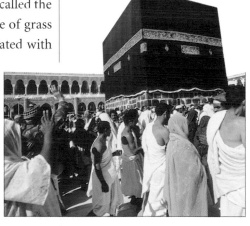

The Ka'ba, *in pre-Islamic times center of a pagan cult, is now the focus of the hajj, the annual pilgrimage to Mecca. Here pilgrims perform the tawaf, seven circuits of Ka'ba.*

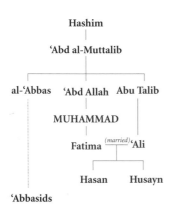

Hashim
|
'Abd al-Muttalib
|
al-'Abbas   'Abd Allah   Abu Talib
|
MUHAMMAD
|
Fatima *(married)* 'Ali
|
Hasan   Husayn

'Abbasids

MUHAMMAD, THE MESSENGER OF GOD

Muhammad ibn 'Abd Allah, the Prophet of Islam, belonged to a clan of Quraysh called Hashim. The date of his birth is generally agreed to have been 570. His father died when he was very young, his mother Amina when he was a boy of six. He was raised first by his grandfather, chief of the clan, then by his uncle Abu Talib. Like the vast majority of his compatriots, he was illiterate. When he was 25 he married a wealthy widow named Khadija, who was involved with the caravan trade and for whom he worked as a commercial agent. Almost nothing else is known of Muhammad's life before he received the first revelation of the Qur'an at the age of 40. He died in 632.

Tradition records the presence in Mecca at this time of a group called *hanif*, men dissatisfied with the prevailing pagan environment who made a practice of going on retreat in caves on the surrounding mountainsides. Muhammad apparently went on retreat to a cave on a nearby mountainside for a month each year, and it was while he was there that the first verses of the Qur'an were revealed to him.

THE FIRST REVELATION

This first revelation occurred on the slope of Mount Hira outside the town of Mecca in western Arabia in the year 610. The archangel Gabriel (Jibra'il) appeared to Muhammad holding a scroll in his hand and commanded him to read it, saying iqra'! (Read!).

Terrified, Muhammad pleaded that he was unable to. Gabriel reiterated his command, and Muhammad repeated the words after him, reciting the first five verses of what is now the 96th chapter of the Qur'an:

> **Recite, in the name of the Lord who created,**
> **Created humanity from a blood clot!**
> **Recite, for your Lord is most generous,**
> **Who taught by the pen,**
> **taught humanity what it knew not.**
>
> **[QUR'AN 96:1-5]**

The archangel Gabriel (Jibra'il)
was the intermediary between God and the Prophet, delivering the Qur'an in a series of revelations between 610 and 632.

Shaken by his experience and doubting his own senses, Muhammad returned to his home and confided in his wife Khadija, who questioned him closely about the circumstances. Had the revelation come from an angel or from a devil? Convinced of the reality of what had occurred, and that the revelation was indeed divine, she reassured her husband. Other revelations followed, at irregular intervals, asserting the Oneness of God, demanding that mankind abandon polytheistic beliefs, warning of dreadful punishments for those who did not hearken. These first revelations are short, densely worded, and urgent. There is only one God. He has no associates. He is the same for all humanity. All humanity must submit to the One God *(Allah)* and repent before the imminent end of the world. It is from the verb meaning "submit" that the noun Islam, meaning "submission (to the will of God,)" is derived.

For a time Muhammad confided the continuing revelations only to his family and closest friends. After Khadija, the first to accept the faith was Muhammad's cousin 'Ali, later to become the fourth caliph *(khalifa)* of the Muslim community. Then followed Zayd, a slave he had freed and adopted as his son. Other early converts were Abu Bakr, 'Umar, and 'Uthman, all to number among the successors to Muhammad at the head of the Muslim community.

Three years after the initial revelation, Gabriel commanded Muhammad to preach openly, and he began to make public attacks on polytheism. He gained new adherents, and news of Islam began to spread throughout Arabia. Leaders of the tribe of Quraysh became worried, for they were the custodians of the Ka'ba and the haram, and while they had no objection to the idea of a new religion, they feared both for their authority and the revenues they derived from the cult center they controlled. Muhammad's followers began to be actively persecuted, and a number of them fled across the Red Sea and took refuge with the Negus, the Christian ruler of Ethiopia. Muhammad himself was protected by his relationship to his uncle Abu Talib, but his humbler followers, like the Ethiopian slave Bilal, the first to give the *adhan*, the call to prayer that summons the faithful to their devotions, suffered greatly. The *adhan* given by Bilal is unchanged to this day:

Tuareg tribesmen *carry palm fronds as part of the annual celebration of* mawlid, *the birthday of the Prophet, held on the 12th day of Rabi' al-Awwal.*

God is the most Great! I testify that there is no god but God. I testify that Muhammad is the Messenger of God. Come to prayer! Come to salvation! God is the most Great! There is no god but God!

THE NIGHT OF POWER

The Night of Power, *Laylat al-Qadr*, the night the Prophet received the first revelation, is traditionally identified as the 27th day of Ramadan, the month of fasting.

Behold, We sent it down on the Night of Power;
And what shall teach thee is the Night of Power?
The Night of Power is better than a few months;
   in it the angels and the Spirit descend,
by the leave of their Lord, upon every command.
   Peace it is, till the rising of dawn.

Quran 97:1-5

THE MUSLIM LUNAR CALENDAR

Muslims regulate time by the Moon, rather than the Sun. The day begins at sunset, rather than dawn. This means that as the Sun sets on Thursday evening, Friday begins.

Months are calculated from crescent moon (*hilal*) to crescent moon. The lunar year is about 11 days shorter than the solar year, so there is a discrepancy between solar and lunar calendars. The lunar year contains 354 days, rather than 365. This means that, in relation to the solar year, the lunar calendar retrogresses through the seasons at the rate of 11 days a year. For agricultural and fiscal purposes, however, a solar year was used, so that it would march in accordance with the seasons.

The names of the months are:

- **Muharram**
- **Rajab**
- **Safar**
- **Sha'ban**
- **Rabi' I**
- **Ramadan**
- **Rabi' II**
- **Shawwal**
- **Jumada I**
- **Dhu al-Qa'da**
- **Jumada II**
- **Dhu al-Hijja**

The festival of *'Id al-Fitr* marks the end of the 30 days of fasting in Ramadan, the seventh month.

THE HIJRA (HEGIRA)

As Muhammad refused to cease preaching monotheism and attacking the pagan gods, his position in Mecca became increasingly untenable. Then his uncle Abu Talib died, and he lost the protection of his clan. The death of Abu Talib was quickly followed by that of his beloved wife, Khadija, also a powerful source of comfort and protection. He considered emigrating to Ta'if, in the mountains near Mecca, but here too there was a pagan cult center and he was driven out by its devotees. Around this time Muhammad met a group of men from one of the Arab tribes from Yathrib. Impressed by his message, they offered him their protection if he should need it. Fearing for the safety of his followers, Muhammad sent them, 70 men and women, to take refuge in Yathrib, an oasis some 215 miles (350 km) to the north.

On the night of July 16, 622, Muhammad and his friend Abu Bakr left Mecca for Yathrib, closely followed by a detachment of Meccans bent on killing them. They passed the night in a cave and while they slept a spider spun its web across the mouth. Spotting the unbroken web the Meccans rode on and Muhammad and Abu Bakr were able to elude their pursuers and reach Yathrib safely.

This exodus from Mecca is known as the *hijra*, a word that means "migration." Those who migrated from Mecca to Yathrib in 622 are therefore called the *muhajirun*, "those who made the hijra." Islamic tradition has lovingly preserved their names, for they are the nucleus of the first Muslim community and a primary source for the deeds and sayings of the Prophet.

The hijra marks the shift from a persecuted minority religion to an organized autonomous Islamic community. Muslims very early recognized the hijra as the turning point in their history, and 622 was taken as the first year of the Muslim lunar calendar, known from the event with which it begins as the *hijri* calendar.

THE CONSTITUTION OF MEDINA

The earliest Islamic political document is known as the Constitution of Medina, for this was the name by which Yathrib would henceforth be known. The full form in Arabic is Madinat al-Nabi, "The City of the Prophet", for it was here that Muhammad resided until his death. The Constitution of Medina, the text of which has been preserved in the biography of the Prophet by Ibn Ishaq,

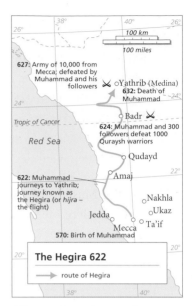

The map shows *the approximate route of Muhammad's journey* (hijra) *from Mecca to Medina in 622.*

regulated relationships between the muhajirun and the inhabitants of the oasis of Medina. Those who extended their hospitality to the immigrants from Mecca and accepted Islam are called the *ansar* or "helpers." The ansar were for the most part from the two Arab tribes which dominated the oasis. Like the muhajirun, they are an important source for tradition. The Jewish tribes formed part of the community, or *umma*, and like the Muslims were required to contribute to the cost of military campaigns and fight against external enemies. A major part of the document concerns what might be termed rules of engagement and division of booty. The Muslims of Medina were on a war footing because of the threat from the Quraysh of Mecca. All disputes were to be referred to God and Muhammad.

This document marks a radical break with the tribal past. Tribal loyalties are replaced by loyalty to the umma. It is no longer blood relationship which defines the group, but faith. All Muslims, whatever their origins, are equal. Those who could not accept this new state of affairs were expelled. Relationships with the Jewish tribes rapidly soured. One tribe was expelled two years after the hijra for doubting Muhammad's mission. Two years later another tribe was expelled for plotting his assassination. Finally, in 627, the men of the last Jewish tribe of the oasis were exterminated for collaborating with the enemies of the umma and their womenfolk enslaved.

The Arab conquerors traveled in much the same way as these present-day Bedouin, covering vast distances on swift camels. However, they fought on foot or from horseback.

It was around this time that tradition places the composition of the letters Muhammad sent to the rulers of Persia, Byzantium, Ethiopia, and the Governor of Egypt, inviting them to embrace Islam, or suffer the consequences.

MUHAMMAD'S WIVES

Soon after reaching Medina, Muhammad married 'A'isha, the daughter of his friend Abu Bakr. She was a very young girl, still playing with dolls, and the marriage was not consummated until two years later. 'A'isha was Muhammad's favorite wife, and tended him on his deathbed. Because of her closeness to him she is the authority for many essential traditions. After the Prophet's death she played a brief political role, taking part in the Battle of the Camel. Although the Qur'an limits the number of wives a Muslim may have to four, the Prophet married many times. Some marriages were political, others love matches. He married Hafsa, the daughter of 'Umar, the second caliph and a daughter of 'Uthman, the third caliph. His own daughter by Khadija, Fatima, married his cousin 'Ali.

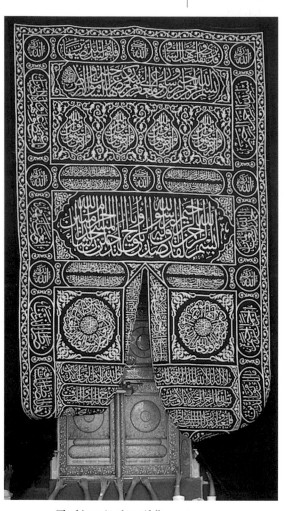

The kiswa is a beautifully embroidered covering that is hung over the Ka'ba in Mecca. The doorway below it in the picture above leads to the chamber where the pagan idols were kept before Muhammad destroyed them in 628.

WAR WITH THE MECCANS

In 624 the Muslims defeated the Meccans and their tribal allies at the Battle of Badr, capturing an important caravan and gaining much prestige among the neighboring tribes for doing so. The Meccans counterattacked the following year, winning the battle of Uhud. It is a tribute to Muhammad's leadership and authority that this defeat did not dishearten his followers. The Meccans besieged Medina for 40 days in 627, but finally withdrew. This was the famous Battle of the Ditch. A Persian convert to Islam named Salman al-Farsi suggested digging a deep trench to stymie the Meccan cavalry, and this was effective.

The Muslims retaliated by moving on Mecca. Quraysh saved their city by negotiating a treaty at a place outside Mecca called Hudaybiyya. The treaty allowed the Muslims to come to Mecca for three days the following year to perform the pilgrimage. A truce of 10 years was agreed upon. Meccan caravans could pass freely through Muslim territory, and in return the Muslim community of Medina was recognized as an autonomous legitimate political entity.

In accordance with the terms of the treaty of Hudaybiyya, the Muslims of Medina made the pilgrimage to Mecca the following year. The prayers and actions of the Prophet during this first Islamic pilgrimage established these rites for all time.

During the course of this pilgrimage Muhammad destroyed the idols inside the Ka'ba, restoring it to its pristine Abrahamic purity.

In 629, the Muslims were strong enough to take Mecca, even though they numbered no more than about 1,500. The city was surrendered by a wealthy leader of Quraysh named Abu Sufyan. His son Mu'awiya would in time become the first Muslim governor of Syria and the first caliph of the Umayyad dynasty. Two of Muhammad's bitterest opponents, 'Amr ibn al-'As and Khalid ibn al-Walid, embraced Islam. This was a momentous event for the faith, for in a few short years these two men were to lead the armies that conquered the Byzantine empire and Sasanid Persia. The rapid rise to prominence in the Muslim community of men of Quraysh (who had recently been bitter enemies) gave rise to natural resentments among the muhajirun and the ansar. It is a mark of Muhammad's skill as a leader and his authority that he was able to overcome these resentments. If Islam was to survive and triumph over its enemies, it needed as many competent supporters as possible.

The taking of Mecca took place without bloodshed. Since the city surrendered, it was granted immunity from looting and only a few executions were carried out. This established a legal precedent for dealing with enemies who did not take up arms against the Muslim armies.

Having consolidated the Muslim grip on Medina and Mecca, the main danger to the umma now came from the tribes. Several of these had been allies of Quraysh, others had already shown their loyalty to Muhammad. Alliances with these nomadic tribes was personal, between leaders, and according to custom such agreements terminated on the death of the leaders who had made them. Some tribes converted to Islam, at least nominally, new alliances were formed with others, some were defeated militarily and submitted to Islamic rule.

THE DEATH OF MUHAMMAD

On June 8, 632, three years after the occupation of Mecca, Muhammad died after a short illness. His death meant the end of revelation and direct divine guidance. The community had suddenly lost its Prophet, leader, friend, guide, and counselor.

Muhammad died at noon. No one knew what to do. Some refused to believe that he could be dead. Finally, Abu Bakr, Muhammad's closest friend, father of his favorite wife 'A'isha, who had been with him when he died, stepped forward and addressed the crowd that had gathered before the humble dwelling in which the Messenger of God had died. "Whoever worshipped Muhammad, let him know that Muhammad is dead, but whoever worshipped God, let him know that God lives and dies not!"

That evening the closest friends and relatives of Muhammad met to discuss the succession to the leadership of the community. Among them were Abu Bakr, 'Umar ibn al-Khattab, 'Uthman ibn 'Affan of the clan of Umayya, and the Prophet's son-in-law, 'Ali ibn Abi Talib. All four of these men were related to Muhammad either by blood or by marriage. At a certain point in the discussion, 'Umar clasped Abu Bakr's hand, signifying that he had been chosen to succeed Muhammad at the head of the Muslim community. The word for "successor" in Arabic is *khalifa*, literally, someone who takes the place of someone else. The fact that during Muhammad's last illness Abu Bakr had taken his place as leader of the communal prayers was a deciding factor.

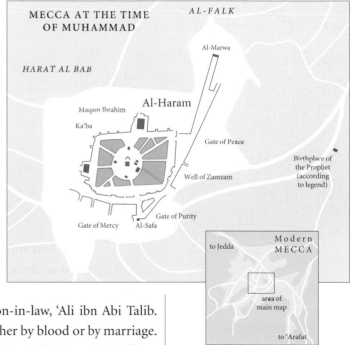

The town of Mecca *in the time of the Prophet was dominated by the Haram, the sacred enclosure housing the Ka'ba. There were also various sites, such as the Well of Zamzam, associated with the life of Abraham (Ibrahim).*

THE QUR'AN

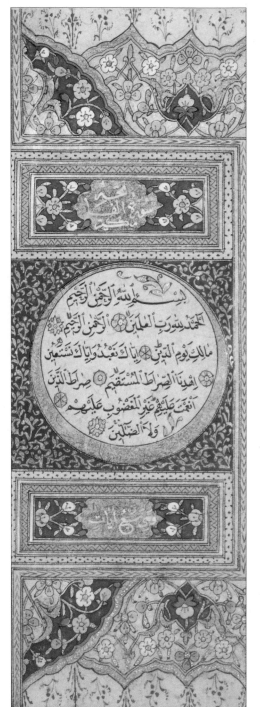

The opening page *of the Qur'an, as in this beautifully decorated Persian example, contains the* Fatiha *(the* Opening*) preceded, as is every sura but one, by the* basmala.

FOR ALL MUSLIMS THE QUR'AN (KORAN) is the word of God. It is the final and perfect revelation revealed in Arabic to His Prophet, Muhammad, through the archangel Gabriel in a series of revelations that took place in western Arabia between 610 and 632.

The word *Qur'an* is derived from the Arabic verb "to recite" or "to read," and means simply "recitations, readings." Islam means "submission," that is "submission to the will of God." A Muslim is one who has so submitted. Faith is *iman*, and hence a "believer" is a *mu'min*. The essence of the Islamic faith is stated in the *Fatiha*, the *Opening* of the Qur'an:

Praise belongs to God, the Lord of all Being, the All-merciful, the All-compassionate, the Master of the Day of Doom. Thee only we serve; to Thee alone we pray for succor. Guide us in the straight path, the path of those whom Thou hast blessed, not of those against whom Thou art wrathful nor of those who go astray.

[QUR'AN: FATIHA]

Islam is the last of the three monotheistic religions, the Qur'an is the final revelation, and Muhammad is the final Prophet. The Qur'an completes and supersedes the scriptures of the two earlier monotheisms, the Jewish Torah and the Christian Gospels. Tawrah and Injil, as they are called in Arabic, are referred to throughout the Qur'an and are accepted by Muslims as inspired.

Islam, Christianity, and Judaism thus share a common body of reference. The Qur'an refers throughout to the prophets and patriarchs of the Old Testament and to Jesus in the New. Adam and Eve, Cain and Abel, Noah, Abraham, Moses, Aaron, Elijah, Isaac, Ishmael, Jacob, Jonah, Zachariah, Benjamin, Joseph, David, and Solomon are as familiar to Muslims from the Qur'an as they are to practicing Jews and Christians. They are all referred to in the Qur'an, sometimes glancingly, sometimes in detail. Sometimes the references to biblical figures coincide with scripture, sometimes the Qur'anic versions differ slightly or substantially. Other prophets, unfamiliar to the Judeo-Christian tradition, are also mentioned, such as Dhu al-Qarnayn, Dhu al-Kifl, Salih, and Shu'ayb.

Since the One God is the ultimate source for all three scriptures, these similarities are not surprising. Differences are accounted for by the partial nature of previous revelations and in some cases their careless transmission or even falsification. There is a fundamental difference between the Qur'an and its predecessors. The Qur'an is not "about" God, it is the very word of God, speaking directly to humanity or addressing His Messenger, Muhammad.

This explains the centrality of the Qur'an to Muslims. The Qur'an is the foundation stone of Islamic society, its constitution, and permeates all aspects of life. To try to live by the Qur'an is to obey God's will, and the ideal society is a society governed by its precepts.

> **Say, He is God, One, God, the Everlasting Refuge, who has not begotten, and has not been begotten, and equal to Him there is not any one.**
>
> [QUR'AN 112]

The central message of the Qur'an is to believe in The One God, and in Him alone. He is All-Powerful and All-Knowing. The word for God in Arabic is *Allah*, literally, "The God." There is no other, and to associate anything with God, thereby detracting from His uniqueness, is *shirk*, "polytheism." Time and again God has sent His prophets to humanity, warning them to abandon unbelief, but the warnings have been ignored, the prophets persecuted and driven away. The Qur'an presents a last chance for humanity to submit to the will of God, for Muhammad is the "Seal of the Prophets", and there will be no more warnings.

Believers will be rewarded with Paradise, while the unbelievers will be sent to Hell. The delights of Paradise and the torments of Hell are graphically described. God's mercy and compassion are infinite, and He guides whom He wills. There is a final judgment, in which humanity will be weighed in the balance and made to account for its sins.

DUTIES OF THE TRUE BELIEVER

Central virtues of the Islamic faith, after true belief in God and the Final Judgment, are charity and keeping one's word.

> **True piety is this: to believe in God, and the Last Day, the angels, the Book, and the Prophets, to give of one's substance, however cherished, to kinsmen, and orphans, the needy, the traveler, beggars, and to ransom the slave, to perform the prayer, to pay the alms. And they who fulfill their covenant when they have engaged in a covenant, and endure with fortitude misfortune, hardship, and peril, these are they who are true in their faith, these are the truly godfearing.**
>
> [Qur'an 2:177]

Providing water *for wayfarers by endowing roadside fountains is a common act of charity in the Islamic world.*

The Qur'an's famous Throne Verse incomparably presents the Islamic concept of God:

God there is no god but He, the Living, the Everlasting, Slumber seizes Him not, neither sleep; to Him belongs all that is in the heavens and the earth. Who is there that shall intercede with Him save by His leave? He knows what lies before them and what is after them and they comprehend not anything of His knowledge save such as He wills. His Throne comprises the heavens and earth; the preserving of them oppresses Him not; He is the All-high, the All-glorious.

[QUR'AN 2:255]

THE TEXT OF THE QUR'AN

Muhammad could not read and write. He proclaimed the revelations he received to his followers, who learned them by heart. Arabian society knew of writing, and several members of the early Muslim community, such as Zayd ibn Thabit, the Prophet's scribe, were literate. They noted down the revelations as they came, using whatever writing materials were on hand – thin flat stones, pieces of leather, potsherds, the flat surfaces of the shoulder blades of camels. Oral transmission was nevertheless thought more reliable. Professional reciters were able to transmit without error large numbers of long, complex poems. Whereas a written document could contain scribal errors or even be forged, a text known by heart by a number of people was a guarantee of accuracy and authenticity. The greater confidence placed in oral rather than written transmission was reinforced by the ambiguities of the early Arabic script.

Even today, many Muslims have committed the entire text of the Qur'an to memory. Someone who does so is known as *hafiz*, "one who has preserved." If for some reason all printed copies of the Qur'an should vanish, the exact text could still be faithfully reproduced from the oral tradition.

Although the first two caliphs, Abu Bakr and 'Umar, were concerned about the possibility of the loss of revelation by the deaths of men and women who had memorized portions of it, it was not until the third caliph, 'Uthman, that all the materials were gathered together to produce a standard written text. This was completed by 650 and all subsequent Qur'ans reflect this text.

THE LANGUAGE OF THE QUR'AN

The Qur'an contains passages of great mystery and beauty, like the following beloved of the mystic orders known as sufi.

God is the Light of the heavens and the earth; the likeness of His Light is as a niche wherein is a lamp (the lamp in a glass, the glass as it were a glittering star) kindled from a Blessed Tree, an olive that is neither of the East nor of the West whose oil well-nigh would shine, even if no fire touched it; Light upon Light!

[Qur'an 24:35]

This mosque lamp *is beautifully decorated with verses from the Qur'an and calligraphy giving the name of the ruler.*

OPPOSITE

A young man *in Mauritania studies a portion of the Qur'an. Writing boards are used in regions where paper is scarce.*

Muslim children throughout the world learn to recite the Qur'an in special schools.

PATRIARCHS AND PROPHETS
The Qur'an makes frequent allusions to the lives of the major figures of the Old Testament and the New.

We raise up in degrees whom We will; surely thy Lord is All-wise, All-knowing. And We gave to him Isaac and Jacob – each one We guided. And Noah We guided before; and of his seed David and Solomon, Job and Joseph, Moses and Aaron – even so We recompense the good-doers – Zachariah and John, Jesus and Elias; each was of the righteous – Ishmael and Elisha, Jonah and Lot – each one We preferred above all beings; and of their fathers, and of their seed and of their brethren; and We elected them, and We guided them to a straight path.

[Qur'an 6: 81-85]

STYLE

The concise, allusive, elliptical style of the Qur'an is very unlike that of the Old or New Testaments. A single *sura* will often contain many different rhythmic modes, sudden shifts from first to third person, equally sudden shifts of subject, verbal and rhythmic echoes of what has gone before or is to come. End rhyme often occurs in linked passages, but the verses do not fit the metrical schemes of Arabic poetry, and are not poetry. Nor are they prose. The depth and range of allusion, both in sound and sense cannot be reproduced in translation, but can be appreciated even by those unfamiliar with Arabic by listening to a recording of a Qur'an recitation.

Although narratives occur, such as the stories of Joseph and Noah, even these are highly allusive and presuppose a familiarity with the story. The Qur'an therefore needed commentary to be properly understood, and commentaries, sometimes of great extent, were produced by scholars from earliest times. Called *tafsir*, they are still a major area of scholarly endeavor today.

The style of the Qur'an is so striking and so different from other literary works that it is characterized as inimitable. The inimitability of the Qur'an is technically termed *i'jaz*, and the concept was elaborated in the 10th century. The Qur'an cannot be imitated, and any attempt to do so is doomed to failure. The Qur'an is also untranslatable. This is why all Muslims, whatever their native language, must learn to read the Qur'an in the original. Versions of the Qur'an in other languages can of course be used to understand the meaning of the text, and there are early examples of Qur'ans written in Iran and Turkey with interlinear versions in Persian and Turkish, but these are simply aids to understanding and not the Qur'an.

FORM

The Qur'an contains 114 chapters, called suras. Each sura is divided into verses, called *ayas*, literally "signs." In modern editions of the Qur'an these are numbered, as in the Bible, but traditionally they were marked off by rosettes and sometimes numbered by fives. The suras are arranged in order of length, with the exception of the first, the *Fatiha*, the "Opening." This sura, repeated five times a day by every Muslim at the beginning of prayers, is the condensation of the message of the Qur'an into eight short verses. After the Fatiha, all the other suras are arranged by order of length, with the longest placed at the beginning of the book and the shortest at the end. This arrangement goes back to the original 'Uthmanic codex of 650.

Each sura has a name, usually chosen from a striking word or expression in one of the verses. Thus the very long second sura of the Qur'an, immediately following the Fatiha, is called the "Sura of the Cow," *surat al-baqara*, after the story of the unblemished cow sacrificed by the Children of Israel in the wilderness at the command of Moses, which occurs in this chapter. Some suras, such as the "Sura of Abraham," have straightforward, self-explanatory names, others are more intriguingly titled, for example the "Sura of the Ant" or the "Sura of the Elephant."

As the revelation of the Qur'an took place over a period of 22 years, during which Muhammad preached first in Mecca, then in Medina, and because very often verses could not be understood without some knowledge of the circumstances that called them forth, it became customary to add, after the name of the sura, the city in which it was revealed – Mecca or Medina.

MANUSCRIPT OF THE QUR'AN

This superb early Ottoman Qur'an with its rich but restrained decoration and meticulously exact calligraphy shows the skill and devotion of the copyist and illuminator. To make beautiful the Word of God is held to be an act of worship and thanksgiving. Because the Qur'an is the Word of God, care is always taken to avoid even the smallest slip in copying.

The need to read *and study the Qur'an in its original language spread literacy throughout the Islamic world.*

The flap protects the manuscript from dust

Glazed and polished, hand-made paper

The heading gives the name of the sura and often the number of verses it contains and whether it was revealed at Mecca or Medina

The script of this Qur'an is naskhi, developed by Ibn al-Bawwab in the 10th century and brought to perfection by Ottoman calligraphers

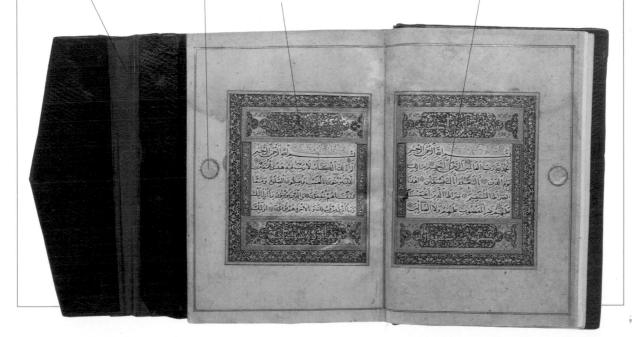

THE SURAS OF MECCA

This short sura of just 12 lines is a good example of the more passionate, mysterious style of the revelations made at Mecca.

By the white afternoon and the brooding night! Thy Lord has neither forsaken thee nor hates thee and the Last shall be better for thee than the First. Thy Lord shall give thee, and thou shalt be satisfied. Did He not find thee an orphan, and shelter thee? Did He not find thee erring, and guide thee? Did He not find thee needy, and suffice thee?

As for the orphan, do not oppress him, and as for the beggar, scold him not; and as for thy Lord's blessing, declare it.

[Qur'an 93: 1-12]

This inscription *is the* basmala, *"In the name of God, the Merciful, the Compassionate," beautifully reproduced on Iznik tiles at the Kılıç Ali Pasha Mosque in Istanbul.*

Generally speaking, the suras revealed in Mecca are short, highly charged and deeply moving. The suras revealed in Medina, where the first Muslim community became a political as well as religious entity, are longer and frequently contain, as well as passages of great beauty, more prosaic passages containing material on marriage, divorce, inheritance, and other subjects of concern to the ordering of a Muslim society.

Every sura but one is preceded by the *basmala*; "In the Name of God, the Merciful, the Compassionate" *(bi-smi llah al-rahman al-rahim)*. This phrase is still written at the head of every document, even personal letters, and is repeated before undertaking almost any activity. The emphasis upon God's mercy and compassion is the quintessence of Islam. Because this phrase occurs with such frequency in written documents, Muslims are always careful not to tread on paper with Arabic script, and will very often pick up scraps of paper with writing upon them and place them in a niche in a wall to guard them from possible desecration.

Copies of the Qur'an can only be touched by someone in a state of ritual purity, that is, who has just performed the ritual washing that precedes prayer. Non-Muslims are naturally never in this state, and should therefore not touch the Qur'an. This prohibition does not extend to translations into other languages, for these of course are not the literal word of God.

The Qur'an is recited, or rather chanted, aloud when read. It is normally placed in a folding wooden support, the *kursi*, in order to elevate it above the knees of the reciter, who is generally seated on the floor.

There are seven traditionally accepted ways of "reading," that is, pronouncing the consonantal text. None of these affect the consonantal text itself, and in only a very few cases do they affect the sense. Early commentaries on the Qur'an will often cite "readings" from one or another of these different traditions, in order to throw light on the meaning of a particular passage and to show different ways in which it can be construed. Very rarely do these affect points of doctrine.

THE SCRIPT OF THE QUR'AN

The Arabic script in which the first exemplars of the Qur'an were written consisted of 14 basic letter forms which represented 28 different consonants.

Short vowels were not indicated at all and long vowels only infrequently. In the course of the 7th century this defective script was perfected, first by the addition of dots above or below letters to differentiate consonants of similar shape but different pronunciation, then by marks above and below the letters indicating the three short vowel sounds of the Arabic language – a, i and u. These aids to pronunciation brought the written text into line with the orally transmitted text, producing a canonical text that was accepted by all Muslims.

An essential difference between the Islamic and the Jewish and Christian revelations can be appreciated at a glance by opening scholarly editions of the Hebrew Bible and the Greek New Testament and comparing them to the Qur'an. The texts of both the Hebrew Bible and the Greek New Testament are accompanied by extensive notes at the bottom of the page, listing large numbers of variant readings from the manuscript tradition. Both have long and exceedingly complex textual histories. The text of the Qur'an, however, is presented with no scholarly apparatus whatsoever; no variant readings from divergent manuscript traditions are listed. The consonantal text has been fixed from the year 650, when the Caliph 'Uthman established the text we have today both from the fledgling written tradition and, more importantly, from the memories of those men and women, contemporaries of the Prophet Muhammad, who had learned verses of the Qur'an by heart as they were revealed.

A young British Muslim *recites from the Qur'an. The text rests on a* kursi, *the traditional wooden stand used to hold the Qur'an.*

KUFIC SCRIPT

The earliest Arabic script takes its name from the town of Kufa in what is now Iraq, though it was in use well before the town was founded. There are a number of regional forms, but all are bold and angular. A modern form of Kufic is used throughout North Africa. This Kufic Qur'an, written on vellum, the finest kind of parchment, dates from the 9th or 10th century.

The red dots indicate vowel sounds. The system used in this manuscript was later replaced by a more accurate notation

The skill of the calligrapher lay in spacing the letters attractively on the page

The letters are widely spaced, rather than closely joined, as in modern Arabic script

Early Kufic Qur'ans are written on parchment, often trimmed to this rectangular shape and size

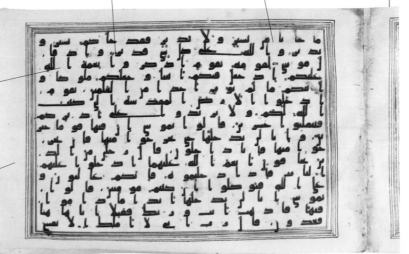

Buraq *is the winged, human-headed beast that carried the Prophet on the Night Journey to Jerusalem and the seven spheres of heaven.*

It is He who has sent His Messenger with the guidance and the religion of truth, that He may uplift it above every religion, though the unbelievers be averse.

[QUR'AN 9:33]

THE MESSENGER

Muhammad was the *rasul*, or messenger, who delivered God's word to humanity. He is also a Prophet, *nabi*. In the Islamic prophetic typology, which as we have seen includes the Prophets of the Old Testament as well as Jesus, the Prophet is in touch with the supernatural, and can perform miracles. Muhammad too was able to multiply food, cause stones to speak, split the Moon. But Islamic tradition does not lay particular stress upon these miracles, with the exception of the Night Journey to Jerusalem (*'isra*). The Prophet's journey to Jerusalem and his ascent into heaven (*mi'raj*) on the back of the miraculous steed Buraq are referred to in the Qur'an, in the sura called "The Night Journey." The "Further Mosque" (*al-masjid al-aqsa*) in the first verse of this sura was located by the commentators in Jerusalem. However, the true miracle of Islam is the Qur'an itself, which eclipses all others.

But Muhammad was not simply the passive receptor and transmitter of the Qur'an. He had total understanding of the meaning of the words he transmitted, and had been in close contact with the divine. He is the exemplar of the perfect man (*al-insan al-kamil*) and the perfect Muslim. Because of his contact with the divine, and the fact that he alone of all mankind was chosen as recipient of the revelation, he is considered free of error (*ma'sum*).

It is thus incumbent upon Muslims to try to model themselves upon him. Unlike the Christian ideal of *imitatio Christi*, this form of emulation is not limited to the spiritual, but for males can include externals, such as dress, comportment, dignity, even physical features such as length of beard.

SUNNA AND HADITH

The men and women of the first generation of Muslims to whom Muhammad repeated the verses of the Qur'an are known as the *sahaba*, "Companions." Since they had direct contact with the Prophet, they were not only sources for the exact wording of revelation itself, but for the day-to-day behavior of the Prophet, his deeds, sayings, and even his

THE PROHIBITION OF IMAGES

Although there is no specific prohibition of human images in the Qur'an, Islamic tradition has been reluctant to accept images of humans or living things. Non-Arabic speaking cultures were more tolerant. Timurid and Safavid Iran, the Ottoman Turks, and Mughal India all had traditions of figural art, but not sculpture. Their manuscript illuminations sometimes include images of the Prophet, but his face is always hidden by a veil.

The Name of the Prophet *can be formed into a decorative design.*

silences. The *sahaba* are thus the source for the *sunna* ("precedent"), an immense corpus of eyewitness reports of the public and private behavior of the Prophet and the men and women who knew him. Each of these reports is known as a *hadith*, a word that is often misleadingly translated as "tradition," but which in fact simply means "news, report." Each hadith is composed of two parts. It is introduced by an *isnad*, or "chain of authorities," the first link of which is the name of one of the sahaba. The succeeding names in the isnad are the names of the men and women who heard the hadith from the previous name in the chain.

The second part of the hadith is the actual report, called the *matn*. This may be a saying of the Prophet on a particular occasion, in which case the exact words are reported, or an account of something he did or did not do.

Because all four schools of law accepted the principal of the primacy of Prophetic hadith as a key source for legal rulings, it became imperative to winnow these from what scholars of the time called "the raging sea of hadith." In the early 9th century, the hadith were collected into six main collections, organized on slightly different principles. This material, gathered from the oral tradition, forms the sunna, and together of course with the Qur'an, is one of the four "roots" *(usul),* or principles, of the *shari'a*, the Holy Law of Islam.

The most famous and earliest collection is the *Sahih* of al-Bukhari. The title, meaning "The Sound," indicates that the hadith it contains are authentic according to the precepts of the hadith collectors. Hadith criticism centered not on the actual report, the matn, but on the chain of transmitters, the isnad.

The names that occurred in the isnad had to be those of reliable, upstanding men and women. Not only that, it had to be shown that they could in fact have coincided in time and place so that the hadith in question could be properly transmitted. On these and other similar critera, the hadith were classified as sound, good, or weak *(sahih, hasan, da'if)*.

Al-Bukhari classifies his material under headings that key into the legal literature. The range of topics shows how comprehensive Islamic law is: Revelation, faith, knowledge, prayer, charity, pilgrimage, fasting, social and economic relations, merits of the Prophets, the Qur'an, marriage, divorce, medicine, manners, apostasy, dreams, the Unity of God.

HADITH AND ISNAD (CHAIN OF AUTHORITIES)

• *Isnad* (chain of authorities):
'Ubayd Allah ibn Musa related to us: 'Hanzala ibn Abi Sufyan reported to us on the authority of 'Ikrima ibn Khalid on the authority of 'Umar (May God be content with them both!): He said the Messenger of God (May Prayers and Peace be upon him!) said:

• *Matn* (text of *hadith*):
"Islam is built on five (things): the testimony (There is no god but God and that Muhammad is the Messenger of God); the performance of prayer; giving alms; the pilgrimage; and the fast of Ramadan."

Ayyub al-Ansari, *the Prophet's Standard bearer and one of the* sahaba, *was killed at the first siege of Constantinople in the 7th century. His tomb (above) in Istanbul was erected in 1458.*

Sira

The Prophet is referred to by name five times in the Qur'an, four times as Muhammad and once as Ahmad, a version of the same name. There are references to the fact that he was an orphan, but otherwise there are no materials in the Qur'an with which to reconstruct his biography. Nor would there be, for the Qur'an is not "about" Muhammad, but is God's message to humanity.

In order to understand that message, however, it was necessary to know, insofar as possible, the circumstances of the revelations of which the Qur'an is composed. It has already been pointed out that early Qur'ans divided the suras into two groups, those revealed in Mecca and those revealed in Medina. Many hadith with isnads reaching back to the sahaba recorded the exact circumstances under which a particular group of verses was revealed. In other words, a biography of the Prophet and the history of the first Muslim community could be reconstructed from the oral tradition. This would also allow a deeper understanding of the background of the revelation of the Qur'an and thus of the precise meaning of specific verses.

The earliest surviving biography *(sira)* of the Prophet is that of Ibn Ishaq, who died in 767. We do not possess Ibn Ishaq's original, but an edited version done in the early 9th century by a scholar named Ibn Hisham. Later biographies, some of which add new material, are for the most part based on Ibn Ishaq.

The *sira* of Ibn Ishaq is thus a primary source for the life of the Prophet. It is based on hadith, but includes poems and even documents, like the "Constitution of Medina," fundamental to an understanding of the earliest Muslim community.

ʿILM AND FIQH

ʿIlm, "knowledge," is the technical term for knowledge of the Qur'an and its exegesis as well as the legal decisions of the Prophet and the sahaba as recorded in the hadith. A scholar who has attained this knowledge through the demanding, lifetime's study required, is an *ʿalim* (plural *ʿulama*). The ʿulama are custodians of the system of divine law which regulates the lives of Muslims. They have not hesitated to correct rulers and try to bring them back on the right course. Today the most revered institution for the training of ʿulama is al-Azhar in Cairo. The rulings of the ʿulama of al-Azhar have great authority throughout the Muslim world.

Fiqh is a Qur'anic term meaning "understanding." It refers to the task of understanding the duties incumbent upon Muslims as revealed in the Qur'an and the sunna, and the implications of these two sources for individual and social action. The specialist in this area of Islamic learning is a *faqih* (plural *fuqaha*). The standard compendia of fiqh are normally divided into two parts, one dealing with religious duties, the other with social duties and human relationships, including political theory.

SHARIʿA

All aspects of the lives of Muslims, public and private, are in theory governed by divine law. The *shariʿa* is the system of divine law that governs worship, ritual, conduct, and legal matters such as commercial contracts, marriage, divorce, and inheritance. The ultimate point of this system is entry to Paradise for the believer. The shariʿa maps the road to salvation.

Like many other key words in Islam, shariʿa has the original sense of "way, path." The systemization of the shariʿa began in Umayyad times and was completed under the early ʿAbbasids, slightly before the compilation of the canonical collections of hadith. The key figure in its elaboration appears to have been al-Shafiʿi, who firmly based the shariʿa on the sunna of the Prophet. Only Prophetical hadith were acceptable as legal proofs, that is hadith whose chains of authority led back to the Prophet himself.

SCHOOLS OF LAW

There are now four major mainstream schools (*madhahib*, singular *madhhab*): Malikiyya, Hanifiyya, Shafiʿiyya, and Hanbaliyya, each named after its founder. Shiʿa Islam follows the Jaʿfariyya, which takes its name from the seventh Imam, Jaʿfar al-Siddiq.

DIETARY LAWS

The four categories of prohibited (*haram*) foods are carrion, blood, pork, and offerings to pagan gods.

> These things only has He forbidden you: carrion, blood, the flesh of swine, what has been hallowed to other than God.
>
> [Qur'an 2:168]

The shariʿa also prohibits the flesh of scavengers and carnivores, animals killed by a blow to the head or strangled, amphibious animals, insects and birds of prey with talons. Wine, and by extension, alcohol and other intoxicating substances are also forbidden. The Hanafi school of law prohibits shellfish. For meat to be lawful (*halal*), it must be slaughtered under hygienic conditions by a mature Muslim of sound mind approved by the religious authorities. The animal's throat must be cleanly cut, severing respiratory tract, esophagus, and jugular. The name of God must be invoked before partaking of a meal.

These young men *are studying the principles of* fiqh *(Islamic jurisprudence) at a madrasa in Inner Mongolia, China.*

The Malikiyya, or Maliki, school is named after Malik ibn Anas, a *qadi*, from Medina, who died in 795. He is the author of the earliest law code, the *Muwatta'*. Malik recognizes four sources, or roots, of Holy Law: the Qur'an, sunna, customary law of Medina, and the consensus *(ijma')* of the jurisconsults *(fuqaha)*

The four schools of law *in a* madrasa *are often arranged around the four sides of a courtyard, as here at the Sultan Barquq madrasa in Cairo.*

of Medina. As the city of the first organized Muslim community, the practice of Medina was held to be closest to the Prophet and his Companions. This school of law is followed in Upper Egypt, North Africa except for Libya, parts of West Africa, the Sudan, Kuwait, and Bahrain.

The second school is named after Abu Hanifa (699–767), a jurisconsult of Iranian origin. The Hanifiyya accepts the principle of reasoning by analogy, *qiyas*, basing a decision, in the absence of specific guidance from the Qur'an or sunna, on a similar case, guided by the principle of *istihsan*, "choosing the best solution." This school was the official school of law under the Ottoman empire. Today it rules the lives of Muslims in China, India, Pakistan, Afghanistan, Central Asia, the Caucasus, Turkey, and the Balkans.

The founder of the third school was al-Shafi'i, who died in Cairo in 820. It was he who established a methodology for deriving law from the sunna, arguing that only Prophetical hadith could be used. Hadith from the Companions were disallowed. He held that the sunna served only to explain the Qur'an, and could not contradict it. He stressed the role of consensus *(ijma')*. Today the Shafi'iyya is the predominant school in Lower Egypt, Palestine, East Africa, and Indonesia.

The Hanbaliyya, or Hanbali, school is named after Ahmad ibn Hanbal (780–855), a student of al-Shafi'i. He was even more rigorous than al-Shafi'i, rejecting all sources but Qur'an and sunna. This school was followed by the Wahhabi reform movement, and is today followed in Saudi Arabia, Oman, and Qatar.

Towards the end of the 10th century it was felt that these four schools had effectively exhausted the possibilities of the Qur'an and sunna for the formulation of the shari'a. Only in modern times have scholars once again turned to the sources themselves with a fresh eye.

THE QADI

The shari'a is implemented by the *qadi* (from the verb *qada*, "to carry out"). The qadi must be learned in the shari'a and of recognized probity. He is appointed by the ruler. The institution took shape in Umayyad times, and was fully elaborated under the 'Abbasids. The Chief Qadi *(qadi al-qudat)*, residing in the metropolis, has authority over those in provincial towns. The qadi is assisted by official witnesses, whose task is to testify that correct procedures are followed. Plaintiffs have the right to be judged by the law of whichever school they follow. The shi'a, however, do not recognize the authority of sunni courts.

Pious men have always been concerned by the lack of separation between the executive and judiciary, fearing political interference. Even more worrying is the possibility of making a wrong judgment, and there are many cases in Islamic history of men refusing from moral scruples to accept the position of qadi.

PUNISHMENT

Human actions are classified by the specialists in Islamic law into five categories: obligatory, recommended, disapproved, forbidden, and permissible. Obligatory actions are those that bring a reward in the afterlife, but punishment in the afterlife for omission. Recommended actions bring reward, but no punishment. Forbidden actions bring punishment, but reward for avoidance. Disapproved actions bring reward for avoidance, but no punishment for performance. Permissible actions are neutral, bringing neither reward nor punishment.

The punishments *(hudud)* for crimes like murder and theft are set out in the shari'a. Voluntary murder is punished by death, although this can be commuted if the offended parties agree to compensation. Involuntary murder or wounding is settled by compensation, theft by cutting off the right hand, brigandage by death, adultery by 100 lashes for both men and women, and the same for drinking wine and spirits. Stoning for adultery is based on the sunna, while the punishment of 100 lashes is Quran'ic. Standards of proof in a shari'a court are rigorous – four adult male witnesses are necessary to prove adultery. As a leading early jurist remarked, "Seldom do four witnesses come together on such a matter."

MARKET INSPECTORS [MUHTASIB]

Despite the comprehensive nature of the shari'a, it is limited by its sources, and there are many areas in which it is silent. The conflict between the ideal of rule by divine law and economic and political reality is a constant in Islamic history. Public order in the great Islamic cities was kept by the police. Markets were regulated by a *muhtasib*, a market inspector, who was responsible for keeping public order, testing weights and measures, and checking the quality of goods. Several medieval manuals for market inspectors have survived, and give fascinating glimpses of urban life in medieval cities.

The market inspector *was in charge of public order and fair trading in the markets of traditional Islamic cities.*

The status of women varies enormously from country to country within the Islamic world. Here a group of young women attend a study group in a mosque in Morocco.

Women

The Qur'an specifically addresses both men and women, and women are as responsible for their actions before God as are men. They are legally inferior, however. A Muslim man may marry a non-Muslim, but the children must be raised in the Islamic faith; a Muslim woman may not marry a non-Muslim. In certain circumstances a woman's testimony in a shari'a court is worth half that of a man. The inheritance rights of women are guaranteed in the Qur'an, but a sister receives only half the portion received by her brothers. A woman's husband is obliged to provide for her and her children, but polygamy is accepted, and a man may take up to four wives, provided he looks after them equally. He may also take an unlimited number of concubines. In the modern world polygamy is rare and concubinage has vanished.

Marriage is a contract, sanctioned of course by divine law. In sunni Islam, the woman's guardian, usually her father, establishes the contract in her name. The shi'i, on the other hand, regard the contracted woman as a legal entity coequal with the groom. The groom pays a dowry, the *mahr*, which is returned to the wife if divorced. The shari'a, following the Qur'an, discourages divorce, calling it "the worst of all possible things," but nevertheless recognizes that sometimes it is unavoidable as a last resort. A man may divorce his wife unilaterally, by pronouncing the *talaq*, the formula "I divorce thee!" three times. The first two pronouncements must be followed by a waiting period, in order to determine that the wife is or is not pregnant. If she is, she will have custody of male children until the age of seven and female till the age of puberty, defined by the various schools of law as 15 or 18. The same rule applies to custody from the form of divorce known as *khul'*, which is divorce instituted by the wife. In this case, the wife forfeits the dowry received from her husband on marriage. This form of divorce can only be validated with the consent of the husband, except under Maliki law, which recognizes the authority of the court in this matter in cases of irreconcilable differences.

There is a famous verse in the Qur'an [4:34] which states that it is licit to beat a rebellious wife. Early jurisconsults softened the natural consequences of the text by concluding that beating was licit, but could only be done with the small stick used to clean the teeth – essentially a toothbrush. They thus brought the verse into line with the Prophet's well-attested kindness toward and respect for women.

The Qur'an contains just one single reference to the veil: "and let them cast their veils over their bosoms and not reveal their adornments save to their husbands" [Qur'an 24:10]. This has been interpreted to mean anything from concealing the hair and obscuring the shape of the body to full concealment. The term *hijab*, veil, is often extended to mean the seclusion of women from the view of non-kin. The modern hijab is often a scarf covering the hair and tied under the chin, plus modest dress. The wearing of Islamic dress, *ziyy islami*, a mark of Muslim identity, is widespread among young Muslim women and men living in Europe.

The imam delivers the Friday sermon from a pulpit called a minbar *as in this illumination from a medieval manuscript showing a preacher in the mosque at Samarkand.*

THE PILLARS OF ISLAM

It is in the Sahih of al-Bukhari that the idea that there are five basic principles of the Islamic faith is first enunciated. They are the profession of faith, prayer, charity, fasting, and pilgrimage. By the 10th century, these had come to be called the Five Pillars *(arkan)* of Islam.

THE PROFESSION OF FAITH [SHAHADA] The *shahada* is the Muslim profession of faith: "There is no god but God; Muhammad is His Messenger" *(la ilaha ila llah; Muhammadun rasul allah)*. The word shahada has a legal sense, "witness," and the pronunciation of this formula in Arabic, prefaced by a statement of intent and before qualified witnesses, is all that it takes formally to become a Muslim. This simple statement expresses total commitment to the message of Islam. Abu Hanifa, the founder of the Hanafiyya madhhab, gives the definition: "Faith is professing with the tongue, counting true with the mind, and knowing with the heart."

PRAYER [SALAT] There are five daily prayers; dawn, noon, afternoon, sunset, and evening. The worshipper faces toward the Ka'ba in Mecca as he prays. The worshipper must be in a state of ritual purity before praying, and this is accomplished by *wudu'*, "ablutions."

The direction of prayer is called the **qibla**, and is indicated in mosques by an empty niche in the wall called the *mihrab*. The correct way of performing ablutions, the wording of prayers, number of bows *(rak'at)*, position of the hands during prayer, are all meticulously laid out in the shar'ia. Worshippers normally repair to the mosque for the noon prayer. On Fridays, prayers are communal. They are led by an imam, literally "one who stands in front," who also delivers a sermon, called the *khutba*.

The mihrab indicates the qibla *or direction of Mecca and worshippers face it when they pray. This mihrab is in the Great Mosque of Córdoba.*

FASTING IN ISLAM

The aim of fasting is to attain, through the discipline of denial, a peaceful, devout state of mind, putting away all evil thoughts.

"O you who believe, fasting has been prescribed for you just as it was prescribed for those before you, so that you will be godfearing."
[Qur'an 2:183]

A crowd of worshippers in Cairo gives thanks at the festival of 'Id al-Fitr, which marks the end of the fast of Ramadan.

OPPOSITE

Pilgrims perform the tawaf, the sevenfold circumambulation of the Ka'ba, one of the key rites of the hajj.

ALMS [ZAKAT] The giving of alms is fundamental to Islam, and charity is a form of worship. The *zakat* is obligatory, as the tithe was in medieval Christianity, and was levied in fixed proportions according to the wealth of the individual. The shari'a stipulated 10 percent of crops, 2 $\frac{1}{2}$ percent of income. In the absence of any duly constituted authority to collect it, the *zakat* should be paid voluntarily. The alms are to be used for the relief of the poor, for the necessities of travelers, to ransom captives, to free debtors, and for other charitable purposes. In addition, all Muslims who can afford to should also give voluntary alms, called *sadaqa*.

FASTING [SAWM] The lunar month of Ramadan is set aside for fasting. The fast lasts from sunrise to sunset each day for 30 days. Adults must let nothing pass their lips during the hours of fasting. This applies not only to food and drink, but to tobacco smoke, for example. They must abstain from sexual contact and from all antisocial behavior. The observance of the fast of Ramadan unites all Muslims in a common enterprise and creates great social cohesion. The object is to subdue the passions and draw nearer to God by purifying one's being through self-denial. The fast is broken after sunset and before dawn by meals, and the streets of any Muslim city are filled with joyous crowds at night during Ramadan. Many people perform *tarawih*, voluntary worship during the night hours. Very often the entire Qur'an is recited. For this purpose, the text is divided into 30 equal portions to correspond with the nights of Ramadan. Ramadan ends with 'Id al-Fitr, the "Festival of Fast Breaking," one of the two major festivals of the Islamic calendar, celebrated on the first day of the month of Shawwal. A special tax called the *zakat al-fitr* is levied to provide food or money to the poor so that they may particpate in the 'Id al-Fitr. This festival is also known as the 'Id al-Saghir, "The Little Festival," as opposed to the 'Id al-Kabir, "The Big Festival," which is celebrated at the completion of the pilgrimage.

PILGRIMAGE [HAJJ] The annual pilgrimage to Mecca reenacts the Prophet's pilgrimage of 630, which in turn enacted events associated with the life of Abraham. It is incumbent upon every Muslim of sound health who can afford to do so to try to make the pilgrimage at least once in his lifetime, and it is the dream of all Muslims to make the hajj. The pilgrimage to Mecca is one of the most remarkable mass pilgrimages in the world, bringing pilgrims from all over the world to the city where the Prophet received the first revelation of the Qur'an. In the course of their lives, all of the pilgrims have faced the Ka'ba thousands of times while performing the daily five prayers, and to finally see the focus of those prayers is an event of tremendous emotional impact.

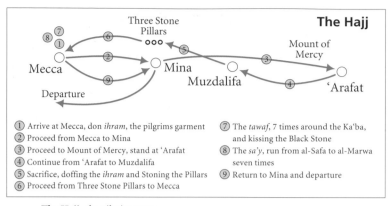

The Hajj

① Arrive at Mecca, don *ihram*, the pilgrims garment
② Proceed from Mecca to Mina
③ Proceed to Mount of Mercy, stand at 'Arafat
④ Continue from 'Arafat to Muzdalifa
⑤ Sacrifice, doffing the *ihram* and Stoning the Pillars
⑥ Proceed from Three Stone Pillars to Mecca
⑦ The *tawaf*, 7 times around the Ka'ba, and kissing the Black Stone
⑧ The *sa'y*, run from al-Safa to al-Marwa seven times
⑨ Return to Mina and departure

The Hajj, *the pilgrimage to Mecca that all Muslims try to make at least once in their lives, takes place in the twelfth month of the Islamic calendar, Dhu al-Hijja. The route taken and actions performed are based on events in the life of the Prophet.*

The Hajj takes place between the eighth and the thirteenth days of the last month of the lunar calendar, Dhu al-Hijja. Mecca is surrounded by a sacred precinct called the *haram*. When the pilgrim approaches the outer limit of the precinct, he must enter a state of ritual purity by bathing, having his hair and nails trimmed, removing jewelry and headgear, and donning two seamless white garments, one wrapped around the waist and the other around the upper part of the body. This is called the *ihram*. As they don the ihram, the pilgrims declare their intention of making the pilgrimage and pronounce the *talbiya*, a phrase that declares their presence before God: "Here I am, O God, at thy service!"

The pilgrims now enter the haram and proceed to the Great Mosque in whose central courtyard stands the Ka'ba. Now they perform the *tawaf*, the circumambulation of the Ka'ba. They move at a rapid pace around the Ka'ba, which is draped in a black embroidered covering called the *kiswa*, seven times counterclockwise. They then perform the *sa'y*, the "Running," between two small hills called al-Safa and al-Marwa, now linked by an arcade.

The Hajj proper begins on the eighth day of Dhu al-Hijja. All the pilgrims proceed to Mina, outside Mecca, where again, following the practice of the Prophet, they meditate overnight. The next day they move on to the plain of 'Arafat, 9 miles (15 km) from Mecca, for the *wuquf*, "The Standing." They assemble at the base of *Jabal Rahma*, the "Mount of Mercy," where the Prophet delivered his farewell sermon. Here they again pray and meditate, from noon to sunset, examining their consciences and seeking God's mercy. The Prophet said: "The best of prayers is the prayer of the Day of 'Arafat," and for Muslims this is the culmination of their spiritual life.

After the Sun has set, they proceed to Muzdalifa, about 4 miles (7 km) on the way back to Mina, where they pass the night. The next morning, the 13th of Dhu al-Hijja, they continue on to Mina, passing three pillars at which each pilgrim casts seven stones. One of the pillars represents

It is the custom *in Aswan in Upper Egypt for returning pilgrims to decorate the fronts of their houses with scenes of Mecca and their pilgrimage.*

Satan. The 'Id al-Adha, "Festival of Sacrifice" now commences. Camels, goats, and sheep are ritually slaughtered and the pilgrims partake of a celebratory meal. (The festival, also called the 'Id al-Kabir, is celebrated throughout the Muslim world, and is the second major festival of the Islamic calendar.) Those pilgrims who have not already done so now return to Mecca to perform the *tawaf* and the *sa'y*. The pilgrimage is now officially over, and to indicate that the pilgrims have passed out of a state of ritual purity the men have their heads shaved and the women a lock cut from their hair.

JIHAD

Jihad is not one of the "pillars" of Islam, although the importance of the concept caused some early scholars to consider placing it among the primary Muslim duties, and it is sometimes considered "the sixth pillar." Jihad means "struggle, exertion." Two kinds are distinguished, the "Greater" and the "Lesser" Jihad. This distinction goes back to a Prophetical hadith. The "Greater Jihad" is the struggle against evil that all Muslims engage in throughout their lives, and it is this that is emphasized in the tradition.

The "Lesser Jihad" is "legal war," which unlike the Greater Jihad, is a collective, rather than personal, activity. The war must be legally declared by the Caliph. The enemy must be unbelievers whose territory borders on Islamic territory. Before the opening of hostilities, they must be invited to convert to Islam. If they accept, they then form part of the community of believers. If not, there are two possibilities. If they are conquered by force, the prisoners of war become the property of the leader. Movable property, after subtraction of the fifth part set aside for the poor, is divided among the warriors. Women and children must not be harmed. Trees must not be cut down, or herds upon which the livelihood of peasants depends driven off. "People of the Book," originally Jews and Christians, but later other groups with scriptures, have a privileged status and maintain the free exercise of their religion on payment of a head tax, the *jizya*. This codification of the rules of legally declared war is based on the practice of the Prophet in his wars against the pagan tribes of Arabia. The Muslim armies that conquered the Byzantine and Persian empires in the 7th century were on jihad. Accounts of their conquests make a point of showing that they observed the stipulations of the shari'a, particularly with regard to the treatment of subject populations and division of booty. At various times in Islamic history, groups within the Islamic community have declared jihad upon each other. The Isma'ilis, for example, declared their sunni enemies "unbelievers" in order to be able to wage war against them legally. So did the Almoravids in the 11th century, who declared the Muslim rulers of Spain "unbelievers" because of their failure to implement the shari'a. Since it is expressly forbidden in the sunna for Muslim to make war on Muslim, both these movements were discredited in the eyes of leading jurisconsults.

Muslims in Delhi *gather to pray at the festival of 'Id al-Adha, which marks the end of the Hajj.*

JIHAD

The duty of the believer is to spread the faith. This stern injunction is softened by the Qur'anic verse: "There is no compulsion in religion." This is taken to refer to the "people of the Book" who have protected status within the *umma*.

> So let them fight in the way of God who sell the present life for the world to come; and whosoever fights in the way of God and is slain, or conquers, we shall bring him a mighty wage.
>
> [Qur'an 4:75]

THE MOSQUE

ALL MOSQUES, however grand in scale and richly decorated, conform to one simple basic pattern. The essential elements of a mosque are highlighted here on the great Selimiye Mosque in Edirne, built in 1569–75.

The muezzin mahfili is a raised platform, on which the muezzin stands when chanting responses to the imam (head of the mosque).

The mihrab, an ornate niche in the wall marks the direction of Mecca. The prayer hall is laid out so most people can see it.

The loge provided the Ottoman sultan with a screened-off balcony where he could pray, safe from would-be assassins.

The minbar is a lofty pulpit to the right of the mihrab. This is used by the imam to deliver the Friday sermon.

AUTHORITY IN ISLAM

Religious authority in the Muslim community resides in the Qur'an and sunna. There is no organized "church," with a hierarchy of authority, and there is nothing comparable to a priesthood, since there are no sacraments. Marriage is a contract. Mosques are places of worship, but are not consecrated ground. Islam is thus a "lay theocracy," and every Muslim is in a sense his own priest, as he himself carries out the obligations of his religion and has access to scripture.

Many mosques have a board outside, giving the times of prayer. These vary through the year with the times of sunrise and sunset

Minarets
The mosque's four slender minarets each have three balconies

Dome
The dome was the proudest achievement of Sinan, the great Ottoman architect. His aim was to surpass the dome of the great Byzantine church, the Hagia Sophia

Sultan's Loge
The loge is supported on green marble columns. It has its own ornately decorated mihrab

Mihrab
The niche is made of carved Marmara marble

Prayer Hall
The Selimiye's interior is exceptionally light because of the number of windows in the dome and surounding arcades

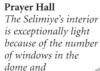

Ablutions Fountain
Intricate pierced carving decorates the top of the 16-sided open fountain.

Supporting Columns
The mosque's dome rests on eight massive pillars arranged in an octagon

Muezzin mahfili
Only very large mosques normally have a rostrum of this kind for the use of the muezzin

After the death of the Prophet in 632, political and religious leadership of the community passed to the caliphs. The word "caliph," *khalifa* in Arabic, simply means "successor." The first four caliphs – Abu Bakr, 'Umar, 'Uthman, and 'Ali – were all related to the Prophet, the first three by marriage, 'Ali by blood. They are known as the "Rightly Guided Caliphs" because all had direct access to the Prophet, and thus to the sunna. All were from the tribe of Quraysh, and all were elected to the caliphate *(khilafa)*. Jurists later codified the qualifications for the caliphate as any member of the tribe of Quraysh, of sound mind and body, who had been elected to the caliphate by his peers. Early divisions within the Muslim community centered on succession to the caliphate. The Shi'a, the "Party of 'Ali," believed that 'Ali was the natural successor to the caliphate by reason of his close kinship to the Prophet, and restricted the line of succession to his descendants.

Before performing *their five daily prayers, Muslims must ritually purify themselves by ablutions* (wudu').

By early 'Abbasid times, the major religious obligation of the caliph was to ensure that the shari'a was carried out. The class of men learned in the shari'a, the 'ulama, became the real authority in the Islamic empire. A scholarly elite, open to anyone with the requisite talents who had followed the grueling course of study under recognized authorities, was formed and it was this elite that elaborated classical Islamic civilization.

THE UMMA

The word *umma* for the community of Muslims goes back to the establishment of the first Muslim community in Medina in 622. The fundamental concept, akin to the Greek idea of an ecumene, is that tribal, national, and ethnic loyalties are subordinate to a larger concept, that of the brotherhood of all Muslims [Qur'an 49:10]. All members of the faith are equal, and this includes members of sectarian movements. This is why the use of words like "orthodoxy" borrowed from the Christian tradition make no sense in an Islamic context. Whatever their differences over the Caliphate, Shi'i and Sunni are equal before God.

The umma *embraces the whole worldwide community of Islam, from the wealthy Gulf states to the people shopping in this humble market in Gambia. The notion of a single Islamic community is in some ways similar to the the idea of Christendom invoked in medieval Europe.*

Outward signs proclaim the *umma*. The performance of the stipulated prayers at the stipulated times, the call to prayer itself, the shared fast of Ramadan, the Pilgrimage, the reading of the Qur'an and saying of prayers in the Arabic language, family structure, legal system, dietary laws, position of women and the custom of veiling, the use of the *hijri* calendar, urban organization and institutions – all these and many more serve to create an unmistakable Muslim identity. The flexibility and pragmatism of Islamic law has allowed great diversity in local practice, clear to anyone who has traveled in Muslim lands.

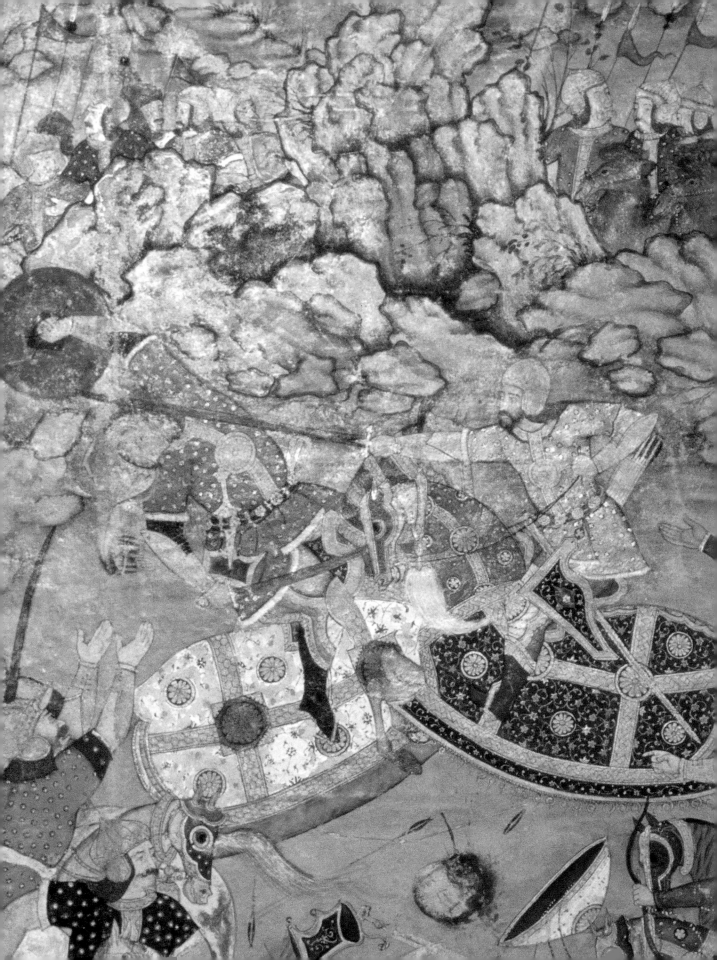

HISTORY OF THE ISLAMIC WORLD

The irruption of Arab armies from the Arabian Peninsula in the 7th century, bearing the message of Islam, remains one of the world's great epics. Within a few decades they had reached the Atlantic coast, entered Europe, and stood on the borders of China and India. The enduring legacy of this achievement is a tribute to the resilience of the Islamic social order.

Much of the history of Islam *is marked by fierce fighting for control of West and Central Asia. In this miniature painting (c.1591) the Mughal emperor Babur does battle with his cousin Tamal.*

THE RIGHTLY-GUIDED CALIPHS [al-Khulafa al-Rashidun]

Abu Bakr 632–634

'Umar 634–644

'Uthman 644–656

'Ali 656–661

Pre-Islamic Arabia

Sasanid Empire

Byzantine Empire

QURAYSH Arabian tribe

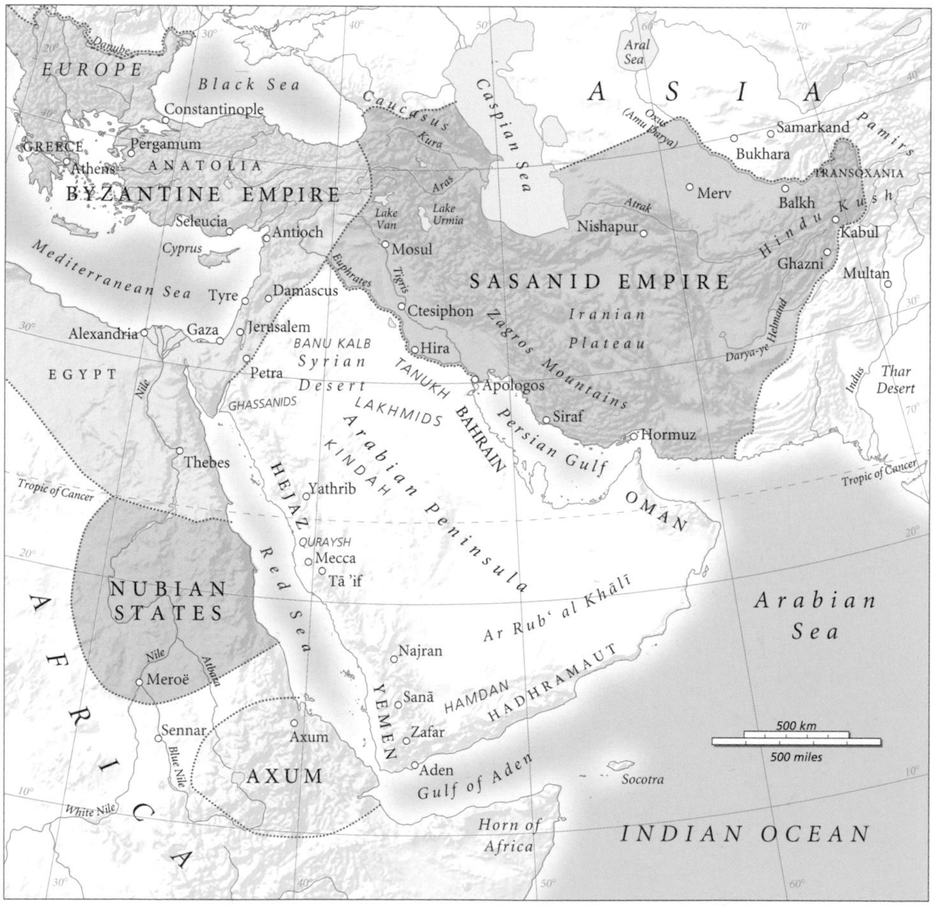

THE CALIPHATE

WHEN MUHAMMAD DIED on June 8, 632, he had no living male heir. There were four candidates to succeed him as leader of the Muslim community: Abu Bakr, 'Umar, 'Uthman, and 'Ali. As things turned out, each served in turn as successor (khalifa) to Muhammad. They are known as "The Rightly-Guided Caliphs" because they all had heard the revelation from the Prophet himself and been guided by his example.

Although 'Ali was most closely related to the Prophet, it was Abu Bakr who was elected Muhammad's successor. By a mixture of force and diplomacy, he brought the tribes of Arabia, who had renounced their allegiance to the Muslims on the death of the Prophet, back to obedience and sought a common enterprise to unite them. Following the Prophet's last wishes, he sent them, under Meccan leaders, against the Byzantine and Persian empires. Abu Bakr received news of the first victory shortly before his death in 634.

Under his successor, 'Umar, the Byzantine army was annihilated at Yarmuk in Palestine. In 638, 'Umar entered Jersusalem, alone and simply clad, astonishing a populace used to the pomp of the Byzantine emperors. He was welcomed by the Patriarch Sophronios and granted lenient terms to the city, guaranteeing that the Christian churches would not be destroyed or taken over by the Muslims. No effort was made to convert Christians and Jews, who enjoyed freedom of worship in protected communities governed by their own laws. While in Palestine, 'Umar set up the administration of the empire, organizing taxation of the conquered lands and pensions for Muslim warriors and their families. He retained local institutions, and for some years Greek in former Byzantine provinces and Pahlavi in former Sasanid provinces continued to be the languages of administration.

In the spring of 637, the Muslims won a major victory over the Sasanids at al-Qadisiyya, near Ctesiphon. In 642, another victory at Nehavend added all of Persia to the Muslim empire. The same year saw the fall of Alexandria, key to naval control of the Mediterranean. The Muslim armies that conquered Egypt were assisted by the Coptic population, who like the Nestorians and Monophysites of Iraq and Syria had suffered under Byzantine persecution.

'Umar was assassinated by a Persian Christian slave in 644. An advisory council chose 'Uthman to succeed him. Under 'Uthman, what is now Libya was added to the growing empire. Armenia was subjugated and Mu'awiya, whom 'Umar had appointed governor of Syria, built a navy and fought a number of naval battles against the Byzantines, at one point besieging Constantinople. 'Uthman's most enduring action was the establishment of the authorized text of the Qur'an. During his caliphate, 'Uthman was accused of showing undue favoritism to his own clan, that of Umayya. Disaffected troops from Egypt went to Medina to present their grievances, but negotiations broke down and 'Uthman was killed. The murder of 'Uthman and the choice of 'Ali to succeed him opened a rift among Muslims that persists to this day.

The Umayya clan, which included Mu'awiya, governor of Syria, refused recognition to 'Ali on the grounds his supporters had been implicated in the murder of 'Uthman. The conflict came to a head in 657 at Siffin, near the Euphrates. 'Ali and his partisans confronted Mu'awiya and his powerful army. Unwilling to spill the blood of fellow Muslims, 'Ali agreed to submit their differences to arbitration. The arbitrators decided against 'Ali, choosing Mu'awiya as caliph.

A 6th-century mosaic map of *Jerusalem, found at Madaba in Jordan, shows the city with its many Christian pilgrimage sites, as it would have appeared when 'Umar entered it in 638. The magnificent colonnaded main street was built by the Roman emperor Hadrian in the 2nd century CE.*

The Byzantines fought *many wars against the forces of Islam, Their secret weapon was Greek fire, the main ingredient of which was naphtha. It was propelled against enemy shipping from the nozzle of a plunger-driven device.*

THE TWELVE SHI'I IMAMS

'Ali 656-661

Hasan 661-669

Husayn 669-680

Zayn al-'Abidin . . .680-712

Muhammad
al-Baqir 712-c.735

Ja'far al-Sadiq 735-765

Musa al-Kazim 765-799

'Ali al-Rida 799-818

Muhammad
al-Taqi al-Jawad . . .818-835

'Ali al-Hadi 835-868

Hasan al-'Askari . . .868-873

Muhammad al-Mahdi
*(The 12th imam vanished.
The shi'a, who call him the
"Awaited One," believe he will
return at the end of time as the
Mahdi to bring peace and
justice to the world.)*

**The Church of St. John the
Baptist** *in Damascus was
transformed into a mosque in
Umayyad times. It is decorated
with magnificent mosaics sent by
the Byzantine emperor to
Damascus for the purpose.*

The supporters of 'Ali believed that he should have been the immediate successor of Muhammad, and that he had three times been unfairly passed over. The schism of Islam into sunni and shi'i dates from Siffin. The sunni, or *ahl al-sunna wa l-jam'a*, "the people of custom and community" believe the caliph is Muhammad's successor only as ruler of the community, and that the caliphate is elective within the Prophet's tribe, Quraysh. The shi'i, (from *shi'at 'Ali* or partisans of 'Ali), believe the caliphate, which they call the imamate, is non-elective, and that the head of the Muslim community must be a descendant of Muhammad. They hold that the imam inherits the Prophet's spiritual knowledge and the ability to interpret Divine Law in its light.

Another faction was born out of the negotiations at Siffin. This was made up of those who refused recognition to either party. They considered the caliphate to be open to any observant Muslim of sound mind and body. They are called Kharijites *(khawarij)*, meaning "those who withdrew". They formed a radical egalitarian sect that for years caused havoc throughout the Muslim world.

In 661, 'Ali was assassinated by a Kharijite in Kufa. The Kufans proclaimed his son Hasan caliph, but Hasan relinquished his rights to Mu'awiya, who had already been accepted by most Muslims as the legitimate caliph.

THE UMAYYADS

Mu'awiya moved the capital from Medina to Damascus, from where he had governed Syria. The abandonment of the apostolic simplicity of the oasis of Medina, city of the Prophet, for a thriving, cosmopolitan city, filled with magnificent classical buildings and with a large Christian population, symbolized a fundamental change in the development of Islam.

Later Muslim historians accused the Umayyad caliphs, with one exception, of being kings, rather than caliphs. The word king, *malik*, had a pejorative sense in Arabic, for the Arabs had no tradition of kingship. Mu'awiya and his successors lived in palaces and built magnificent hunting lodges in the Syrian steppe. The ruling Arab military elite was proud of its Arab origins, cultivating the poetry and song of pre-Islamic times, at the same time adopting the luxuries of the civilizations they had conquered.

Mu'awiya maintained the unity of the empire, but could not eradicate the simmering discontent of the shi'i or the threat of the growing numbers of non-Arab voluntary converts to Islam *(mawali)* who felt excluded from the privileges enjoyed by Muslims of Arab descent. Before his death in 680, Mu'awiya obtained with great difficulty recognition from his advisory council of his son Yazid as his heir.

The shi'i refused to recognize Yazid as caliph, and urged 'Ali's son Husayn, grandson of the Prophet, to claim the caliphate by force. Yazid's army met him and his small band of followers at Karbala, not far from Kufa. Husayn lost his 10-year old nephew, two sons, and six brothers, before he too, the last to die, met his fate. In 683, an Umayyad army invaded Arabia to crush another claimant to the caliphate. They sacked Medina and attacked Mecca. During the battle the Ka'ba caught fire, and Mecca was only saved from destruction by the death of Yazid.

In 685, the caliph 'Abd al-Malik came to power. He ruled for 20 years, creating an administrative structure, based on Byzantine models, that lasted, with modifications, throughout classical Islamic civilization. He made Arabic the language of administration, set up a postal system and issued the first Islamic coinage. He had the irrigation canals in the Tigris-Euphrates valley restored and introduced the Indian water buffalo to the Iraqi marshes. During his reign, Muslim armies reached the borders of Chinese territory, while in the west, the conqueror 'Uqba ibn Nafi' founded Kairouan and rode all the way to the Atlantic.

DOME OF THE ROCK

The earliest extant work of Islamic architecture, the Dome of the Rock was built in 688–91 CE by the Umayyad caliph 'Abd al-Malik. It is probable that he intended this glorious building to be a visible confirmation of the success of Islam, superimposed as it was on the site of what was believed to have been the Temple of Solomon. Although there are classical precedents for many of its features, it displays a style and confidence which is entirely Islamic.

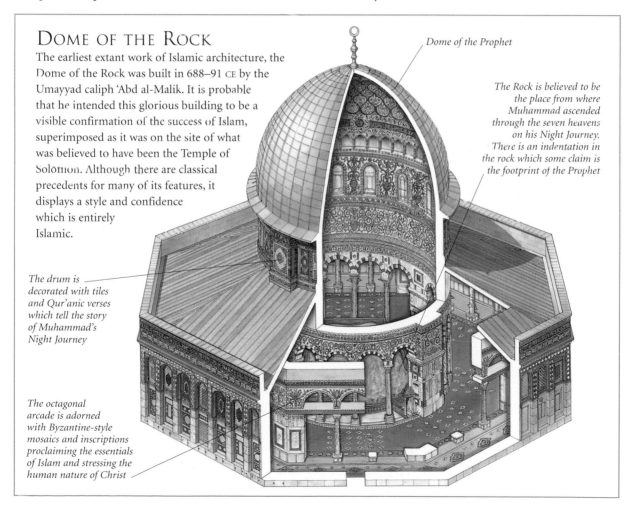

Dome of the Prophet

The Rock is believed to be the place from where Muhammad ascended through the seven heavens on his Night Journey. There is an indentation in the rock which some claim is the footprint of the Prophet

The drum is decorated with tiles and Qur'anic verses which tell the story of Muhammad's Night Journey

The octagonal arcade is adorned with Byzantine-style mosaics and inscriptions proclaiming the essentials of Islam and stressing the human nature of Christ

THE UMAYYAD DYNASTY

Mu'awiya 661-680

Yazid I 680-683

Mu'awiya II 683

Marwan I 684-685

'Abd al-Malik 685-705

al-Walid 705-715

Sulayman 715-717

'Umar II 717-720

Yazid II 720-724

Hisham 724-743

al-Walid II 743-744

Yazid III 744

Ibrahim 744

Marwan II 744-750

THE SECOND WAVE OF CONQUESTS

The pacification of the central lands of the caliphate meant attention could be turned once more to conquest. The armies that had so recently been engaged in fighting each other, were now unleashed on North Africa, Spain, and the lands beyond the Oxus. In these regions, the Arabs were entering unfamiliar territory, far from the heartlands of the empire, and far from their supply bases.

In 710, a small group crossed the Strait of Gibraltar on reconnaissance. Meeting no opposition, the decision was taken to invade Visigothic Spain the following year. Led by a Berber convert to Islam named Tariq, a larger army crossed over in 711 and crushed the Visigothic army in a single battle. He was followed by his commander-in-chief, Musa ibn Nusayr, and by 713 all Spain, with the exception of Asturias in the far north, was in Muslim hands.

While the conquest of Spain was underway, another army, far to the east, crossed the Jaxartes River, having first subdued all of Transoxania, and fought all the way to Kashgar, on the borders of China. The year was 712. Simultaneously, yet another army reached the Indus and took Multan in the Punjab. It is said that the caliph received news of all three conquests on the same day. The territory of the empire had been doubled, and stretched from the Atlantic to the Indus.

In 718, Muslim forces crossed the Pyrenees and took Narbonne. In 725, they sacked Lyon and Vienne. A large force of Arabs and Berbers crossed the Pyrenees once more in 732, intent on sacking the shrine of St. Martin at Tours, one of the richest religious foundations in Gaul. They were finally turned back outside Poitiers by Charles Martel.

The conquest of Byzantine lands had not been completed. In 717, the year before the Muslims crossed the Pyrenees into Gaul, the Umayyad caliph Sulayman mounted a combined land and sea assault on Constantinople which ended in failure, due to the superb fortifications of the city, a bitter winter, and the use of Greek fire by the defenders.

Umar II succeeded Sulayman on the latter's death in 717. He is the one Umayyad caliph of whom later chroniclers approved. He made a concerted effort to resolve the most serious social conflict in the empire, the position of the non-Arab converts to

This coin issued *by 'Abd al-Malik shows the caliph imitating Byzantine usage. Later in his reign, 'Abd al-Malik removed images from coins, retaining only Arabic legends.*

British Isles

FRANKISH EMPIRE

732: Frankish army under Charles Martel halts Arab advance

✕ Poitiers 732

ATLANTIC OCEAN

KINGDOM OF ASTURIAS Toulouse ✕ 721

Oviedo ○ ✕ Covadonga 718 Narbonne 720

Pyrenees 710

KINGDOM OF THE VISIGOTHS Saragossa 714

Lisbon ○ 711 Mérida ○ Toledo 712

Iberian Peninsula Cordova 711

Rio Barbate ✕ 711 Tahert

711: Berber general Tariq leads troops across Strait of Gibraltar (Jabal al-Tariq, the Rock of Tariq) Strait of Gibraltar

Rabat ○ Fez ○ *Maghreb*

Atlas Mountains

Islam. Despite the fact that they had accepted Islam, they were still forced to pay the taxes levied on non-Muslims. Umar rectified this situation, and ordered that they should be treated as equals of the Arabs. Those who had fought against the pagan Turks in Transoxania were granted state pensions. Unfortunately, these reforms, and others, came too late to stop the tide of discontent that was sweeping the empire. Umar II died after a reign of only three years, before his thoughtful and wide-ranging reforms could take effect.

In the last years of the Umayyads, a secret organization rallied to its cause various groups hostile to the ruling dynasty, among them many shi'i and non-Arab Muslims. In 747, the black flags of rebellion were unfurled in Khurasan in the name of a descendant of the Prophet's uncle, 'Abbas. The army of the last Umayyad caliph was defeated and all members and clients of the dynasty hunted down and exterminated. Only one young prince survived the debacle, 'Abd al-Rahman, who escaped to Spain, where he founded the brilliant dynasty of the Spanish Umayyads.

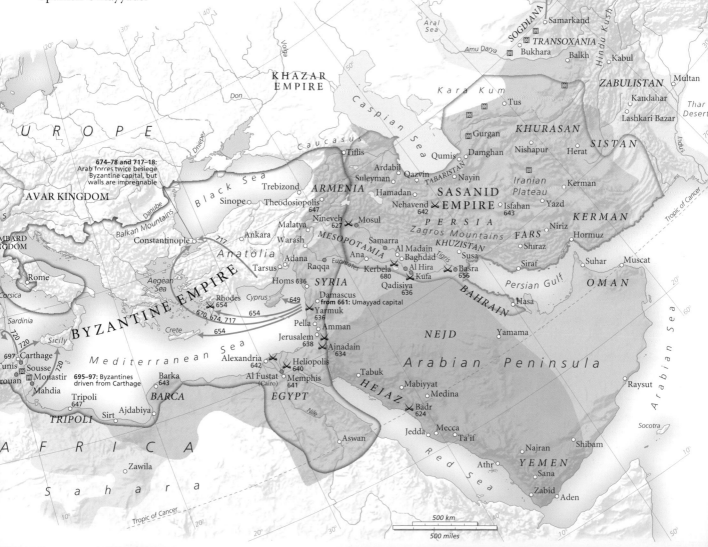

The growth of the Islamic world

- Muslim lands by 634
- Muslim lands by 656
- Muslim lands by 756
- → Muslim raid, with date
- • new city founded by Muslims
- ▣ Muslim fortress
- ✕ Muslim victory, with date
- ✕ Muslim defeat, with date
- 649 date of Muslim conquest
- Byzantine Empire c.610
- Sasanid Empire c.610
- Frankish Empire c.610

THE 'ABBASIDS

The 'Abbasids transformed the Arab empire of the Umayyads into a multiethnic Muslim empire. The government was no longer a *mulk*, a temporal kingdom, but a theocracy ruled by the caliph, who was now styled as "The Shadow of God Upon Earth." The cohesive factor in the empire was Islam, and all believers were equal. The *mawali* had finally come into their own, their original ethnic and cultural identity submerged in the *umma*. The power of the Arab aristocracy was over in the heartlands, although many of the older ways continued at the neo-Umayyad court in Cordoba. 'Abbasid society was dominated by Muslims of non-Arab origins, largely Persian.

BAGHDAD

To symbolize the change, the center of power was shifted from Syria to Iraq, and a new capital built, Baghdad. The name of the city, significantly, is Persian, and means "Gift of God." It comes from the name of a small village that stood on the site of the new city. Baghdad is on the banks of the Tigris, not far from the Sasanid capital of Ctesiphon. Al-Mansur, the caliph who founded the city, chose the site because of the good air and the fact that the Tigris was a major commercial artery, linking the city to the Gulf and ultimately to the sea route to China, already opened by Muslim traders.

Baghdad was founded in 763, with due attention paid to the conjunction of the planets so the first stone could be laid on a propitious day. The core of the city, housing the caliph, his administrators, slaves, and personal guard, was laid out according to cosmological principles, probably of Persian origin. It was circular, with concentric circuits of walls marking off the different quarters. In the center was the caliph's palace. The walls were pierced by four gates, orientated to the four points of the compass. Beyond the outer wall of the Round City, suburbs grew up, and Baghdad shortly became one of the largest cities in the world, with a population larger than that of Constantinople. It was conventionally referred to as Madinat al-Salam, "The City of Peace".

The Umayyad caliphs had ruled like exalted Arab tribal leaders, and even the most autocratic of them had consulted councils of tribal and military leaders before taking important decisions. The 'Abbasid caliphs radically broke with Arab tradition in this and all other ways. The caliphs of Baghdad were absolute monarchs, holding the power of life and death over their subjects. Like the Sasanid Shahs, they were remote from the people, appearing only on ceremonial occasions, to lead the Friday prayers and the army on major campaigns.

The 'Abbasid caliphs all assumed throne names when they came to power, and these names all proclaim their dependence upon God, and at the same time divine support for their authority. They were descended from al-'Abbas, the

Prophet's uncle, and were therefore of the same clan, Hashim.

THE WAZIR

The *wazir*, anglicized as vizier, was the head of the bureaucracy, the *diwan*. The institution itself is almost certainly of Iranian origin, as is the word. The principal function of the vizier was to raise money and oversee the workings of an ever-expanding and complex bureaucracy. In early 'Abbasid times, the vizier was almost always a non-Arab. The famous Barmakid family, which provided a succession of viziers to the early caliphs, originated in Balkh, where they had been custodians of the famous Buddhist temple of Nawbahar.

This bureaucracy was staffed by clerks, *kuttab*, largely of Persian origin, and these formed an elite literate class that played an important cultural role, both producing and consuming the literary works that accompanied the 'Abbasid cultural renaissance. It was in early 'Abbasid times, coinciding with the foundation of the dynasty, that the Chinese technique of making rag paper was introduced first to Samarkand, then to Baghdad. The presence of a cheap, readily available writing material not only contributed to the growth of the bureaucracy itself, but to general literacy among the public. Baghdad and other metropolitan areas had well-stocked libraries, bookshops, popular authors, and avid readers.

The army was formed largely of Persians and other non-Arabs, later predominantly of Turks. The volunteer tribal armies of the conquests were a thing of the past, and the commander-in-chief of the army, the *amir al-'umara*, became a powerful and often dangerous figure in the government.

The administration was modeled on that of Sasanid Persia, with many elements taken over from the Umayyads. The postal system, similar to the pony express of the American West, was used for official communications. Urgent messages were sent via pigeon post. The postal system doubled as an intelligence service, for it linked all the provinces of the enormous empire to Baghdad and its agents regularly reported to central government on everything from the activities of dissident sects to the state of the harvest.

The noria (Arabic na'ura), a device for lifting water from one level to another, is only one of the technologies that revolutionized agriculture in Islamic times.

The inner city of Baghdad c.800

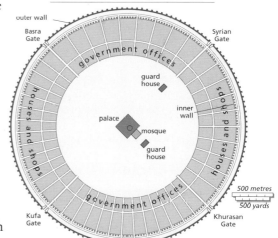

outer wall
Basra Gate
Syrian Gate
government offices
guard house
houses and shops
shops
inner wall
palace
mosque
guard house
houses and shops
government offices
Kufa Gate
Khurasan Gate
500 metres
500 yards

Founded in 763, *the new 'Abbasid capital of Baghdad quickly became the commercial and cultural hub of the empire. The city was planned in every detail, with the caliph's palace and government offices at the center.*

This 10th-century plate *from Nishapur, decorated with elegant Kufic script, shows the sophistication of 'Abbasid ceramics. Baghdad and other major cities had special quarters devoted to the various crafts: leatherworkers, metalworkers, bookbinders, jewelers, weavers, dyers, druggists, and papermakers.*

TRADE AND PROSPERITY

Baghdad became the largest and wealthiest city in the world, rivaled only by Constantinople and far-off Xian, capital of T'ang China. The caliphate was ideally situated for the creation of a global trading network. Islamic shipping dominated both the Mediterranean and the Indian Ocean and colonies of Muslim merchants were established in the ports of western India, East Africa, Indonesia, and China. Gradually Islam spread far beyond the political confines of the 'Abbasid empire.

The founding of the caravan city of Sijilmassa in southern Morocco in 757 opened up a trans-Saharan trade in the gold, ivory, slaves, and ostrich feathers of sub-Saharan Africa, and this gold, together with silver and gold from mines in Central Asia, fueled the economy of the empire.

Trade was encouraged by a stable bimetallic currency, the silver dirham and the gold dinar. These two coins, with a fixed weight that scarcely varied, became the standard for later European coinages and have been found in great quantities in archaeological excavations as far north as Scandinavia.

New ideas, technologies, plants, and crafts flowed along the complex of land and sea routes which led to Baghdad and the provincial capitals. The expansion of commercial activity led to the development of sophisticated banking and exchange techniques. A letter of credit issued in Baghdad could be honored in Sijilmassa or Samarkand. Trade stimulated crafts and craftsmen organized mutual-benefit societies which offered social services, caring for orphans, endowing schools, and lodging travelers. Hospices for lodging travelers were built not only in cities, but along major trade routes.

During the reigns of Harun al-Rashid and his son al-Ma'mun Greek scientific and philosophical texts were systematically translated into Arabic, stimulating the development of Islamic science.

THE CALIPHATE IN DECLINE

Political decline, however, was already apparent even during the reign of Harun al-Rashid. Two years after he came to the throne in 786, an independent shi'i regime was established in far-off Morocco. The founder, Idris, was a great-grandson of Hasan. In 800, Harun al-Rashid granted another western dynasty, the Aghlabids in what is now Tunisia, virtual autonomy against an annual cash payment. This meant that the caliphate had virtually no authority west of Egypt, and in 868 a Turkish warlord, Ahmad ibn Tulun, seized that wealthy province.

Turkish slaves captured in Central Asia filled the ranks of the 'Abbasid army. Superb fighting men, they were indispensable but hard to control. As time went on they made and unmade caliphs at their will. They were so unruly in Baghdad that the caliph al-Mu'tasim built the city of Samarra to escape their violence.

OPPOSITE

The Mosque of Muhammad Ali, *the 19th-century ruler of Egypt, dominates the skyline of Cairo. The city was founded by the Fatimids in 963. With the eclipse of Baghdad, Cairo became the leading cultural, commercial, and religious center of the Arabic-speaking world.*

THE BREAK-UP OF THE 'ABBASID DYNASTY

In the 10th century, because of a combination of poor administration, inability to maintain the irrigation system upon which the agricultural prosperity of Iraq was based, growing salinity of the soil, and above all the proliferation of independent dynasties, the revenues of the caliphate were much reduced.

In 945, an Iranian shi'i dynasty, the Buyids, occupied Baghdad. They were a Persian-speaking military elite, whose leaders only learned Arabic subsequent to their occupation of Baghdad. They took all economic and political power to themselves, even issuing coins in their own names with shi'i slogans.

Independent states proliferated: Tahirids, Saffarids, Samanids, Buwahids, Ziyarids, and Ghaznavids in the east; Hamdanids in Syria; Tulunids followed by Fatimids in Egypt. Although this trend may have been regrettable from the point of view of Baghdad, it was beneficial for the spread of Islamic culture. Each of these dynasties emulated the court at Baghdad, attracting scholars, poets, musicians, architects, and craftsmen. Under the Samanids, in Khurasan, Persian, written in the Arabic alphabet, reached the level of a literary language.

The idea of the caliphate, a united Islamic world, survived until 1926 when it was formally abolished. However, already in the second half of the 9th century political power was starting to pass from the caliph in Baghdad to dynasties of local rulers.

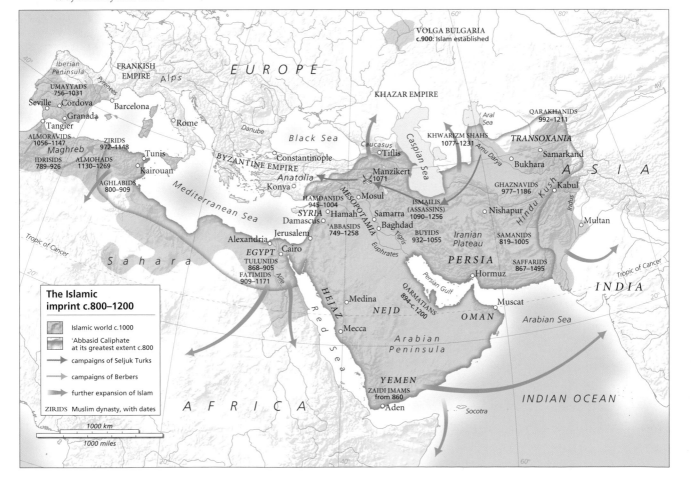

The Islamic imprint c.800–1200

- Islamic world c.1000
- 'Abbasid Caliphate at its greatest extent c.800
- → campaigns of Seljuk Turks
- → campaigns of Berbers
- → further expansion of Islam
- ZIRIDS Muslim dynasty, with dates

1000 km
1000 miles

THE FATIMIDS

The sixth imam of the Shi'a, Ja'far al-Sadiq died in 765. His death led to a division in the Shi'a community that has lasted till the present. Ja'far had two sons, Isma'il and Musa. Isma'il was the elder, but his father disinherited him and appointed Musa heir to the imamate. The majority of shi'i recognized Musa, but a minority thought Isma'il was the legitimate imam. They are therefore known as Isma'ilis – one of the earliest, strangest and most successful of the dynasties that broke away from 'Abbasid control. They are also sometimes known as "Seveners," because Isma'il was the seventh in the line of succession that went back to 'Ali and Fatima, daughter of the Prophet, who gave her name to the Fatimid dynasty they founded.

The movement succeeded in establishing itself in Yemen, and from there sent agents to North Africa, where they mobilized a powerful army among the Berbers and in 903, in Kairouan, installed 'Ubayd Allah al-Mahdi as the first Fatimid caliph. The assumption of the title of succession to the Prophet was a direct challenge to the 'Abbasid caliphate.

'Ubayd Allah founded the port of Mahdiya, on the Tunisian coast, from where he and his followers almost succeeded in conquering the Islamic world. They took over much of North Africa and Sicily, then turned their eyes to Egypt. In 969, Jawhar, the general of al-Mu'izz, the fourth Fatimid caliph, conquered Egypt with an army of 100,000 men and began the construction of a splendid new capital: Cairo (al-Qahira).

In 868, Ahmad Ibn Tulun, the governor of Egypt, declared his independence from the 'Abbasids. The mosque he built at Fustat, now part of Cairo, is one of the glories of early Islamic architecture. When the Fatimids conquered Egypt in 969, they sited their capital al-Qahira (Cairo) nearby.

Under the Fatimid caliph al-Aziz (975–996) and his exceptionally competent wazir, Ya'qub ibn Killis, Egypt became the richest and most stable land in the Islamic world. The Fatimid navy dominated the Mediterranean, and Alexandria became once more the great market of the East. They also opened up the Red Sea route to India, diverting lucrative trade from the Gulf and Baghdad.

Al-Aziz was succeeded by his son, al-Hakim, whose cruel and erratic reign was marked by savage persecution of Jews and Christians and stern ordinances forbidding women to leave their homes. Some radical groups considered him semi-divine, and one of these has survived, the Druze of Lebanon and Syria.

The high point of Fatimid power was reached with the caliphate of al-Mustansir (1036–94). In 1057, a Fatimid general even briefly took Baghdad. Toward the end of al-Mustansir's long reign, Fatimid power decreased and overtaxation of the Egyptian population led to serious upheavals.

This ivory pyx depicting the pleasures of courtly life is from 10th-century Córdoba and is inscribed with the name of a son of the caliph 'Abd al-Rahman III.

THE UMAYYADS IN SPAIN

The only survivor of the 'Abbasid massacre of the Umayyads, 'Abd al-Rahman, called "The Immigrant," reached Spain, and in 756 was accepted by the various Arab factions as their ruler. Under the Umayyads al-Andalus, as the Arabs called the Iberian Peninsula, became the most heavily urbanized and richest country in Europe. They encouraged trade and agriculture, introducing sophisticated irrigation systems and new cash crops such as sugar, cotton, saffron, and indigo.

In 929, 'Abd al-Rahman III took the title of caliph, an act of supreme defiance towards his 'Abbasid enemies. During his reign, his capital Córdoba became the richest and most sophisticated city in Europe, with a population of perhaps 500,000, at a time when Paris numbered some 38,000. Córdoba was famous for its mosques, palaces, and libraries, one reportedly housing 500,000 manuscripts.

In the late 10th century, the brilliant and devious chamberlain *(hajib)*, al-Mansur, led biannual campaigns against small Christian kingdoms in the north of the peninsula. In 997, he sacked and destroyed the shrine of Santiago de Compostela, the principal pilgrimage site in Europe, "the Mecca of the Christians." Al-Mansur died in 1002, and with him the military glory of the Umayyads. In 1018, Córdoba was sacked and burned by disaffected Berber troops. The dynasty effectively came to an end in 1031, when a group of prominent Córdobans simply abolished the Umayyad caliphate. Al-Andalus fragmented into numerous small kingdoms, each based on a provincial capital, some Arab, some Berber, and at least one Slavic – for numerous Slavs had served in the caliphal armies.

This scene of chess players is from a manuscript of the 13th-century Cantigas de Maria, a collection of songs in praise of the Virgin by Alfonso X, who set them to popular Arab melodies.

THE RECONQUISTA

By the 11th century, however, a small pocket of Christian resistance had begun to grow. Alfonso VI took Toledo, the former capital of the Visigoths, in 1085. It was the beginning of the period the Christians called the Reconquest *(Reconquista)*, and it underlined a serious problem that marred this refined and graceful era: the inability of the numerous rulers of Islamic Spain to maintain their unity. This so weakened them that when the various Christian kingdoms began to pose a serious threat, they were forced to ask the Almoravids, a North African dynasty, to come to their aid.

The Almoravids *(al-murabitun)* were Sanhaja Berbers of the Sahara. Like their modern descendents the Touareg, the men of the Sanhaja veiled their faces, which contributed to the fear they instilled in their enemies. They were a puritan, refoming movement dedicated to jihad. In the years before they crossed into

Spain they had conquered large areas in Ghana. They then moved north and swept through Morocco. In 1086, led by the fearsome Yusuf ibn Tashufin, founder of Marrakesh, they crossed the Strait of Gibraltar and drove back the Christian armies. They then killed or exiled the Muslim rulers who had summoned their aid and established themselves in the splendid cities of al-Andalus, where the luxurious life quickly tempered their puritan zeal. The dynasty came to an end in 1147 at the hands of another Berber reforming dynasty, the Almohads.

*The **Christian victory** over the Almohads at Las Navas de Tolosa in 1212 marked the beginning of the end for the Muslim kingdoms of the Iberian Peninsula.*

This movement was founded by Ibn Tumart, a Masmuda Berber who proclaimed himself the Mahdi, "The Guided One." The Almohads (*al-muwahhidun*, "those who proclaim the unity of God") strove to restore Islam to its original purity. Ibn Tumart passed the torch of leadership to his companion and friend, 'Abd al-Mu'min, who took the title of caliph and declared jihad against all who opposed him. In 1146, he annihilated the Almoravid army at Tlemcen and the following year took Marrakesh, the Almoravid capital. His empire soon stretched from Spain to the Egyptian border.

In 1170, the Almohads chose Seville as their capital, and it is here that they produced two of their finest works of architecture, the Torre del Oro and the Giralda, transformed from minaret to bell tower when the city was reconquered by the Christians in 1248. Like the Almoravids, the Almohads did not last long. Their army was virtually annihilated in the battle of Las Navas de Tolosa in 1212 by a coalition of Christian kings. The surviving Almohads fled Spain, and the *Reconquista* moved relentlessly forward.

GRANADA

In the last two centuries of their rule, the Muslims of Spain created the kingdom for which they are most famous: Granada. It seems as if they suddenly realized that they were a people without a country, and set about building a memorial: the Alhambra. This magnificent palace was begun in 1238 by Muhammad ibn al-Ahmar who, to buy

*The **Alhambra**, built during the 13th and 14th centuries, is one of the most beautiful architectural complexes in the world, a fitting monument to the Muslim presence in Spain.*

safety for his people when King Ferdinand of Aragon laid siege to Granada, offered to become the king's vassal in return for peace.

His loyalty to Ferdinand eventually purchased another two and a half centuries for the kingdom of Granada. The last Muslim stronghold in Spain finally fell in 1492, the same year the New World was discovered by Columbus.

THE SELJUK TURKS

The arrival of the Seljuks in Islamic lands in the 11th century saved the caliphate of Baghdad from succumbing to the Isma'ilis. The Seljuks were Oghuz Turks, whose original homeland lay in the vast steppe north of the Caspian and the Aral Sea. The Muslims had encountered the adept Turkish-speaking horsemen and archers of this region when they first crossed the Oxus in the 7th century. Many were recruited to the caliphal armies and some Turkish commanders were powerful enough to establish their own dynasties. The powerful Ghaznavid dynasty, whose most famous ruler was Mahmud of Ghazna, conqueror of northern India, was founded by a military commander who had served the Samanids.

The Ince Minare Madrasa in Konya, built in 1260, is so called for its "slender minaret", partly destroyed by lightning in 1900. Konya was the Anatolian capital of the Seljuk Turks. The facade of the madrasa is remarkable for its almost baroque decoration of intertwined stone ribbons bearing calligraphic inscriptions.

Around 960, a group of Oghuz clans abandoned their shamanist beliefs and embraced sunni Islam. Their ancestral, semi-legendary leader was named Seljuk (Saljuq). After his death, power over the clans passed to his son Arslan, who began to push into the territory of Mahmud of Ghazna. Arslan's nephews, Tughril and Chaghri Beg crossed the Oxus and seized the key garrison town of Merv. In 1040, they defeated the armies of Mahmud of Ghazna. This victory marked the beginning of Seljuk power.

Between 1040 and 1060, the Seljuks fought bitterly against the Buyids, winning and then losing Baghdad several times. The Buyids went so far as to ally themselves with the Fatimids, their former enemy, but to no avail. The power of the sunni caliphate was restored and the staunch support of Tughril Beg and his troops put an end to Fatimid dreams of universal dominion.

In 1058 the caliph crowned Tughril Beg "King of the East and West", delegating the defence of the empire to him. His title was Sultan, a word that simply means "power". This power, and with it the responsibility of defending the Muslim community both from attack from without and schism from within, remained in the hands of Turkish-speaking peoples until the abolition of the caliphate in 1926.

The enemy without was the Byzantine empire, which had taken advantage of the weakness of Buyid rule to regain important territory in Anatolia, Armenia and Syria. The Byzantines were catastrophically deafeated at the battle of Manzikert in 1071, and the emperor taken prisoner. The Byzantine defeat changed the demography of Anatolia forever. It ceased being a land of Greek speech, as Turkoman tribes and other Turkish groups sought new pastures in the wake of the Seljuk conquests, settled and eventually founded local dynasties. The loss of their richest territory was a blow from which Byzantium never recovered.

THE CRUSADES

Arab historians at the time considered the Crusades a minor irritant, dwarfed by the demographic, political and social transformation triggered by the coming of the Seljuks and the devastation wrought by the Mongols in the 13th century.

Threatened by Seljuk expansion after the battle of Manzikert, the Byzantines appealed to Pope Urban II for military aid. The Seljuk victory and the Almoravid invasion of Spain that occurred not long afterwards created a Christian reflex: Holy War. In 1095, Pope Urban II declared a "Truce of God", urging Christian leaders to lay aside their quarrels and unite in a crusade to recover the Holy Land.

The difficulty of the enterprise was daunting. The Christian armies, drawn from all over Europe, made up of volunteers, younger sons of noble houses, mercenaries, kings, adventurers and camp followers, had to cross thousands of miles of unfamiliar, hostile country to face an enemy of which they knew almost nothing. Yet these motley armies, driven by a combination of faith, greed and a desire for adventure, succeeded in taking Jerusalem in 1099. By this time, Seljuk power was waning, due to infighting over the succession, their inability to produce a durable political structure, and the invasion of yet another group of steppe nomads, the Kara Khitai, on their eastern frontier.

The crusaders were able to establish principalities along the Levantine coast, based in cities whose names still resound with romance: Aleppo, Antioch, Edessa, Tripoli and Acre. The Muslim response was at first confused and limited. When they did counter-attack, besieging Edessa in 1144 and retaking Aleppo, the Second Crusade was launched. It was a disaster. An attempt to take Damascus was repulsed, and the Emperor Conrad and King Louis VII returned in ignominy to Europe.

One of the leaders to oppose the crusaders was a Turkish commander, Zangi, who retook Edessa in 1144. His son Nur al-Din, famous in Arabic annals as a model of the just ruler, united Syria and Iraq, blocking the advance of the crusaders.

THE CRUSADES

• 1st Crusade (1096–9): Capture of Jerusalem.

• 2nd Crusade (1146–8): Siege of Damascus fails.

• 3rd Crusade (1189–92): Crusaders take Acre, but fail to retake Jerusalem.

• 4th Crusade (1202–4): Crusaders take Constantinople.

• 5th Crusade (1217–21): Attack launched on Egypt.

• Crusades of St. Louis (1248–54 & 1270): On first Louis IX of France is captured while attacking Egypt: on second he dies outside Tunis.

The capture of Jerusalem *by the crusaders in 1099 was a bloody affair, in which the mostly Christian population was put to the sword.*

Saladin was the most brilliant general to oppose the crusaders. His victory at Hattin in 1187 effectively broke crusader power.

The Ayyubids, *the dynasty founded by Saladin continued for some 60 years after his death in 1193, but as was often the case with military dynasties, in fragmented form.*

Nur al-Din had two trusted Kurdish generals, Shirukh and Ayyub. Ayyub was the father of perhaps the most famous Arab ruler of the time, Salah al-Din, "Saladin." When the crusaders, whom the Arab chroniclers always referred to as "Franks," a portmanteau term for all Europeans, decided to wrest Egypt from the hands of the now decadent Fatimid caliphate, Nur al-Din sent Shirukh and Saladin to prevent this. On Shirukh's death in 1169, power passed to his nephew, Saladin, founder of the Ayyubid dynasty. In 1171, Saladin abolished the Fatimid caliphate and restored the name of the 'Abbasid caliph in the public prayers. Sunni Islam was once more the official faith of Egypt.

With Egypt as his base, Saladin took the offensive against the crusaders. In 1187, he invaded Palestine, destroying the crusader army at the battle of Hattin. Jerusalem was occupied, and except for the coastal city of Tyre, the Holy Land was once more in Muslim hands. He eventually ruled not only Egypt, but also Yemen, much of North Africa, Palestine, Syria, and Armenia. He actively encouraged trade, which had declined during the last years of Fatimid rule, allowing Genoese and Venetian merchants to trade freely in Alexandria and other ports. The Red Sea route to India was under his control, and taxes on imports and exports formed an important part of his revenues. Saladin became a byword in medieval Europe for chivalry and bravery, often depicted as the bosom friend of Richard the Lionheart. Indeed much of the chivalric tradition, including heraldry, was brought to Europe by returning crusaders.

THE ASSASSINS

Isma'ili influence did not disappear with the Fatimids, but took a new form. At the death of the Fatimid caliph al-Mustansir, in 1094, another schism occurred, one group following his younger son, who succeeded him, the other his older, who had been put to death. Those who followed the older son, Nizar, formed a new, radical movement dedicated to destabilizing Seljuk rule by a campaign of assassination. These Nizari Isma'ilis, known to the crusaders as "Assassins," conducted a terror campaign, targeting for the most part sunni leaders. Their base was Alamut, in northern Persia, from where they sent agents to assassinate prominent sunni leaders. They twice made attempts on Saladin's life. The sect was led by Rashid al-Din Sinan, "The Old Man of the Mountain."

Saladin and the Ayyubid Sultanate 1169–1193

- maximum extent of Crusader states 1144
- Saladin's advance 1174–84
- other Ayyubid campaigns 1174–90
- routes of Third Crusade 1188–92
- Zangids 1127–1222
- dominions of Saladin 1193
- other Muslim states 1193
- Crusader states 1193
- other Christian states 1193

THE MONGOLS

In the 13th century, the Islamic heartlands faced yet another invasion of steppe nomads, more terrible than any that had gone before. These were the Mongols, led by Genghis Khan. They were a confederation of tribes, some Mongol and some Turkish, united by Genghis Khan in 1206. By 1218, he had succeeded in subduing the steppe peoples and turned west. The Mongols invaded the lands of the Kara Khitai, which brought them to the northern borders of Islamic territory, held by the Khwarizm Shahs. The following year, the Muslim Turkish Shah of Khwarizm massacred a party of 450 merchants on their way back from Mongolia. Genghis Khan considered this an attack on his own authority, and in 1220 led his armies into Khwarizm territory, taking Samarkand and Bukhara, then the two great cities of Merv and Nishapur.

Genghis Khan died in 1227, and two years later his son Ögödei was chosen as Khan of the Golden Horde. A new invasion of Muslim lands was launched, and by 1240 the Mongols had occupied western Iran, the Caucasus, and much of Iraq. Three years later they defeated the Seljuk sultan of Anatolia.

In 1255, another Mongol army led by Hülegü Khan, grandson of Genghis, crossed the Oxus. He had been ordered to conquer Islamic lands as far as Egypt. In 1258 he sacked Baghdad, massacred the inhabitants, and put the last ʿAbbasid caliph, al-Mustaʿsim, and all the members of his family to death. Baghdad was looted, then burned to the ground. The ancient systems of irrigation were destroyed. The devastation was so complete that in many areas agricultural recovery is still incomplete.

In 1260, the Mongols turned toward Palestine and Egypt. Here they encountered the Mamluks, now the ruling dynasty of Egypt. Alerted to the danger facing them by a chain of signal fires stretching from Iraq to Egypt, the Mamluks had time to marshal their forces. They confronted the Mongols in Palestine, at ʿAyn Jalut, "The Well of Goliath" and defeated them – the first time a Mongol army had ever met defeat in the field.

A Mongol dynasty, the Il-Khans, ruled Iran until 1380, when they fell before yet another invasion from the steppes, that of Timur. With time, the Il-Khans embraced Islam and became patrons of art and architecture. The assimilative powers of Islam were as strong as ever.

MONGOL RULERS

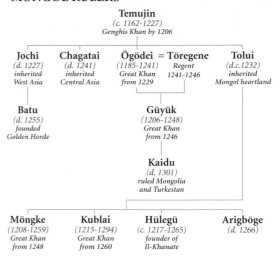

Temujin
(c. 1162-1227)
Genghis Khan by 1206

Jochi	Chagatai	Ögödei = Töregene	Tolui
(d. 1227) *inherited West Asia*	(d. 1241) *inherited Central Asia*	(1185-1241) *Great Khan from 1229* — Regent 1241-1246	(d.c.1232) *inherited Mongol heartland*

Batu
(d. 1255)
founded Golden Horde

Güyük
(1206-1248)
Great Khan from 1246

Kaidu
(d. 1301)
ruled Mongolia and Turkestan

Möngke	Kublai	Hülegü	Arigböge
(1208-1259) *Great Khan from 1248*	(1215-1294) *Great Khan from 1260*	(c. 1217-1265) *founder of Il-Khanate*	(d. 1266)

Genghis Khan and his sons *all led conquering armies westward into Central Asia. This illustration is from a manuscript of Rashid al-Din's detailed history of the Mongol conquests.*

*The **Mamluks** learned much
from Mongol methods. Their
displays of archery from the back
of a galloping horse were
particularly impressive. This
illustration is from a Mamluk
manual of the equestrian arts.*

THE MAMLUKS

The Mamluks who defeated the Mongols at 'Ayn Jalut in 1260 are remarkable for reasons other than just military prowess. Mamluk means "possessed," hence "slave," and the rulers of this dynasty were of non-Muslim origin, purchased as slaves and often bearing the names of their owners. They were converted to Islam, educated, and trained in the martial arts. Most were of Turkish, Mongol, or Circassian origin and retained their native languages.

There were two dynasties of Mamluks, which ruled in succession. The first were the Bahri Mamluks, who ruled from 1260, when Baybars took power after the victory of 'Ayn Jalut, until 1382. The Burji Mamluks who succeeded them were typically Circassian in origin, and ruled until their defeat by the Ottomans in 1517. The words *Bahri* and *Burji* (Nile and Tower) refer to the position in Cairo of the garrisons that housed them.

Baybars was perhaps greatest of the Mamluk rulers. He is one of the few Muslim rulers to be the subject of a romance, the *Sirat Baybars*, which can still, just, be heard recited in the coffee shops of Damascus. His many campaigns against the crusader states led to the final expulsion of the crusaders from Muslim territory under his successors. He repeatedly defeated Mongol assaults, but exchanged embassies with the Khan of the Golden Horde in his native Kipchak territory north of the Black Sea, and he and his successors forged commercial treaties with European monarchs, encouraging trade, which they taxed heavily.

In 1261, Baybars brought an uncle of the last 'Abbasid caliph to Cairo in order to confer legitimacy upon his reign. These shadow caliphs were given a pension and the task of supervising pious endowments *(awqaf)* and their income. Their presence was merely symbolic, and they were without power.

The Mamluks ruled Egypt and Syria, uniting them into a single state and the cities of Cairo, Jerusalem, and Damascus are still studded with fine examples of Mamluk architecture. Baybars' magnificent tomb in Damascus still stands, as do his school and mosque in Cairo. The destruction of Baghdad and devastation of the Tigris-Euphrates valley shifted the focus of the Arabic-speaking world from Iraq to Egypt, with Cairo replacing Baghdad as the main center of commerce and learning.

***Timur invaded India** in 1398,
sacking Delhi in the same year.
Babur, the 16th-century founder
of the Mughal dynasty claimed
descent from Timur, and through
him from Genghis Khan.*

TIMUR

Timur Lang ("Timur the Lame") was born in Transoxiana in 1336, into a Mongol tribe that had embraced Islam. He claimed, falsely, to be a descendant of Genghis Khan, although he did marry a princess related to the great conqueror. He led the last of the great Turko-Mongol nomad invasions – in many ways the most destructive of all. In 1380, having formed a coalition of Tatar, Mongol, and Turkish nomads, he began a series of far-reaching campaigns that led him east as far as Delhi, where he massacred 80,000 people, and as far west as Russia.

Before putting the populations of the cities he conquered to the sword, he carefully set apart all those with special skills, and sent them to Samarkand, which was transformed into one of the loveliest cities in the world. Scholars, musicians, poets, and artisans, brought to Central Asia to beautify Timur's capital, established a courtly style that spread throughout the region, reaching Afghanistan and India.

Timur's motives are hard to assess. He called himself the scourge of God, sent to punish men for their sins. He died in the town of Otrar in 1405, where the Khwarizm Shah had murdered merchants traveling under Mongol protection and unleashed the fury of Genghis Khan. At the time of his death, he was on his way to conquer China. The descendants of Timur were passionate lovers of architecture and science. Ulugh Beg, his grandson, founded a magnificent observatory at Samarkand and prepared a catalog of the coordinates of the stars that was the most accurate yet to appear. The Mughal rulers of India traced their descent from Timur, and through him to Genghis Khan. They venerated their ancestor not only as world conqueror, but as a spiritual master.

Timur destroyed what was left of *Baghdad in 1393, then sacked cities, killing their entire populations throughout Iraq. In 1400, he destroyed Aleppo, and many other of the principal cities of Syria, making huge towers of the heads of the dead, as was his custom. The following year Damascus fell, and the Umayyad mosque, one of the earliest and most beautiful Islamic buildings, was burned. 1402 found Timur in Anatolia, where he defeated and captured the Ottoman ruler Bayezid in the battle of Ankara.*

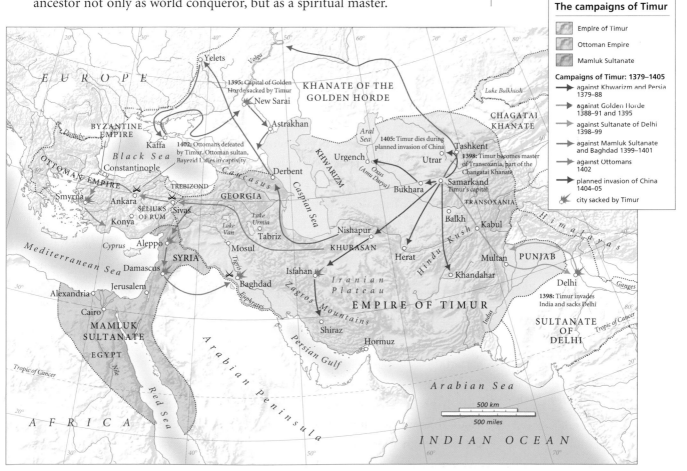

The campaigns of Timur

Empire of Timur
Ottoman Empire
Mamluk Sultanate

Campaigns of Timur: 1379–1405

→ against Khwarizm and Persia 1379–88
→ against Golden Horde 1388–91 and 1395
→ against Sultanate of Delhi 1398–99
→ against Mamluk Sultanate and Baghdad 1399–1401
→ against Ottomans 1402
→ planned invasion of China 1404–05
✕ city sacked by Timur

Mehmed II, *conqueror of Constantinople, painted by Sinan Bey in about 1480.*

(cont. p.70)

THE OTTOMANS

The Mongol invasions damaged the Seljuk empire in Anatolia beyond repair. Turkish nomadic tribes, fleeing before the Mongols, migrated into former Seljuk territories and small Turkish principalities arose in Anatolia, each centered on a former Byzantine city, and each dedicated to war against the Byzantines. The warriors who raided across the Byzantine frontier were called ghazi (raiders), but the word came to be almost an honorific, meaning a man who had risked his life and possessions to expand the Dar al-Islam, the Abode of Islam.

The westernmost of these principalities was founded in the early 14th century by Osman, whose name is commemorated by the empire that grew from this small beginning: Osmanli in Turkish, Ottoman in English.

The Ottomans captured Bursa in 1326 and this became their first capital. It became a major commercial center, especially for the silk trade. Osman's son Orhan invaded Europe in 1354, taking Gallipoli. From this beachhead the Ottoman armies moved on to Adrianople, which became their European base for further expansion. They reinforced their position by transferring Turkish nomads and villagers to the European side of the Bosphorus Strait. By 1372, the Ottomans had reduced the king of Bulgaria to vassalage and controlled the main routes through the Balkans.

It was during this period that the Janissaries, the elite corps of the Ottoman army, were formed. It was made up of Christian prisoners of war who embraced Islam and was under the command of the sultan himself. The name comes from the Turkish *yeni çeri* (new troops). The Janissaries were not allowed to marry, and were bound together through membership of the mystical Bektashi order. Personal mystical belief had been part of Islam since the beginning, but the formation of mystical sufi brotherhoods coincided with the rise of the Turkish ruling dynasties. These orders, devoted to mystical union with the divine through ecstatic practices, organized in strict hierarchies, proliferated and spread rapidly throughout the Islamic world.

One by one the Balkan rulers were reduced to submission, retaining their positions against payment of a yearly tribute. They formed part of the Ottoman empire, and had the duty of defending it against its enemies. Meanwhile, the empire continued to expand in Anatolia at the expense of rival Turkish dynasties.

Under Bayezid, "The Thunderbolt," uprisings in the Balkans forced the elimination of many vassal states, and a centralized empire began to take shape. At the battle of Nicopolis in 1396, Bayezid crushed a coalition of European princes sent to oppose the expanding empire. The flower of European chivalry was left dead on the field, mostly French knights who charged straight into Bayezid's army of 60,000 men. Ten thousand prisoners were decapitated.

The growth of the Ottoman empire

- Ottoman Empire and vassals 1512
- conquests of Selim I, 1512–20
- conquests of Sulayman I, 1520–66
- Ottoman conquest, 1566–1639
- Austrian Habsburg possessions
- Spanish Habsburg possessions
- Venetian Republic and possessions
- –·–·– vassal border
- ——— frontiers 1600
- ••••• frontiers 1913
- ——— Holy Roman Empire
- ⚔ battle, with date
- 1538

The Ottoman empire *expanded most rapidly in the course of the 15th and 16th centuries, notably under Selim I and Sulayman I (the "Magnificent").*

The euphoria of victory was short-lived. A new, more formidable enemy had appeared on the eastern border of Ottoman dominions. Timur invaded Anatolia and defeated the Ottomans at the battle of Ankara in 1402. Bayezid was taken captive and committed suicide shortly afterward. Ottoman lands were reduced to the nucleus from which they had started just a short time before.

Remarkably, Bayezid's son Mehmed and his successor Murad II were able to piece the empire together again. By the time of the death of Murad in 1451, the empire had been restored to its former territorial extent.

In the interval between the suicide of Bayezid and the death of Murad, an event of enormous consequence had occurred. Efficient cannon and arquebuses had been developed in Europe. These revolutionized warfare, military architecture, battle formations, and above all society.

Selim "the Grim" *(1512-1520)*
conquered Mamluk Egypt, greatly
expanding Ottoman territory and
the tax base of the empire. Much
of the new wealth was spent on
public buildings in Istanbul.

THE CAPTURE OF CONSTANTINOPLE

The Ottomans were a military state and quick to borrow and improve new technology. By 1453, when Mehmed the Conqueror camped beneath the walls of Constantinople, artillery had been perfected, and his huge cannons were able to breach the walls that had withstood Muslim sieges since the 7th century.

With the conquest of Constantinople, Mehmed ruled a Muslim empire from the city of Constantine, the first Christian emperor. One of his first acts on entering the city was to transform Hagia Sophia into a mosque. Constantinople was now Istanbul, and would remain the Ottoman capital for the next 469 years.

The capture of Constantinople was a watershed of European history, marking the division between medieval and modern history. Greek scholars fleeing the Ottoman advance contributed to the rebirth of classical learning in Europe, and the rediscovery of Greek philosophical and political texts radically transformed European society and thought. At the same time, blocked to the east by the now vast Ottoman empire, Europe began to look west to the Atlantic.

Mehmed had learned the importance of sea power during the siege, and took steps to create an Ottoman navy, with shipyards at Gallipoli. Naval control of the eastern Mediterranean and the Black Sea was of vital strategic interest.

Mehmed died in 1481, and immediately dissatisfaction that had been hidden while he lived welled up into open revolt. The Janissaries were tired of continual war and wanted to enjoy the fruits of their estates. The coinage had been repeatedly debased and Mehmed had alienated the 'ulama by confiscating property administered as pious endowments. His two sons, Jem and Bayezid, disputed the succession, and fought a bitter war, Jem ending his life an exile in Europe. Bayezid II consolidated the empire formed by his father, but in 1512, old and ill, he was deposed by his son Selim. A new wave of Ottoman conquest began, this time in the east.

In 1500, Shah Isma'il had come to the throne of Iran, the first ruler of the Safavid dynasty. He made Shi'ism the religion of the state, despite the fact that the majority of the population were sunni. Conflict with the Ottomans was inevitable, for they were the upholders of sunni Islam. At the battle of Çaldiran in 1514, Selim defeated the Safavids, but conflict between the two states continued.

Selim then turned his attention to the Mamluks. In 1516, he led his armies against Syria and Egypt. He confronted the Mamluk army outside Aleppo and defeated it, killing the sultan al-Ghawri. He then marched on to Egypt, and in 1517 won another victory outside Cairo. True to their chivalric traditions, the Mamluks refused to use firearms and were cut down by Selim's cannons. Selim received the submission of

the Sharifs of Mecca and Medina, and was now protector of the Holy Cities. Control of the Red Sea and Aden, emporium of the Indian Ocean trade, greatly increased the revenues of the empire. In the 1530s, fleets were dispatched from Basra against the Portuguese. Muslims as far away as Indonesia and India looked on the sultan as their protector. The Ottoman Sultanate was recognized by all but the Safavids of Iran as the successor to the caliphate.

Selim was succeeded by Sulayman "The Magnificent." With the Middle East pacified, he turned once more towards Europe. The victory at Mohács in 1526 opened the way to Hungary, and 1529 found the Ottoman army camped beneath the walls of Vienna. The army retreated three weeks later, but the point was made: the Ottomans had become a world power.

The jade-handled ceremonial dagger of Sulayman the Magnificent. Sulayman was known in the West as "The Magnificent", but to the Ottomans he was Kanuni, "The Law Giver."

The first major Ottoman defeat at Christian hands was at sea, the naval battle of Lepanto in 1571. The Ottoman fleet was demolished, but it was rebuilt within a year, to the consternation of Europe.

Many 16th-century European observers considered the Ottoman empire the model modern state: an efficient military machine ruled by an absolute monarch, with no hereditary aristocracy, a meritocracy in which any man of talent could rise.

Yet the cost of maintaining and employing such a huge military apparatus was one of the reasons for the decay of Ottoman power after the death of Sulayman in 1566. The practice of tax farming to raise revenues, the increasing use of slave armies rather than the traditional backbone of the army, the cavalryman living on a land grant in return for military service, also contributed to the decline.

The economy was severely affected by inflation. Rural unrest spread and religious fanaticism increased. The Ottomans had always been very tolerant of Christian and Jewish communities and receptive of Western innovations in science and technology. However, in response to the worsening economic situation and to modernization, reactionary puritanism flourished. One populist religious movement rejected all innovations introduced since the time of the Prophet; they were opposed to the sufi orders, to music, dance, mathematics, science, philosophy, coffee, and tobacco.

The highly organized Ottoman army *under the command of Sulayman the Magnificent marched on Vienna in 1529.*

SAFAVID PERSIA

The peoples of the steppe, Turks and Mongols, changed the demographic face of Iran as they had done in Anatolia. Concentrated particularly in the north, they formed some 25 percent of the population. These Turkish-speaking peoples were influenced by various heterodox religious brotherhoods as well as Shi'ism. The Safavid dynasty that ruled Persia from 1500 to 1722 originated in this milieu. It takes its name from the Safawiyya order, founded in the 14th century by Shaykh Safi al-Din. The center of the order was Ardabil in Azerbijan. When the order declared jihad against the Christian populations of eastern Kurdistan and Georgia, its raids were carried out by the Qizil Bash, followers of the order. Their name means "red heads," so-called because of the red caps they wore.

The Shah Mosque *(now called the Imam Mosque) in Isfahan was begun by the greatest of the Safavid rulers, Shah Abbas, in 1611 and completed by his successor Safi in 1630.*

The Safawiyya order had originally been sunni, but some time in the 15th century turned to an extreme form of Shi'ism. In 1500, the head of the order, Isma'il, embarked first on the conquest of neighboring chieftaincies, then of Iran proper. In 10 years, he brought the entire country under his rule. He declared shi'ism the national religion, but not the extreme form professed by his followers. Instead, he adopted *ithna 'ashari*, or "Twelver Shi'ism," a less radical variety. Shi'a 'ulama were imported from all over the Islamic world and organized into an administration, headed by a state-appointed official, the *sadr*. The 'ulama were given estates and lived off the income, thus forming a religious aristocracy.

The Safavid shahs, for they used this old Iranian title, pursued just as radical a program on the cultural front. They sponsored the revival of ancient Iranian traditions, harking back to the pre-Islamic Sasanid past in both literature and art. Their first capital was at Tabriz, close to the Ottoman border. This was occupied by the Ottomans after the Safavid defeat at Çaldiran in 1514, and the capital transferred first to Qazvin, then finally to Isfahan, which was transformed into one of the most glorious cities in the east. The long wars with the Ottomans continued with great savagery on both sides. Much of the hatred that divides sunni from shi'i dates from this time.

Safavid power reached its apogee under Shah Abbas (1587–1629). The Safavids had previously resisted the introduction of firearms, but Shah Abbas modernized his army, forming corps of artillerymen and musketeers. It was Shah Abbas who moved the capital to Isfahan, where he encouraged the establishment of an Armenian merchant colony. An alliance with the East India Company allowed the recapture of Hormuz from the Portuguese in 1622, providing Persia with a key port in the Indian Ocean trading network. Many of the institutions developed by the Safavid shahs persist in Iran to this day, but the dynasty declined after the death of Shah Abbas and came to an end in 1722.

OPPOSITE

Shah Jahan *ruled the Mughal empire from 1628 to 1658. In 1639-48 he built Shahjahanabad as his new seat of government in Delhi. The walls enclosed a population of 50,000, almost all engaged in supplying the needs of his fabulously opulent court.*

The Babur Nama, *the memoirs of the founder of the Mughal dynasty, give an unusually detailed picture of every aspect of the author's life and times. In this illustration Babur demonstrates his love of gardens.*

THE MUGHAL EMPIRE

In 1496 a young descendant of Timur, Babur, set siege to Samarkand. He won the city, but soon lost it again. Only 13 years old, he was unable to handle the older and more ferocious warlords of the region. He was to gain and lose Samarkand again before his 18th birthday, but in 1504 managed to take the wealthy city of Kabul. Sometime in the 1510s he acquired guns and in the 1520s revived Timur's claim to northern India.

In 1526, Delhi and Agra were taken. After victory at the battle of Panipat against a coalition of Hindu princes, he took the title of *ghazi* – warrior of Islam. He was now in control of the heart of Hindustan. Babur's interest in his new domains was lively: he laid out gardens and introduced new plants, and carried out research into artillery techniques. However, his hard life, the Indian climate, and indulgence in drugs and alcohol had undermined his constitution, and he died in 1530.

Babur's son, Humayun, inherited a difficult situation. The Mughals – the word comes from the Persian for Mongol, although the family preferred to think of themselves as Turks – were the military occupiers of India and their position was based on Babur's personal reputation. Humayun did not have his father's personality and Afghan infighting followed him to India. He soon found himself at odds with one of the warlords, Sher Shah, as well as with his brothers. Defeated, Humayun fled to Persia.

Humayun eventually returned to Afghanistan where, after much fighting, he retook Kandahar and Herat. He reentered Delhi in 1555, but died the following year. His son Akbar, aged 13, successfully claimed the throne. By the age of 19, he was firmly in control and began to put into practice the policies that were to mark his reign: religious tolerance and the attempt to find a path whereby the different groups within his empire could cooperate and coexist. Akbar's tolerance did not imply pacifism. His campaigns were ceaseless and he pushed back the boundaries of his empire in all directions. He made Agra rather than Delhi his capital. All the arts were encouraged, and at Akbar's sumptuous court everything from manuscripts to jewels were raised to their highest level in the imperial workshops.

Thanks largely to Sher Shah, India had a good infrastructure of roads and postal systems. Building on these foundations, Akbar also instituted reforms to increase the amount of land under cultivation and improve the lot of the peasant. He reigned for some 50 years and gave Hindustan prosperity and internal peace. However, the latter part of his reign was marked by uprisings and rebellions, not least by his sons.

The defensive walls *of Shah Jahan's Red Fort in Delhi enclosed his new capital, Shahjahanabad, built in 1639-48. The fort remains largely intact in the heart of Old Delhi.*

Akbar's eldest surviving son, Salim, came to the throne in 1605 and, lest he be confused with Selim, the Sultan of Turkey, took the throne name of Jahangir, "World Seizer." He proved less weak and disastrous than his father had feared. He shared his father's interest in the arts, and manuscript production and painting reached new heights. Two figures dominate his reign; Jahangir's wife, the intelligent and politically astute Nur Jehan, whose father and brother were Jahangir's chief advisers, and Khurram (later Shah Jahan), his eldest son, who, following the usual Mughal pattern, rebelled against his father.

Like his father, Jahangir loved Kashmir, but in 1627 even its favorable climate could not restore his health, undermined by years of the family addiction to alcohol and opium, and he died in the fall of the year.

When Shah Jahan succeeded to the throne, he showed a passionate interest in the arts, and the luxury of the court was maintained in all its splendor. However, he never fully recovered from the death of his wife, Mumtaz Mahal in 1631. The empire meanwhile was stagnating. Campaigns to the south were a drain, but produced no new lands or spoils and most revenue came from evermore corrupt and oppressive tax collectors.

*The **Taj Mahal** was built between 1632 and 1643 by Shah Jahan as a tomb for his beloved wife, Mumtaz Mahal, who had died giving birth to their fourteenth child. It remains the consummate example of Mughal architecture in South Asia.*

There was tension too between his sons Dara Shikoh and Aurangzeb. The former, Shah Jahan's favorite, followed the family traditions of syncretic mysticism, tolerance, intellectual curiosity, and sympathy for his non-Muslim subjects. Aurangzeb indulged in none of these things, which endeared him to the orthodox 'ulama. Fighting broke out between the brothers and in 1658 Aurangzeb defeated Dara Shikoh near Agra. Shah Jahan was captured and imprisoned (he was to die in jail). Declaring himself emperor, Aurangzeb hunted down and killed his brother. He placed India under a strict form of the shari'a and persecuted the "infidel" into accepting Islam. Laws against non-Muslims were implemented with full severity, music was banned, and the writing of literature and history discouraged. Aurangzeb did not object to painting, and portraits of him survive, usually dressed in the austere manner of a holy man. He attacked non-Muslim neighbors, such as the Rajputs, with politically disastrous results. Successful guerrilla campaigns proved to the Hindus that their Muslim overlords were by no means invincible and that to throw them off was not an impossible dream.

After Aurangzeb, the Mughal dynasty declined rapidly. It came to an end in 1738, when Nadir Shah, a Turk from Central Asia, who had just displaced the Safavid dynasty in Iran, crossed the Indus, defeated the emperor, and sacked Delhi.

THE LATER OTTOMAN EMPIRE

In the 17th century the Ottoman sultans ceased to wield absolute power, delegating authority to the grand vizier, while the wives and mothers of sultans often took informal charge of financial affairs. The modern army – large contingents of infantry armed with guns – was more expensive to maintain than the traditional cavalry, and tax farming was introduced to raise the money to pay the troops. Already in the second half of the 16th century, the Janissaries had received the right to marry. By the 17th century membership in this elite corps had become first hereditary, then open to purchase, with an inevitable decline in fighting ability. They formed an increasingly unruly element, deposing sultans who did not meet their approval. Power shifted to civilian elites with private funds, while provincial authorities, military and civil, built up power bases through marriage and joint commercial ventures, founding local dynasties.

It was against this background that in 1683 Grand Vizier Kara Mustafa led the Ottoman armies once more to the walls of Vienna. They were put to flight after a siege of 60 days. This was the first major defeat of an Ottoman army, and the sultan was forced to accept humiliating terms by the Treaty of Karlowitz in 1699.

Between 1683 and 1718, the Ottomans fought three more wars against the Habsburgs, and lost them all.

In the 18th century Russia also expanded into Ottoman territory. In the course of three major wars the Ottomans lost the Crimea, Podolia, and Bessarabia, and the lucrative Black Sea trade passed into Russian control. The greater part of the Balkans having been lost to the Habsburgs, large Muslim populations now lived under non-Muslim rule.

Another threat to the territorial integrity of the empire came from an unexpected quarter. In the mid-18th century, Muhammad ibn 'Abd al-Wahhab launched an Islamic reform movement in Arabia, advocating the suppression of sufi orders and the elimination of all practices not expressly sanctioned by the Qur'an and sunna. He forged an alliance with the Sa'ud dynasty, and despite eventual military defeat, the movement resurfaced in the 20th century and was instrumental in the founding of modern Saudi Arabia.

In July 1799 *Napoleon's army invaded Egypt, defeated an Ottoman army twice its size and captured Aboukir near Alexandria. This defeat convinced the Ottomans of the need for further military reforms.*

In 1798, Napoleon invaded Egypt and made it clear to the Arabic-speaking provinces of the empire that Ottoman invincibility was a thing of the past. The ruling sultan, Selim III, was himself influenced by Enlightenment ideas. He fought against corruption and made sweeping reforms of the army, but in 1807 he was deposed by the Janissaries and put to death. His successor, Mahmud II, broke the power of the Janissaries forever by massacring them in 1826. He set up a European-style cabinet and a state school system and actively promoted the study of medicine, science, and technology. He also abolished traditional dress, replacing the turban with the fez, which became a symbol of reform.

The subject populations of Serbia and Greece fought wars for independence during the first three decades of the 19th century, and in 1830 France occupied Algeria, the first of a succession of French and English colonial adventures in Islamic lands.

The Ottoman governor of Egypt, Muhammad Ali Pasha, who effectively ruled the country from 1805 to 1848, severed his links with the sultan, and took drastic steps to modernize the country. He turned Egypt into an autonomous secular principality, which his descendants continued to rule until the middle of the 20th century. He disestablished the 'ulama and confiscated for the state the pious endowments they controlled. He massacred the Mamluks, the conservative military elite that had ruled Egypt before the Ottomans, and trained a modern army, which fought with great success in the Sudan and against the Wahhabi movement in Arabia.

Muhammad Ali *made Egypt into an autonomous principality where the Ottomans had no authority. He even threatened to overthrow the Ottoman sultan. Here he entertains a British delegation sent to dissuade him from such action.*

The Ottoman sultan 'Abd al-Majid made yet another effort at institutional reform in 1839, reorganizing the army and establishing a legal system based on French models. These and other government-sponsored reforms were known as the *Tanzimat*, "reorganization." They were resisted on the one hand by the traditionalist 'ulama and on the other by the new technically trained elite, who thought them insufficient and called for more political participation.

England and France supported the Ottomans against the Russians during the Crimean War of 1854–56. The "Eastern Question" – which of the great powers would get what provinces of the weakening Ottoman empire – dominated European politics for the rest of century and was a contributory cause of World War I. By 1875, the empire was virtually bankrupt. The following year 'Abd al-Hamid II promulgated a constitution which guaranteed freedom of the press and individual rights. The University of Istanbul was founded as well as schools for women. But in 1877, the sultan brought the Tanzimat reforms to an end and suspended parliament.

In 1908, a nationalist group called the Young Turks seized power, supported by the army. They reestablished the constitution, reconvened parliament, deposed 'Abd al-Hamid, and chose his brother, Mehmed V as sultan. In 1914, the Young Turks brought the empire into the war on the side of Germany, effectively sealing the fate of the Ottoman empire.

THE TWENTIETH CENTURY

The Ottomans entered World War I on the German side, and at the end of the war her former provinces were distributed by the League of Nations to the Russians, French, and British. The year following the end of the war, a young Turkish officer named Mustafa Kamal saved Anatolia, the heartland of the Ottoman Empire, from being divided among the victors. He first drove foreign forces from Anatolia, then repudiated the harsh peace treaty the sultan had been forced to sign.

Turkey has *absorbed many Western influences in the last 100 years. This view of Istanbul c.1900 shows that Western fashions were already taking hold in the old Ottoman capital.*

Mustafa Kamal, later called Atatürk, set about the radical secularization and modernization of the new nation. In 1924 he abolished the sultanate. In 1926 he abolished the caliphate. The abolition of these two institutions, however shadowy they had become, deprived the Islamic world of potent symbols of unity. The end of the Ottoman empire and the division of its provinces among the colonial powers were blows to the widespread pan-Islamic movement. Atatürk led the first nationalist revolution in the Islamic world. He defied the Western powers and defeated European troops on the battlefield. This seemed to show that nationalism was the means to independence and freedom from foreign intervention. At the same time, the abolition of the Arabic alphabet and its replacement with the Latin, seemed to Muslims to renounce the Islamic past entirely and align Turkey with Europe.

In the years following the end of World War II, all the countries of the Arabic-speaking heartlands gained their independence from the colonial powers. The last to do so was Algeria in 1962. The colonial period transformed the Islamic world, even those countries like Turkey, Iran, Saudi Arabia, and Yemen that had not been mandates, protectorates, or colonies. The Muslim world now consists of independent nation states, many with secular governments and legal systems based on European models *(see map, page 9).*

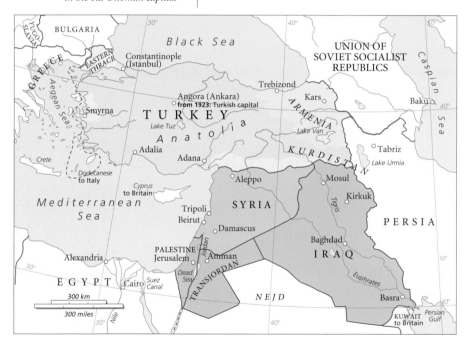

Southwest Asia after the First World War

- ▢ British mandate
- ▢ French mandate
- ▢ Turkey after Treaty of Sèvres (1920)
- ▢ area annexed by Turkey 1921
- ▢ area restored to Turkey by Treaty of Lausanne (1923)
- — international border 1926

Relations with the West have dominated the recent history of many other Muslim countries, in particular the powerful oil-exporting states of the Middle East and Indonesia. Originally developed by Western concessionary companies, these states now control their own resources. Saudi Arabia, Kuwait, and the United Arab Emirates have modernized within traditional frameworks, while Saddam Hussein's Iraq has a socialist military secular regime with a Stalinist-style leadership cult. The savage 1980–88 war between Iraq and Iran, was the latest expression of ancient regional and ethnic rivalries, exacerbated by territorial disputes over oil-rich lands in southern Iraq. In 1990, Iraq invaded Kuwait, and this time a coalition of the United States, Britain, and Saudi Arabia and other Arab states intervened and liberated Kuwait. The subsequent sanctions against Iraq, continued bombing, and the presence of American troops on Saudi soil all fueled resentment against the West.

In oil-rich Iran, the Pahlavi dynasty, founded in 1925 by the radically secularizing Reza Khan, came to an end in 1979. The Islamic revolution that toppled the shah had a profound effect throughout the Muslim world. This broad-based revolution took place not in the name of any socialist or nationalist ideology, but in the name of Islam. The initial excesses of the regime have given way to a successful attempt to govern through Islamic institutions and by Islamic law. Despite the fact that it took place within a particular shi'a context, the Iranian revolution has inspired Islamist movements everywhere in the Muslim world.

THE PALESTINIAN SITUATION

The Balfour Declaration of 1917 promised British support for a national home for the Jewish people in Palestine, provided nothing be done that might "prejudice the civil and religious rights of the existing non-Jewish communities." Muslim and Christian Arabs formed 92 percent of the population. When the state of Israel was formed on the British withdrawal in 1948, the war that followed ended with three-quarters of a million Palestinians displaced from their homes. Most Palestinians have lived in refugee camps ever since, and subsequent wars in 1956, 1967, and 1973 have added to their numbers. Muslims regard uncritical Western support for Israel and indifference to the plight of the Palestinians and the essential justness of their cause as motivated by deep antipathy to Islam. Spiraling violence on both sides bodes ill for the future, and has driven many former moderates into the arms of militant Islamist groups.

Many Jewish immigrants *arrived in Palestine during the British mandate, some legally, some illegally. Even so, the Jewish population was still much smaller than that of the Palestinian Arabs. Israel's victory in the 1948 war drove about 725,000 Palestinians out of the country.*

ISLAMIC ART AND SCIENCE

Despite, or perhaps because of, a nonfigurative tradition in the visual arts, Islamic architects, craftsmen, and calligraphers have generated a rich and wholly distinctive tradition, one underpinned by a clarity of vision reflected in Islamic writing, education, and philosophical and scientific enquiry.

The Great Mosque (Mezquita) *in Córdoba is one of Islam's greatest architectural legacies to Europe. This part of the prayer hall, with its forest of red marble columns topped with a double arcade, was built under al-Hakam II in 962–966.*

THE ARTS

ARCHITECTURE AND CALLIGRAPHY are the two great Islamic art forms and are often intimately linked, as in the brick and tile work of Iran and Central Asia, or the magnificent inscriptions, carved in wood and stone, or worked in mosaic, all across the Muslim world.

The Dome of the Rock *in Jerusalem is the oldest surviving Islamic building* (see also p.51). *Its architecture includes many Byzantine features, but the use of calligraphy as one of the principal decorative elements marks it instantly as an Islamic building.*

Architecture is the most visible mark of a culture, proclaiming its aspirations and identity. Islamic architecture is frequently pictured in terms of a fairly standard Irano-Indian style, rich in domes and slender minarets, with turquoise, green, and gold predominating. This is, however, quite a recent development. Early Islamic architecture varied greatly according to local influences in the conquered lands. But certain unifying factors soon coalesced into a style that made it instantly recognizable.

Islam inherited the urban expectations of both the Byzantine world and Iran. Cities were therefore planned from an early date and, besides the mosque, certain basic elements of infrastructure were assumed: defensive walls, a citadel, bath houses, and hence systems for supplying the water, markets and caravanserais for merchants to stay and store their goods. The giving of alms led to the establishment of hospitals on the Byzantine-Iranian pattern, hospices, mental homes, and orphanages. All these provided opportunities for architectural innovation and display.

THE FIRST MOSQUES

The earliest mosques were of great simplicity, but very soon, through contact with Byzantine architectural traditions, they began to change. The Dome of the Rock in Jerusalem, for example, or the Great Mosque in Damascus, once the Church of St. John the Baptist, whose head was buried there, are still decorated with sumptuous Byzantine-style mosaics.

The first mosques built for that purpose to have survived, however, such as the minaret in Samarra, echoed in the great 9th-century Mosque of Ibn Tulun in Cairo, have a bold simplicity which has survived in the architecture of North Africa. There, mosques, such as the Great Mosque in Kairouan, enormous in size, have a stark unadorned grandeur that suggests a fortress – an appropriate statement for a profoundly military faith in a town that was founded as a military base for the conquest of North Africa. The square minarets of the al-Zaytuna Mosque in Tunis, or the Kutubbiya in Marrakesh, follow the tendency to highly geometric forms, and these uncompromising patterns were carried by the Almohad invaders into Spain. The finest surviving example of this style is the Giralda in Seville. The tendency to bold simple shapes built up of cubes and half spheres has continued to the present in North Africa, in the tombs of holy men and even in domestic architecture.

This dramatic eschewing of unnecessary outer decoration reappears in another medium – mud brick – south of the Sahara, in such buildings as the mosque at Jenne, or the Yaana Mosque, which has recently received the Aga Khan Award.

*The **Great Mosque** in Kairouan, Tunisia, dates in its present form from the 9th century. The triple-towered minaret resembles a classical lighthouse.*

PERSIAN INFLUENCES

As Islam penetrated Iran, another ancient culture with a magnificent architectural tradition, a new fusion occurred. Few of the early brick mosques have survived – the 8th-century one at Damghan being a rare example. Later mosques such as the 9th-century Fahraj Friday Mosque outside Yezd, show very clearly the simple and austere pattern of the early days. Many of the Seljuk buildings such as the Friday Mosque at Isfahan with its superb calligraphic brickwork were subsequently "modernized" in response to a growing taste for decoration or to repair damage caused by the frequent earthquakes in the region.

The rich architectural tradition of Iran ranges from this early simplicity, through the superb tile work of the Timurid mosque at Yezd to the 19th-century mosque at Shiraz, known familiarly as "the rose bowl" for the predominance of pink and the motif of roses in its decoration.

Many of the mosques did not stand alone, but formed part of a complex with madrasas, schools, and libraries. There are also, as elsewhere in the Islamic world – for example the Mamluk tombs in Cairo – splendid examples of funerary architecture, most typically a square building surmounted by a dome. This basic shape became more elaborate with time and in India developed into perhaps the most famous example of Islamic architecture for the world at large: the Taj Mahal.

*The **Friday Mosque** in Isfahan was built in the 11th century under the Seljuks. This detail shows the sophisticated blending of structural and decorative elements.*

Islamic culture expected certain amenities of cities and city planning. From the Round City of al-Mansur's Baghdad, built in 763, to the great central maydans of Isfahan and Samarkand, city planning was an important art. Iran is particularly rich in practical examples of architecture from the numerous great caravanserais – for example, the Seljuk Rebat Shaif between Nishapur and Merv – to the humble pigeon towers, where the birds provided both a source of food and natural fertilizer for the melon fields. The khans and caravanserais were vital for the protection of merchants and the continuance of external trade, but there are also superb examples of covered markets, hospitals, and other public buildings.

Engineering joins with architecture in the question of water. Islam, born in the desert, was profoundly conscious of its importance and a great deal of thought and ingenuity went into developing the earlier Iranian and classical water technology in new ways. The *qanat* system of underground aqueducts to reduce evaporation is a spectacular example of this and came to influence agricultural techniques as far away as South America. Another example of experimentation with water is the Safavid development of the multistoried bridge dam, such as the Khajo Bridge in Isfahan.

Water was needed, of course, not only for agriculture and to support a growing population, but also to fulfill the ritual obligation to wash before prayer.

Another area where engineering and architecture meet is military construction. This is a subject of great complexity, partly because fortifications were constantly updated and hence rarely survive in their original form, and partly because the constant borrowing of new military technology means that a mixture of elements is almost the norm.

The Khajo Bridge in Isfahan, built in 1650, shows the ingenuity of Safavid architects. It serves not only as a bridge and a dam, but also as a recreation area and shopping center.

TURKISH ARCHITECTURE

The Turks were also great builders – and it is striking how many groups of nomads from the steppes, within a generation of settling, produced the most magnificent and innovative architecture. As the Seljuk Turks penetrated the Byzantine empire from about the year 1000, they are generally credited with bringing west the Gothic arch, the first example of which is in the mosque at Van. Their style of building, plain and austere – moved across Anatolia with their conquests, Konya providing some especially fine examples, such as the Ince Minare.

The Turks were also moving east. By the end of the 14th century Timur, whom the West knew as Tamerlane, had set out to conquer the world, reaching the borders of Europe in the west and China in the east and penetrating northern India. After wreaking appalling devastation on many of the cities he conquered,

Timur decided that he needed a capital worthy of his power and set out to make Samarkand the most beautiful city in the world. Craftsmen were brought from countries he had conquered, the city was redesigned, and the finest examples of Central Asian architecture erected in a remarkable short space of time. Samarkand, largely inspired by Iran, is characterized by the Persian use of external tiles, predominantly blue and turquoise, with bold calligraphy as the dominant motif.

AESTHETIC ARCHITECTURE

The rise of the Ottoman dynasty and the fall of Constantinople, the old capital of the eastern Roman empire, Byzantium, brought the Turks into contact with the splendors of late classical architecture – hundreds of magnificent churches and monasteries, mosaics, statues, and works of art. Unlike the Frankish crusaders, who sacked the city in 1204, Mehmet the Conqueror insisted that this artistic treasure house should be respected, converting many of the churches, including the Hagia Sofia, into mosques.

Soon, a new Ottoman style of architecture was flourishing, based on the Byzantine, characterized by its clusters of spreading domes and slender soaring minarets. The outsides were relatively undecorated, as a rule, but the inside was often tiled, particularly with the famous Iznik ceramics, with their patterns based on foliage and flowers, predominantly blue, turquoise, and sealing-wax red.

The greatest Ottoman architect was Sinan (1491–1588). Originally an engineer, he solved difficult problems of road- and bridge-building with an originality and elegance that have survived to the present day. In his 97 years, he built 131 mosques and over 200 other buildings all over the empire, many commissioned by the sultan. They are all characterized by a particular architectural elegance and a skill at using any shaped piece of land to its greatest advantage. Perhaps his most famous work is the Sulaymaniye Mosque in Istanbul, where Sulayman the Magnificent is buried.

DOMESTIC ARCHITECTURE

Domestic architecture, traditionally had much more variety of styles than "official" architecture, which was designed to impress on the populace the glory of God, the power of the sovereign, or the generosity of the donor and therefore needed to be in the latest fashion of the time. The classical model of the courtyard house, grand or humble, tends to predominate, but there are numerous

MINARETS AND DOMES

MINARETS, THE ELEGANT TOWERS attached to mosques can be square-based or round, plain or ornately decorated. Domes are a feature of most mosques and these too vary enormously in style and decoration, which may consist of tiling, gilding, or carved stonework.

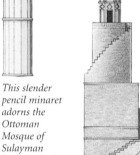

Brass crescent over a pear-shaped bulb.

A pavilion of eight columns supports a crown of stalactites.

Simple wooden railings and modest stalactite decoration were favored by the Ottomans.

Pepperpot caps are found on many early square-based minarets.

This slender pencil minaret adorns the Ottoman Mosque of Sulayman Pasha (1528) in Cairo.

The three-tiered spire of the Qaitbey Mosque (1474) in Cairo features ornate Mamluk stonework.

The minaret of the Ibn Tulun Mosque in Cairo (879) was inspired by the Great Mosque at Samarra in Iraq.

The dome on the Mamluk Qaitbey Mosque combines geometric and floral designs.

The dome of the Great Mosque, Kairouan (c. 900) is classical in its simplicity.

Iranian-style mosques are famous for their rich external decoration.

other local models, from the farmhouses of the Balkans to the towers of Hadhramaut, the caves of Matmata or the yurts of the steppe.

Until the late 20th century, in areas where Islam was the minority religion, or shared its hegemony with another faith, mosques would generally be built in the style of the country – for example the ancient and beautiful Xian Mosque, several of the mosques of Beijing, those of Malacca, Sri Lanka, and many other regions. The buildings were made in the local style and materials, in the first place because the builders did not have the skills or the option to work in the Indo-Persian tradition, but also for the safety of a minority group: it was not wise to be too conspicuous. Also Islam did not have to have a particular "look" – a Muslim could also be culturally African, Chinese, or Bosnian. It was not necessary to renounce the culture for the faith. More recently, this has started to change. Traditional mosques in many areas are being replaced by a more standardized pattern, often funded from the Gulf, indicative of a narrowing of what the Muslim world considers aesthetically acceptable.

THE ISLAMIC STYLE

What, then, are the elements that make an Islamic building recognizable, even when it is not built in the Irano-Indian style? The lack of paintings and images, of course, is one factor, with the concomitant tendency for all decoration to be highly stylized, geometric, floral or calligraphic, and hypnotic rather than emotional. Domes, often flattened, following the Byzantine model, or in some areas ribbed, became characteristic of Islamic architecture. Doors, and such windows as there are, tend to be of great beauty, lovingly decorated and interesting in shape, whether in a palace or a simple house.

Buildings both public and private are turned inward, with high defensive walls or heavily shuttered windows, to segregate the women, as Islam demands, and to protect the inhabitants in an unsettled world. Similarly, the ancient classical plan of building round a courtyard is preferred, the space enriched with water and flowers wherever possible.

It is hard to analyze what exactly marks a building as Islamic – perhaps for many centuries it was the importance of basic structure and function rather than decoration. Where it existed, decoration was part of the function, as in the name of God worked into the brickwork of a mosque. Be that as it may, it is remarkable that within a century, a group that had no strong indigenous architectural tradition had managed to forge a "look" which is instantly recognizable and has lasted to the present.

The Sulaymaniye Mosque *in Istanbul was built by Sinan, the great Ottoman imperial architect, in 1550–57. This view is from beneath the great central dome toward the mihrab.*

*This **basmala** in the hand
of the great calligrapher
Ibn al-Bawwab is written in
the elegant* rayhani *script.*

LITERATURE

Classical Islamic culture was expressed in three unrelated languages, Arabic, Persian, and Turkish. All three have enormously rich literatures. The primary document of Arabic literature is the Qur'an. It is the first Arabic book and the supreme and inimitable example of the Arabic language. Its concise, vigorous, and allusive style deeply influenced later compositions in Arabic.

The other great source for the development of the Arabic literary language was pre-Islamic poetry, which was collected from the oral tradition by the scholars of Basra and Kufa in the 9th century. At the Umayyad court in Damascus a genre of prose literature developed called *adab*. The most famous exponent of the genre was the genial al-Jahiz (d.868), whose *Book of Animals*, the earliest Arabic treatise on zoology, aside from fascinating discussions of things like animal mimicry, contains jokes, satirical anecdotes, and learned etymologies.

World, dynastic, and local history were assiduously cultivated throughout the classical period. These histories ranged from the huge compilation of historical hadith by the 'Abbasid historian al-Tabari, to the one-volume overviews of world history by Ibn Qutayba and al-Dinawari, both produced in the 9th century. The most original of Muslim historians was Ibn Khaldun, whose *Muqaddima* (Introduction to History) is the first attempt to discern the underlying laws governing history and society.

Arabic popular literature includes the *1,001 Nights*, familiar to everyone, as well as tales of adventure and romance less familiar in the West, like the Arabic *Romance of Alexander the Great*, the *Romance of Sayf ibn Dhi Yazan* and most popular of all, the *Romance of 'Antar*. These are similar to the medieval European chivalric romances.

In the 10th century the New Persian language, based on the court language of the Sasanids enriched with large numbers of loan words from Arabic, became a vehicle of literary expression at the wealthy Samanid court in Khurasan. The earliest examples that have survived are the poems of Rudaki, but the cornerstone of New Persian literature is the national epic of Iran, the *Shahnama* of Firdowsi, who died in 1020. This heroic epic of the shahs of Persia and their perennial wars with the Turanians contains 60,000 lines. The subject is the pre-Islamic past of Iran but the meter is based on Arabic metrics and the language is New Persian.

Perhaps because of the influence of the *Shahnama*, Persian literature is one of poetry and verse romances. Nizami lived in the 12th century and is perhaps the most profound and difficult of Persian poets. His *Khamsa* is a collection of five verse romances totaling 30,000 couplets. Omar Khayyam, Hafiz, and Sa'di

ADAB

'Abd al-Hamid ibn Yahya al-Katib, an Umayyad official credited with the creation of this genre, defined its aims as follows: "Cultivate the Arabic language so that you may speak correctly; develop a handsome script which will add luster to your writings; learn the poetry of the Arabs by heart; familiarize yourself with unusual ideas and expressions; read the history of the Arabs and Persians and remember their great deeds."

wrote shorter lyrics that are considered the finest in any of the three Islamic languages. Jalal al-Din al-Rumi's *Mathnawi* is one of the most profound mystical poems in any language.

Like Arabic, Persian has a very rich historical literature. The 12th-century historian Rashid al-Din wrote a history of the Mongols, using Mongolian and Chinese sources, which is one of our main sources for the history of their conquests. Because Persian became the court language of Mughal India, there is a rich Indo-Persian historical and literary tradition as well.

The earliest Ottoman Turkish literature is written in simple language, without the rhetorical flourishes and flowery style that came into vogue later. The *Mewlid* of Süleyman Çelebi, a poem on the life of the Prophet, including a description of the Night Journey and Ascent to Heaven *(mi'raj)* was very popular.

During the 14th and 15th centuries, an intensive effort was made to translate into Turkish the principal works of Arabic and Persian literature. Murad II in particular sponsored and encouraged this effort. Throughout the Ottoman period, educated men read the three languages of Islamic culture, and some could write in all three. Many of the early Ottoman sultans were poets, often writing under pennames. Murad II wrote under the name Muradi, while Mehmed II, conqueror of Constantinople, wrote verses under the name 'Awni.

The two most famous Ottoman poets were Fuduli, who died in 1556 and Baqi, who died in 1600. Baqi attained technical perfection in the handling of complex metrical forms, and his work is still read. He was the court poet of Sulayman the Magnificent. Fuduli came from Baghdad, and unusually, wrote all his poetry in Azeri Turkish.

The Ottomans produced a long line of official historians. Perhaps the most famous is Mustafa 'Ali, who died in 1599. He was the first to introduce critical methods into Ottoman historiography. The objectivity and honesty of Ottoman historians, and the freedom with which they criticized the bad decisions of the great and powerful, including the sultan, are notable.

CALLIGRAPHY

Arabic calligraphy is used not only for documents and books, but also as decoration on porcelain and metalware, for carpets and textiles, on coins and, above all, as architectural ornament.

MAQAMAT

In the 10th century a new literary genre was created by al-Hamdhani, called "The Wonder of the Age." His *Maqamat* ("Sessions"), written in rhymed prose, recounts the adventures of a confidence trickster who takes on different personalities in each "session" and always succeeds in bilking his victim. He was imitated by al-Hariri a hundred years later, and this genre had many imitators, in Hebrew as well as Arabic. This genre may well have influenced the development of the Spanish picaresque novel.

This beautiful illustrated manuscript *of the Persian epic, the* Shahnama, *is written in the* nasta'liq *script. Legend says that the scribe who created this style of writing based it on a flying bird that appeared to him in a dream.*

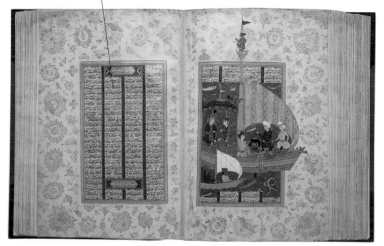

THE ARABIC ALPHABET

The Arabic alphabet has 28 letters. Each may have up to four forms, depending upon its position in the word. All the letters are, strictly speaking, consonants. There are three vowel sounds in Arabic, a, i, and u. Each exists in a short and long form. The long form can be indicated in the script, but not the short. A system of indicating the short vowels was developed in the 8th century, and is used for texts, such as the Qur'an, but not ordinarily in every-day writing.

This page of the Qur'an *is written in the flowing* naskhi *script. Scribes made it their duty to convey the words of God as perfectly as possible.*

At the start of the Islamic era two types of script seem to have been in use: one was square and angular and was called *kufic* (after the town of Kufa in Iraq). It was used for the earliest copies of the Qur'an, and for architectural decoration in the first period of the Islamic empire. The other, called *naskhi*, developed by the famous scribe Ibn al-Bawwab, was rounded and cursive and was used for letters and business documents. By the 12th century, kufic was no longer used for ordinary purposes. In conservative North Africa, however, it developed into the handsome *maghribi* style of writing still used today.

In the first half of the 10th century, the calligrapher Ibn Muqla established the rules of shape and proportion that have been followed by calligraphers since his time. He developed the traditional classification of Arabic writing into the "six styles" of cursive writing: *naskhi* (from which most present-day printing types are derived), *thuluth* (a more cursive outgrowth of naskhi), *rayhani* (a more ornate version of thuluth), *muhaqqaq* (a bold script with sweeping diagonal flourishes), *tawqi* (a somewhat compressed variety of thuluth), and *ruq'a* (the style commonly used today for handwriting in most of the Arab world). From these six, and from kufic, later calligraphers developed and elaborated a range of new scripts. A particularly graceful and delicate script called *ta'liq* came into use in Iran. The horizontal strokes of the letters are elongated, and the words often written at an angle across the page. Another script called *nasta'liq* combines the Arabic naskhi and the Persian ta'liq into a beautifully light, legible script.

Once the early creative flowering had faded elsewhere in the Middle East, the Ottomans took up the art with passion. A popular saying was that "The Qur'an was revealed in Mecca, recited in Egypt, and written in Istanbul." Ottoman styles include *diwani*, so called from the word diwan (state council or government office). It was at first used primarily for documents issued by the Ottoman Council of State. It is an extremely graceful and very decorative script, with strong diagonal flourishes, though less easy to read than some other styles.

Calligraphy is still very much alive wherever the Arabic alphabet is used. Advertisements, newspaper headlines, book jackets, wall posters, and shop signs all display fine examples of the various styles.

THE DECORATIVE ARTS

Because Islam spread into areas with highly developed traditions in many different crafts, it is impossible to do full justice to the richness and variety of the decorative arts across the whole Muslim world. Traditionally Islam has excelled in woodworking, ceramics, textiles, and metalwork and a few of the most important examples of work in these fields will be discussed here.

Many of the areas where Islam spread were poor in forests, with the result that wood tended to be treated as a precious material, skillfully carved and fretted – and also because it helps to prevent warping in extreme climates, Islamic woodwork is often made in small panels, fitted together with consummate art.

Some of the earliest examples are carved wood panels dated to the 7th century from Egypt, which show Coptic influence, with designs of vines and fruit. The oldest large-scale example is the minbar of the Great Mosque in Kairouan (863), made of teak, indicating the breadth of commercial contacts. Other splendid examples are the 11th-century Kairouan *maqsura* and the Mamluk minbar (late 13th century) in the Mosque of Ibn Tulun in Cairo and the Fatimid palaces provide secular examples. Fine wood carving occurs all across the Islamic world and is characterized by its geometric and stylized floral patterns and by the frequent use of calligraphy. Wood was also used for a particularly Muslim item of interior decoration: the *mashrabiyya* or elaborate screens used to cover the windows to guard the privacy of the women, while allowing them a glimpse of the outer world.

Inlay work, particularly associated with Egypt and later Syria, is again typical of Islamic use of small quantities of wood. The marquetry may be done with other woods, or with tortoiseshell or mother-of-pearl, both very popular in the later period. Western Islam also made considerable use of painted woodwork, both in architecture and furnishings. A word should perhaps be said here about ivory carving, of which some fine examples survive, generally in the form of small panels or caskets, or occasionally boards for games such as *mankala*, many of them from Muslim Spain.

The Islamic world has produced a wealth of ceramics of every kind of the highest quality, and for everyday use. Early examples include the faience excavated at Susa and the yellowish-gold wares of Fustat and Samarra. The blue-green and deep green wares of Iraq also appear at an early date and shards are found at numerous points on the eastern coasts of Arabia, as are shards of Iranian wares: clear evidence of trade.

Iran and Central Asia in particular produced the widest range of styles – often influenced by Chinese styles – from the supremely elegant 10th-century plates and bowls with cream grounds and black kufic inscriptions to the exuberant 13th-century Rayy ware often with figurative decoration or the 14th-century Sultanabad wares with their delicate shades of blue and gray.

Tile-making reached the highest level of skill, becoming an intrinsic part of the internal and external architecture of many mosques – for example whole walls covered in gigantic calligraphy – and also palaces. One of the places particularly known for its tiles was Kashan in Iran.

This fine 14th-century Mamluk mosque lamp *is enameled with the name of the ruler and a phrase from the Qur'an.*

This 16th-century Iznik plate, *with its splendid decoration of Mediterranean ships, represents a new departure for Islamic art.*

The Iznik potters *were at first influenced by Chinese blue and white ceramics, then experimented with colors such as tomato red and sage green. This tankard reflects the Ottoman love of flowers.*

Perhaps because of the Muslim prohibition on the use of gold vessels, potters experimented with ways to produce glazes that looked like gold. The Hispano-Mauresque ware of al-Andalus is a well-known example of such experiments.

One of the last great flowerings of Islamic ceramic art was in Turkey, where Iznik produced plates, bowls, and jugs as well as tile revetments with beautifully clear and dramatic floral designs which decorate some of the finest Ottoman mosques.

Less Islamic glass than pottery has survived, but there are, in particular, exquisite mosque lamps of enameled glass from Egypt and Syria, in a style that was copied in Muslim Spain.

Islamic textiles, carpets, and furnishings are important for several reasons. First, the areas where Islam first spread had long been famous for their textiles – the linen of Egypt, for example, and the brocaded silks and carpets of Iran. The historian al-Mas'udi tells the story of the army of the Conquest dividing the magnificent "carpet of the spring of Chosroes," too unsophisticated to appreciate the treasure they were destroying. This soon changed. The Islamic world became a major textile producer, and clothes and textiles then, as now, were of the greatest importance to the economy.

Textiles were important as raw materials, woven cloth and finished goods. All three were traded and probably caused more money to change hands on the international market than anything except metals and arms. Skilled weavers were highly prized and were generally men, but much embroidery was done by women, a way of supplementing the family income, working in leisure moments at home, as Palestinian refugees do to the present day. For wealthier women, it was one of the few means of self-expression for the illiterate, and some of the most charming Islamic embroidery was produced in the Ottoman harems.

Textiles were not only of economic importance, they were also social indicators. In the past, decoration normally had purpose: to indicate a person's wealth, rank, place of origin, job, or religious affiliation. Robes were bestowed as a mark of favor in the Muslim, Christian, and Far Eastern worlds alike. Muslim rulers formalized this practice by setting up workshops producing official textiles – *tiraz* – normally worked with the ruler's name, or auspicious or pious phrases, which were bestowed as a mark of honor on foreign ambassadors and those in favor about the court. Such highly prized pieces found their way into the treasuries of churches and monasteries around Europe, and often feature in medieval European paintings.

A way of judging the impact of one culture on another is the number of loan words. In the field of textiles (as in that of basic foods), the West owes Islam a considerable debt: damask from Damascus, muslin from Mosul, tabby (as in tabby cats) from the at-Tabiyya quarter of Cairo, seersucker from the Persian "milk and sugar" and, of course, cashmere from Kashmir, to name but a few.

For the West, the art form most associated with the Islamic world is the carpet. These seem to have been exported in quantity rather later than silks, probably because of their weight. From the 15th century, however, they were everywhere, but like the silks have often survived only in paintings.

There are several reasons for this emphasis on textiles within the Islamic world. In the case of carpets, since it was required that a person should have a clean place to pray, it was natural that the prayer rug should develop early and also that fine carpets should be made to adorn mosques – although strictly for both purposes a reed mat is adequate. The oldest surviving Islamic carpets have come to light beneath layers of floor coverings donated over the centuries to mosques. These carpets are knotted, of silk or wool, but there is another type – the kelim. Kelims are woven carpets, normally of wool, and are particularly associated with nomads in various parts of the Islamic world. The simplest looms are stretched out on the sand and, as well as for kelims, the woven cloth is used for tents, bags, tent dividers, cushions and bedding, men's cloaks, and sometimes women's clothes. Where there are so few possessions, textiles take on enormous importance, making up the bulk of a family's material goods and also being one of the few ways for women of the household to show off their skills.

Men naturally lavished great care on possessions on which their life might depend, so metalwork is primarily seen in weapons and armor, such as the splendid Irano-Indian sets of etched steel from the 17th and 18th centuries. Another important form of metalwork is jewelry. Under Islamic law a woman's possessions were unalienably her own (unlike in the Christian West) and she kept much of her wealth in gold or silver about her person. However, since styles change, old pieces are frequently melted down by succeeding generations so relatively few pieces from the past have survived. Styles range from enormous archaic silver brooches and great necklaces of amber and coral worn for "good luck" by the Berber women of Morocco to exquisite pieces of enamel, filigree, and gold rich with gems worked for the Mughal courts of northern India.

The third area of metalworking is probably the one with which the West is most familiar: domestic vessels, for cooking and serving food, ewers for water or scent, and decorative objects of various kinds.

Early Islamic textiles, *such as this 11th-century silk cloth, are sometimes found in Christian churches in Spain. This example, decorated with harpies and griffins, was found in the tomb of San Pedro de Osma in Burgo de Osma cathedral.*

SCIENCE

THE PRESERVATION, ELABORATION, AND TRANSMISSION of the scientific tradition of late antiquity is one of the great achievements of classical Islamic civilization. The essential process of translation into Arabic and assimilation to an Islamic cultural context took place in Baghdad between the 8th and the 10th century.

This 9th-century brass astrolabe *was made in what is now Iraq by the instrument-maker 'Ahmad Ibn Khalaf.*

These translations established the framework for original speculation, generating debate about the relationship between reason and revelation that persists to this day. These texts, embedded in their Arabic commentaries, were ultimately transmitted to Europe, beginning in the 11th century, and formed the basis for premodern Western science and philosophy.

There were three scientific traditions in late antiquity: the Greek, the Indian, and the Chinese. The conquests gave Muslim scholars access to the first two of these, but Chinese science remained beyond the ken of the Islamic world, although some Chinese technologies percolated into Islamic lands along the Silk Road and in the wake of the Mongol conquests.

The first concerted efforts to incorporate the body of Greek scientific thought into an Islamic context are conventionally supposed to have begun with the establishment of the 'Abbasid dynasty. Yet even in Umayyad times there is evidence of interest in both Greek and Indian learning. The little Umayyad audience hall and bath of Qasr 'Amra, built in 711, the year Muslim armies invaded Spain, contains a painted representation of the zodiac on the inside of the dome. It is made on what appears to be a stereographic projection, as described by Ptolemy. The same room contains paintings of personifications of History, Philosophy, and Poetry. Each figure is labeled in Greek. The interest in Greek science hinted at in the frescoes of Qasr 'Amra is confirmed by references in the early historians to alchemical experiments made by Khalid ibn al-Yazid, the grandson of the first Umayyad caliph, Mu'awiya. Astronomy, astrology, and alchemy were thus the first sciences to preoccupy Muslim scholars. Toward the end of the Umayyad period, the first literary work in Arabic appeared. This was *Kalila wa Dimna*, an Arabic translation of a Pahlavi version of a lost Sanskrit original done by a Zoroastrian convert to Islam, Ibn al-Muqaffa'. This serpentine line of transmission is typical. This little work is not a slavish translation of the original, a version of the well-known mirror for princes in the form of animal fables called the Panchatantra, but an elegant recreation for a Muslim audience in a language that had never before been used for secular prose literature. So already in Umayyad times influences from Greece and India were beginning to be felt. These increased exponentially with the founding of the new capital, Baghdad, in 763.

The position of Baghdad at the crossroads of Asia and its multiethnic population made it the ideal clearinghouse for ideas as well as merchandise. It was located very near the town of Gondeshapur, in the Ahwaz, where a school of medicine had flourished since Sasanid times, staffed largely by Nestorian Christians who had sought refuge in Persia from persecution by the Byzantines after the Council of Ephesus in 431 excommunicated Nestorius. The Nestorians brought with them a knowledge of two sciences later to be intensively cultivated by Muslim scholars: medicine and astronomy. A physician from the academy at Gondeshapur named Jirjis ibn Bakhtishu cured the caliph al-Ma'mun of an ailment, and became court physician. For almost five generations, members of this Christian family practiced as physicians and produced medical works, melding the Indian and Hellenic traditions.

The Nestorians, like much of the population of Iraq and Syria, spoke Aramaic and the more learned had Greek as a second language. The written form of Aramaic used by the Christian communities of Iraq and Syria was Syriac. Greek science reached the Arabic-speaking world largely through translations into Syriac, although there are notable cases of Arabic-speakers learning Greek in order to read the sources in the original.

The two rabbinical academies of Sura and Pumbedita were very near Baghdad, and indeed, the Gaons of these academies were confirmed in office by the caliphs. Jewish scholars played an important role, particularly in the fields of medicine and pharmacy.

There was yet another source of specialized knowledge in the region of the Islamic heartland. This was in Harran, ancient Carrhae, where the last pagan community to survive in a sea of monotheism still held out. They were star worshippers, and had inherited not only Hellenistic traditions, but had also preserved some of the mathematical legacy of ancient Babylonia.

The constellation of Andromeda *is one of many attractive illustrations in* The Book of the Fixed Stars *compiled by Abd al-Rahman ibn Umar al-Sufi in the 10th century. The individual stars forming the constellation are shown in red.*

Aristotle teaching *in an illustration from* Choice Wise Sayings and Fine Statements *by 11th-century Egyptian writer Mubashshir ibn Fatik.*

This community produced a number of scholars, including the famous Thabit ibn Qurra, who made significant contributions to mathematics and astronomy.

Al-Mansur, the founder of Baghdad, sent embassies to the Byzantine emperor asking for Greek mathematical texts, in particular the *Elements* of Euclid. His son Harun al-Rashid acquired a number of other Greek texts as booty in raids on Byzantine territory. The fact that the Arabic annals often mention diplomatic embassies sent to find specific works is an indication of how rare they were.

Al-Ma'mun created the Bayt al-Hikma, "House of Wisdom" and staffed it with Christian and Muslim scholars. Remarkably like a modern research institute, it was dedicated to the systematic translation of Greek scientific works into Arabic. Some 57 scholars were associated with the House of Wisdom, and its running costs ran to 500 gold dinars a month. These original versions underwent continual revision, as new texts were translated. In the process, all the procedures of modern scholarship were developed, such as collating a number of manuscripts to establish a critical text, glossaries, marginal commentaries, and the compilation of dictionaries of technical terms. Scholars working in the House of Wisdom encountered Arabic numerals in translations of Indian astronomical works, as well as the place-value system that allowed all numbers to be expressed by means of nine figures plus zero (Arabic *sifr*).

Muslim scholars loved to quote the legend Aristotle inscribed above the door to his house: "Let no one enter who does not have a knowledge of mathematics," and it was in mathematics and logic – considered the basis for all other sciences – that Muslim scientists made their most lasting contributions.

The copy of Euclid brought back from Constantinople was translated twice, once for Harun al-Rashid and once for al-Ma'mun. These translations were used to prepare a critical edition by Ishaq ibn Hunayn and Thabit ibn Qurra. A commentary on Euclid by Hero of Alexandria was also translated. In the 13th century, the standard commentary was written by Nasir al-Din al-Tusi. This was one of the earliest Arabic texts to be printed in 16th-century Europe, using Arabic type designed especially for the Vatican Press. Many other works by Euclid or attributed to him were translated, along with at least eleven works by Archimedes, as well as later Greek authors including Nichomachus of Gerasa, Theodosius of Tripoli, Menelaus, and Apollonius of Perga.

Nasir al-Din al-Tusi's *observatory at Maragha in Iran was the most advanced in the Islamic world in the 13th century.*

These, together with a number of translations of Indian mathematical works inspired al-Khwarizmi's *Addition and Subtraction in Indian Arithmetic*, translated into Latin in Toledo in the 11th century under the title

Algorismi de numero indorum, introducing Arabic numerals to the West and giving us the word algorithm, the Latin version of the author's name. His other fundamental work was the *Kitab al-Jabr wa l-Muqabala*, the first book on algebra. The Latin translation of this work was the standard text on the subject in some European universities well into the 16th century.

Translations of Ptolemy's *Almagest* laid the foundations of mathematical astronomy, and well into the 18th century Islamic observatories like the famous Jantar Mantar in Delhi were engaged in revising and perfecting his stellar coordinates.

Several Arabic translations of Ptolemy's *Geography* were done, including one by al-Khwarizmi. As with the *Almagest*, this generated an enormous interest in mathematical geography. The length of a terrestrial degree was accurately measured and used to correct Ptolemy. The study of Ptolemy culminated in the work of al-Idrisi, whose maps and accompanying description of the known world were produced at the request of the 12th-century Norman ruler of Sicily, Roger II.

A doctor cups a patient *in front of a crowd of curious onlookers in an illustration from a 13th-century Arabic manuscript.*

Not all major translation efforts were government sponsored. The famous Banu Musa (The Sons of Musa) not only commissioned translations from the Greek but wrote a number of impressive original contributions to science. Muhammad ibn Musa wrote on celestial mechanics, the origin of the Earth, the atom, and an essay on the Ptolemaic universe. His brother Ahmad wrote an important treatise on mechanics while another brother, al-Hasan, studied the geometrical properties of the ellipse. Sometimes the Banu Musa collaborated, and several of their joint productions, translated into Latin by Gerard of Cremona in the 11th century, influenced Fibonacci.

Two other men who played a key role in the transmission of Greek learning were Hunayn ibn Ishaq and Qusta ibn Luqa. Hunayn, a Jacobite Christian, was known in Europe in the Middle Ages as Joanitius. He was the son of an apothecary, whose father sent him to Baghdad. He was financially supported by the Banu Musa, who urged him to learn Greek. He set about translating almost the entire corpus of Greek medical works into Arabic, including all of Galen and Hippocrates. Many of the works of these two authors now only exist thanks to Hunayn's translations.

Al-Idrisi *(c.1099–1165) wrote a comprehensive world geography illustrated with maps for Roger II of Sicily. This world map based on his work is oriented to the south, in keeping with Islamic cartographic tradition.*

Hunayn also translated the famous Hippocratic oath, which became obligatory for Muslim physicians. He also wrote 29 original works on medical subjects. The most important of these is a collection of 10 essays on opthalmology which cover in systematic fashion the anatomy and physiology of the eye and the treatment of various eye diseases. It is the first Arabic medical

OPPOSITE

Takyuddin and other astronomers *make observations at the Galata observatory founded in 1557 by Sulayman the Magnificent.*

THE HOUSE OF WISDOM

When the Byzantine emperors conquered Syria, the scientific works of the Greeks were still in existence… as time went on, and the Muslim dynasty flourished, the Muslims developed an urban culture which surpassed that of any other nation. They began to wish to study the various branches of philosophy, of whose existence they knew from their contact with bishops and priests among their Christian subjects. The Caliph al-Mansur therefore sent an embassy to the Byzantine emperor, asking him to send him translations of books on mathematics. Muslim scholars studied these books, and their desire to obtain others was whetted. When al-Ma'mun, who had some scientific knowledge, assumed the caliphate, he wished to do something to further the progress of science. For that purpose, he sent ambassadors and translators to the Byzantine empire, in order to search out works on the Greek sciences and have them translated into Arabic.

Ibn Khaldun, 14th-century
North African historian

work to include anatomical drawings. It was translated into Latin and for centuries remained the most authoritative work on the subject.

Qusta ibn Luqa wrote 40 original works on the most varied subjects: medicine, politics, insomnia, "burning mirrors" (convex mirrors used to focus the sun's rays and set fire to things), hair diseases, fans, anecdotes from the lives of the Greek philosophers, a study of dyes, a little essay on nutrition, and a study of paralysis.

The greatest of the 9th-century physicians was al-Razi. He wrote more than 184 works, 56 of them on medical topics. Deeply versed in Greek medicine, his originality lay in his open advocacy of experimental observation. Many of the works of Plato and Aristotle were also translated, along with the commentaries that had grown up around their works. The late classical philosophers had tried to reconcile the two, and this neo-Platonic tradition was inherited by the Muslim world through the commentaries that accompanied their texts.

In the 12th century, Ibn Rushd (Averröes) and al-Ghazali embodied the conflict between reason and revelation. The rationalism of Ibn Rushd, his separation of philosophy from theology was violently antipathetic to al-Ghazali, whose intuitive and mystical sense of the Divine rejected scholasticism. Normative Islam follows al-Ghazali, and Ibn Rushd found no following in Islamic lands, but his commentaries on Aristotle, translated into Latin, had a profound effect on European thought.

Many of the scientific works produced by the House of Wisdom and the succeeding generations of Muslim thinkers were translated into Latin and gave birth to European science and philosophy. The Christian conquest of Toledo in 1085 allowed firsthand contact between European and Muslim scholars. Avid for learning, men from all over Europe flocked to Toledo, where another great movement of translation occurred. Arabic works were translated into Hebrew and thence into Latin. Some Christian scholars even learned Arabic, as Hunayn ibn Ishaq had set about learning Greek long before. After the conquest Seville in 1248, another intense period of translation and adaptation ensued. Works by Muslim agronomists like Ibn al-Awwam were translated and were still being used in one form or another in the 16th century.

The task performed by the scholars associated with the House of Wisdom involved nothing less than the transfer of the philosophical and scientific legacy of the ancient world, first into the Arabic language, then into the conceptual framework of Islam. For one of the few times in human history, a culture with its own language, religion, and customs embarked upon the extraordinary task of fitting an alien intellectual tradition into its own language and conceptual framework. In the process the experimental method, the basis of all scientific progress, was clearly enunciated.

MODERNITY & TRADITION

The Islamic world was profoundly affected by the economic, political, and social changes that swept the world in the 19th century, responding to European expansion and economic and military dominance in a variety of ways. Now all Muslim countries are politically independent, but still seeking a balance between tradition and modernity that will allow them to develop on their own terms.

Modernity is not incompatible *with tradition, as this photograph shows. Oil-producing countries like Saudi Arabia have created modern infrastructures and educational systems within a traditional social framework.*

MODERNITY

IT IS EASIER TO LIST THE ELEMENTS that make up the condition of modernity than it is to define the term. The condition itself is relatively new in historical terms, dating back a mere 200 years. It was the outcome of two European revolutions, the Industrial Revolution and the French Revolution. The complex of techniques and ideas they generated are loosely grouped under the label "modernity."

Throughout the Middle Ages *and well into modern times, textiles were the major trade goods of the Islamic world and silk, cotton and linen were introduced wherever climatic conditions allowed. These modern silks from India continue an ancient tradition of craftsmanship.*

Industrialization created the need for an educated workforce, and this led to mass education and consequent social and economic mobility and new social groupings, such as labor unions and political parties. Representative government was found to be the most efficient form of government. The accumulation of capital led to reinvestment and the ability to replicate resources. The need for new markets and new sources of raw materials spurred colonial expansion. Industrial expansion was based on scientific advances, which gave rise to the idea of progress and in time seriously undermined accepted religious beliefs. Secular nation states with constitutional and democratic governments were formed. As the colonial period ended following World War II, the present global system of sovereign national states, often cutting across former ethnic and tribal divisions, was in place.

The very concept of the nation state was alien to Islam, for Muslim identity is not based on nationality, but faith. Nor, traditionally, do Muslims link ethnicity to territory. The ideal of a single Muslim community, defined in spiritual rather than territorial terms and guided by a caliph, persisted as an ideal even after the formal abolition of the caliphate by Atatürk in 1926 and the formation of sovereign nation states in Islamic lands.

EAST AND WEST

Throughout the European Middle Ages, Islamic lands were the home of technological innovation and intellectual creativity, particularly in the sciences and philosophy. The movement of ideas, like the movement of spices, was from east to west. Highly developed agricultural production, urban crafts, and commerce created great wealth and permitted the growth of large and splendid cities. The position of Islamic lands astride the great Eurasian trade routes, their overland and maritime commerce with India, the Indonesian archipelago, China,

Africa south of the Sahara and East Africa, gave the great cities of the Middle East access to the silks, spices, and other luxury goods in such demand in Europe. Muslim merchants controlled the land routes, as well as the maritime commerce in the Indian Ocean.

The commercial expansion of Europe beginning in the 13th century eventually led, in the 15th, to economic and technological parity with Islamic lands. The combination of political power and private finance generated European expansion, as it did the growing capitalist economies of Europe.

When the Portuguese reached India in 1498, the technological gap between the newcomers and the civilization they found was narrow. Aside from having better guns – and no inhibitions about using them on unarmed shipping – the Portuguese were not obviously more technologically advanced than the cultures they encountered. The Samorin of Calicut was appalled at the cheap trade goods Vasco da Gama offered to exchange for pepper, and advised him that if he wanted to participate in the Indian Ocean trading network to bring gold on his next voyage.

The Portuguese plan of dominating Indian Ocean trade by force was countered by local Muslim principalities, which quickly adopted new-model European firearms and were able to withstand them. The Portuguese survived by becoming one among many such trading principalities and gradually being absorbed into the preexisting network. By the time the Dutch reached the Indian Ocean a century

A complex interlocking system *of overland and sea routes linked Islamic lands with northern Europe, China, and Africa. Ideas, technologies, and luxury goods flowed along these routes, whose maintenance a primary responsibility of Muslim rulers.*

Trade in Medieval Eurasia

——	Arab trade route
——	Silk Road ⎫ routes opened during the
- - -	other route ⎭ 'Mongol Peace' c.1250–1350
——	Chinese trade route
——	Genoese trade route
——	Venetian trade route
——	main Hanseatic trade routes
——	other trade route

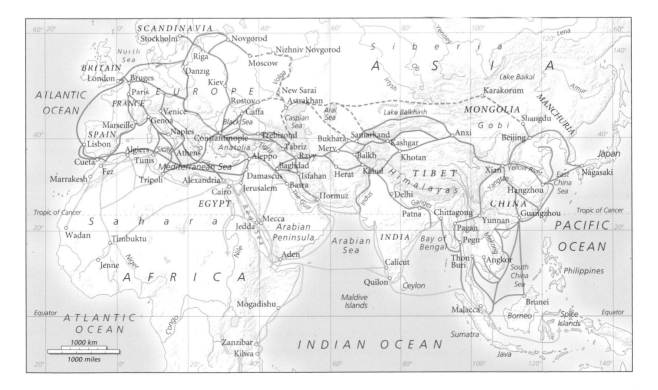

later, Europe was already in its pre-Industrial stage. The Dutch were able, mainly by force, to gain control of all the sources of supply of the spices, and by the middle of the 17th century established a monopoly over all the goods of Asia exported to European markets. Maritime Southeast Asia was thus the first region to experience premodern European commercial practices. The network of Muslim shipping that had plied the waters of the Indian Ocean since the 8th century was severely disrupted.

Over the next three centuries, Islamic lands increasingly bore the brunt of European colonialism. Between 1798 and 1814, the British occupied almost all of India; by 1850 they controlled the entire subcontinent. In 1830, France occupied Algeria. In 1839, the British occupied Aden. France took Tunisia in 1881, Britain Egypt the following year. The Sudan was occupied in 1889. The Italians occupied Libya in 1912, the same year the French marched into Morocco. Following World War I, and the defeat of the Ottomans, the former Ottoman provinces of Syria, Lebanon, Palestine, Iraq, and Transjordan were all placed under French or British mandates or protectorates, while Muslim populations in Central Asia were absorbed into the Soviet Union.

The arrogance *of European colonialism is unwittingly captured in this painting of a Moroccan shaykh humbling himself before a French colonel.*

REFORM

The Ottoman defeat before the walls of Vienna in 1683, and the humiliating terms of the Treaty of Karlovitz made the necessity of reform obvious.

In 1726, a young reformer in Constantinople, Ibrahim Muteferrika, received permission from the religious authorities to establish the first printing press in the Ottoman empire. Among the books he issued was a history of the discovery and conquest of the New World. More importantly, he published a work called the *Nizam al-Umam*, "The Ordering of the Nations," intended to convince the sultan of the necessity of introducing European tactics and organizational methods into the Ottoman army. European advisers were hired and a school of geometry opened soon afterward. These reforms met resistance from the corps of Janissaries, as did later attempts to form a new style army.

Another, different sort of reform movement also occurred in the 18th century, this time in Arabia. A reformer named Muhammad ibn 'Abd al-Wahhab set forth a program to renew and purify Islam, cleansing the faith of non-Qur'anic accretions. The rulers of central Arabia, the Al Sa'ud, embraced this movement, and although defeated by the Ottoman army, this Unitarian puritanical movement continued to flourish.

In 1798, Napoleon invaded Egypt. The ease with which the French army occupied the country, the printing press that produced propaganda broadsheets and newspapers in Arabic, his claim to be a Muslim, his entourage of indefatigable savants who carried out a meticulous description of the country, the artists who drew everything from the pyramids to pairs of sandals, his scientific laboratory which was demonstrated to the 'ulama – all this amazed and astonished the inhabitants, as it was designed to.

As well as soldiers, Napoleon's ships carried ideas. Nationalism, representative government, patriotism, liberty, and equality – including sexual equality – were incendiary concepts. Even more than the Ottoman defeat outside the walls of Vienna, the brief Napoleonic occupation of Egypt caused men to reflect on the reasons for European military and technological superiority.

In 1826, the Sultan abolished the Janissaries and reorganized the army. This reorganization involved various political and institutional reforms as well, but these were not far-reaching enough to halt the decline of Ottoman power. The introduction of a code of civil liberties in 1839 was another important break with the past.

The Ottoman governor of Egypt from 1805 to 1848, Muhammad Ali, made a brutal concerted effort to modernize the administration, the economy, and the army, using European advisers and officers. His successful campaigns in Arabia against the puritan movement launched by Muhammad ibn 'Abd al-Wahhab, his conquest of the Sudan and victories against the Ottomans in Syria, appeared to justify his military reforms. He made himself the *de facto* independent ruler of Egypt. His massacre of the Mamluks, the hereditary military elite which – like the Janissaries in Istanbul – resisted all attempts at military reform, was his most symbolic act, a drastic removal of a survival from the past.

Napoleon set up *French and Arabic printing presses in Egypt in 1798, first in Alexandria, then in Cairo. This attractively printed broadsheet gives the text of a speech by Napoleon on the eve of war with Austria.*

He confiscated the lands and property administered as pious endowments (*awqaf*), control and administration of which had traditionally been in the hands of the 'ulama. This was a major blow at the Islamic infrastructure of the country and was followed by another. The 'ulama were divested of what remaining power they had, a radical assault on tradition which confirmed many in the belief that modernization was incompatible with Islam. Muhammad Ali authorized the establishment of a printing press, which played an important role in the spread of learning. Muhammad Ali's grandson Ismail was even more extreme in his attempts to transform Egypt into a modern state, building the Suez Canal and setting up an ambitious educational program. But in doing so Egypt was bankrupted, and in 1882 the British took over the financial administration of the country.

The Suez Canal, *opened in 1869, was one of the greatest engineering feats of the 19th century. It reduced the length of the sea route to India by 9,700 miles (15,600 km), but bankrupted Egypt. Britain bought a controlling interest in the canal in 1875.*

But the most far-reaching transformation of a Muslim country was in Turkey itself, at the hands of Mustafa Kemal, "Atatürk." The Arabic alphabet, with all its religious associations, was abolished and replaced by the Latin script. This was an act of tremendous symbolic significance. It was followed by the closing of Islamic schools and legal institutions. The 'ulama were disestablished. The mystical Sufi orders, to which most adult males belonged, were suppressed. In 1926, the institution of the caliphate itself was abolished. Turkey is today officially a secular state, although the population is overwhelmingly Muslim in faith.

The most extreme attempt at secularization, accompanied by great brutality, occurred in Iran, under Reza Shah. A civil law code was introduced and the administration of the pious endowments taken from the hands of the 'ulama, as they had been in Egypt and Turkey. Islamic schools were closed, Islamic dress, even the veil, forbidden. The pilgrimage to Mecca, one of the "Five Pillars of Islam" was prohibited. Reza Shah's successor, Muhammad Reza Shah, continued the anti-Islamic policies of his father, and the result was the Islamic Revolution under Ayatollah Khomeini.

The establishment of secular regimes led to the loss of status and power by traditional elites. Almost everywhere the shari'a was replaced by law codes imported from the West, although the shari'a typically continued to rule family law. The disestablishment of the 'ulama by Muhammad Ali, Atatürk, Reza Shah, and more recent leaders, created a crisis of authority. Traditionalist scholars, represented by the 'ulama, were the custodians of Divine Law and its interpretation. They formed the elite from which high ranking government officials, muftis, qadis, and administrators had always been drawn. Their removal

The Turkish Republic *was founded by Mustafa Kemal, later known as Atatürk ("Father of the Turks"), who drove foreign armies from Anatolia and established a modern secular state.*

from positions of authority affected the stability of society and one of the traditional checks on power. The spread of literacy, without the safeguard of supervised study and certificates of qualification *(ijaza)*, democratized access to religious learning. The consequences of this, both positive and negative, resonate throughout the Muslim world.

RESPONSES TO MODERNITY

Beginning in the 19th century, generations of Muslim intellectuals responded to the challenges posed by modernity and secularizing regimes, articulating a wide

spectrum of analyses and programs that are roughly grouped under the headings of reformists and modernists. Nineteenth-century modernists held that the only way for Muslims to regain control of their destinies was through the modernization of institutions, particularly education. This was normally a position taken by elites, military or civil, who had had direct contact with Western civilization. Many of these men were enthusiastic about certain aspects of modernity, although all warned against the superficial adoption of Western practices. Many modernists thought religion should be a private matter. If properly understood, they maintained, there was no conflict between Islam and modern science. The modernist suggestion that social change should be reflected by changes in the interpretation of Divine Law was a new departure and attracted controversy.

Tehran in the 1950s, following the reforms of Reza Shah, began to resemble a European city. All forms of traditional dress were banned under the Shah's unpopular modernization program.

The reformists assumed a traditional posture and argued that Islam must be renovated from within to withstand modernity from without. The purification of Islam by the elimination of practices not sanctioned by the Qur'an and sunna would lead to unity and triumph over their adversaries. Although they vigorously opposed Westernization, reformists recognized the need for institutional reform and the value of education, science, and technology. Reformist movements like the Muslim Brotherhood, founded by Hasan al-Banna in 1928, actively tried to improve the lot of the people by building schools, clinics, and factories. The Muslim Brotherhood and similar reform movements have broad popular support throughout the Islamic world and many adherents among the professional classes.

Islamism was born out of opposition to corrupt secular regimes, particularly that of the late shah in Iran, but its emphasis on return to the sources of Islam, the Qur'an and sunna, and rejection of all other authority harks back to reformers like Muhammad ibn 'Abd al-Wahhab. It represents the radical militant wing of Islam and has had notable success in the burgeoning cities of the Islamic world, providing networks of social services to the urban poor in return for militant support. Islamists emphasize the simplicity of Islam, which must inform every aspect of personal life and society. Only rule by Divine Law can guarantee a just society. Like Christian fundamentalists, they reject modernist metaphorical interpretations of the Qur'an. Modernity is rejected, although not technology, which has greatly aided the spread of Islamist ideas. Western civilization is the enemy, and America is identified with the Qur'anic Satan, who tries to seduce humanity from the straight path to salvation.

Rule by secularizing military elites *has been a feature of a number of modern Islamic states. This poster vividly illustrates the leadership cult fostered by Saddam Hussein in Iraq.*

Ayatollah Khomeini *was able to reverse decades of secularization in Iranian society when he came to power through the 1979 revolution that ousted the shah.*

OPPOSITE

All over the Islamic world *children learn to read the Qur'an in the original Arabic. These Indonesian boys are reading from large, legible copies of the Qur'an.*

GLOBALIZATION

The process of modernization that began in the early 19th century and in the 20th century culminated in the creation of a system of nation states locked into an international economy has evolved into a global system marked by extreme mobility which has already transcended the structure from which it grew. Muslim communities now exist in almost every country in the world, and the border between the "Abode of Islam" and the "Abode of War" can no longer be mapped.

The classical shari'a, elaborated in the wake of the triumphal expansion of Islam, did not contemplate the possibility of permanent Muslim communities dwelling in non-Muslim lands. These communities are challenged by difficult questions. Can a practicing Muslim fully comply with civil laws that conflict with the shari'a? Can he or she participate fully in political processes? Does loyalty to Islam transcend loyalty to the state? Should Muslims assimilate to the dominant society or remain separate? What are the limits of tolerance of the host community? Many of these are questions first posed with the rise of secular regimes within the Muslim world itself, but they have been given added urgency for European and American Muslims by the events of September 11 and their aftermath. The Muslim extremists who hijacked four airliners, crashing two of them into the World Trade Center in New York and one into the Pentagon, had been living in the United States for a long time in order to plan this symbolic terrorist assault on the West and its values.

Just as territorial borders have been transcended, the revolution in information technology has eliminated internal barriers. It is no longer possible for states or elites to control access to information. Educational systems established during the period of modernization have created widespread literacy, and Muslim men and women have direct access to the foundation texts of their faith as well as to secular literature. This has displaced or marginalized traditional elites, and created, on the one hand, broadly-based reform and revivalist movements and, on the other, increasing secularization. It has led to productive and dynamic dialogues with the past that have already resulted in reassessments of the nature of the shari'a, the relationship between religion and politics, and the traditional role of women in Islamic society. There is no doubt that Muslims throughout the world will continue to formulate responses to the challenge of globalization from within the tradition that has proved so creative and dynamic in the past.

THE ISLAMIC WORLD TODAY

COUNTRY PROFILES

THIS DIRECTORY IS INTENDED to provide a range of up-to-date reference material covering the leading Muslim nations of the world today. The criterion for inclusion was quite simply any nation with a majority (i.e. more than 50%) of the population professing Islam as their religion. It is recognized that this criterion excludes India, which is the country with the second largest Muslim population today, and China with its unreported and unrecorded Islamic peoples. The selection of data is intended to provide a general portrait of each nation through its social, political, economic and cultural characteristics. One of the key features is comparability – the data has been assembled to allow direct comparison of any one nation with any other. Naturally, every attempt has been made to ensure accuracy and validity at the time of going to press (December 2001). For more detailed analyses of the Islamic nations, the *DK Financial Times World Desk Reference* is recommended.

 Date of independence or formation

 Date when current borders were established

 National day

 Vehicle identification code

 Time zone: hours plus or minus from GMT

 International telephone dialing code

 Internet country identifying code

POLITICS

 Dates of last and next legislative elections

 Name of head of state. In many cases this is a nominal position and does not indicate that this is the country's most powerful person

 System of government

WORLD AFFAIRS

 Membership of international organizations. A selection of principal organizations; countries may have membership status within numerous other organizations

 Date of entry into the United Nations

PEOPLE & SOCIETY

 Population density: people per square mile

 Percentage of population living in urban/rural areas

 Religious affiliation

 Use of death penalty

ECONOMICS

 World Gross National Product ranking

 Balance of payments

 Gross National Product per capita

 Annual rate of inflation

MEDIA

 Level of political censorship

 Television ownership

 Main national newspapers/ total daily circulation

 TV/Radio stations State-owned/independent

SPENDING

 Vehicle ownership: vehicles per thousand people

 Defense spending: percentage of annual GDP

 Education spending: percentage of annual GDP

 Health spending: percentage of annual GDP

RESOURCES

 Total electric power capacity

 Electricity generation by energy source

 Estimated livestock resources

 Oil production: barrels per day/total oil reserves: barrels

EDUCATION

 Literacy rate: percentage of total population

 Students in tertiary education

 School leaving age

 Percentage of each age group enrolled in each education sector

DEFENSE

 Annual defense budget

 Requirement for compulsory military service

 Nuclear capability

 Total combined forces personnel

HEALTH

 People per doctor

 Average life expectancy

Birth rate: births per thousand people

Infant mortality: deaths per thousand live births

Sources of statistical data

Cambridge International Reference on Current Affairs (CIRCA)
Europa World Yearbook
European Bank for Reconstruction and Development (EBRD)
Food and Agriculture Organization (FAO)
International Atomic Energy Agency (IAEA)
International Institute for Strategic Studies (IISS)
International Labor Organization (ILO)
International Monetary Fund (IMF) World Economic Outlook
International Union for Conservation of Nature (IUCN)
Organization for Economic Cooperation Development (OECD)
OECD Development Assistance Committee (DAC)
Organization of Petroleum Exporting Countries (OPEC)
United Nations: *Demographic Yearbook, Energy Statistics Yearbook, Industrial Commodity Statistics Yearbook, International Trade Statistics Yearbook, Statistical Yearbook, Children's Fund (UNICEF), Development Program (UNDP)*
United States Central Intelligence Agency (CIA)
World Bank: *World Development Indicators, World Development Report, World Bank Atlas*
World Conservation Monitoring Center (WCMC)
World Economic Forum
World Health Organization (WHO)

ALBANIA

OFFICIAL NAME **Republic of Albania** **CAPITAL** **Tirana**
POPULATION **3.1m** **CURRENCY** **Lek** **OFF. LANG.** **Albanian**

LYING AT THE southeastern end of the Adriatic Sea, opposite the heel of Italy, Albania is a mountainous country which became a one-party communist state in 1944. It held multiparty elections in 1991, but economic collapse provoked uprisings in 1997, which were only stabilized by OSCE troops. Still poverty-stricken, Albania has been more stable since the return home of the ethnic Albanian refugees who flooded in from war-torn Kosovo in 1999.

POLITICS

 2001/2005   President Rexhep Mejdani   Multiparty republic

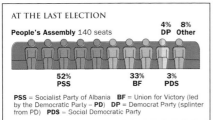

AT THE LAST ELECTION

People's Assembly 140 seats

4% DP   8% Other

52% PSS   33% BF   3% PDS

PSS = Socialist Party of Albania   **BF** = Union for Victory (led by the Democratic Party – **PD**)   **DP** = Democrat Party (splinter from PD)   **PDS** = Social Democratic Party

Albania was dominated for more than 40 years by communist ruler Enver Hoxha, who died in 1985. An exodus of Albanians in 1991 finally persuaded the succeeding regime to call multiparty elections. The resulting center-right coalition failed, however, to create a Western-style liberal state.

Many people were ruined by investing in "pyramid" savings schemes which collapsed in 1997, prompting a rebellion in the south and forcing the government to resign. A new coalition led by the socialist PSS won elections held that year. They won a further term in the mid-2001 elections, as socialist leader Ilir Meta claimed credit for restoring a measure of security and hope.

WORLD AFFAIRS

 CE, PfP, WTO, OSCE, OIC   UN 1955

Foreign policy in the 1990s was dominated by the fate of Kosovo, the predominately ethnic Albanian region in neighboring Yugoslavia. Separatism also erupted in Macedonia in 2001, although Albania's own influence is small. Membership of NATO and the EU is a long-term goal.

PEOPLE & SOCIETY

 293 people per sq mile   39% urban 61% rural

Sunni Muslim 70% Greek Orthodox 20% Roman Catholic 10%   Death penalty not used

Official statistics admitted the existence of ethnic minorities in Albania only in 1989. The Greek minority strongly contests these statistics, which state that 98% of the population are Albanian. Located mainly in the south, the Greeks claim to make up 10% of the population. They suffer considerable discrimination.

Total Land Area :
27 400 sq. km (10 579 sq. miles)

POPULATION
⊚ over 100 000
○ over 50 000
● over 10 000
• under 10 000

LAND HEIGHT
2000m/6562ft
1000m/3281ft
500m/1640ft
200m/656ft
Sea Level

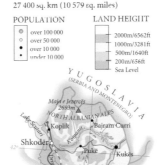

ECONOMICS

 131st $-155m

$930   0.4%

Oil and gas reserves. Significant economic growth achieved since 1997 collapse. Progress with privatization. Rudimentary public services and energy, transportation, and water networks.

RESOURCES

5.7bn kwh   Comb. 100% Hydro 0% Nuclear 0%

Sheep 1.94m Goats 1.12m Cattle 720,000   7,218 b/d (reserves of 181.8m bbl)

Albania needs huge capital investment to develop its minerals and to create a modern electricity supply system.

DEFENSE

 $140m   Compulsory

 None   47,000

The armed forces reestablished officer ranks in 1991, and in 2000 were in the process of being reconstructed. The Kosovo crisis prompted Albania in 1999 to make its airspace available to NATO.

MEDIA

 Censorship   Medium

4 daily 37 per 1,000 people   TV: 1/75 Radio: 1/30

Media freedom has improved, but newspaper sales are in decline; the independent *Koha Jonë* has the largest circulation. Fewer dailies are party run.

EDUCATION

 84.7%   34,257 students

14 years   Primary 100% Secondary 38% Tertiary 12%

Albania's education system is derived from the Soviet, Chinese, and Italian models. There are four universities throughout the country.

HEALTH

 1 per 714 people   73 years

16 per 1,000 people   24 per 1,000 people

The health service is rudimentary, and is heavily dependent on aid from the West for most drugs and medical supplies.

SPENDING

 29 per 1,000 people   3.6%

3.1%   3.5%

Wealth is limited to a few private-sector entrepreneurs. Poverty is worst in northern rural areas but also acute in slum settlements around Tirana and other cities.

MOROCCO

1956	1956	July 30	MA	0	+212	.ma

OFFICIAL NAME **Kingdom of Morocco** CAPITAL **Rabat**
POPULATION **28.4m** CURRENCY **Moroccan dirham** OFF. LANG. **Arabic**

MOROCCO IS SITUATED IN northern Africa, but at its northernmost point lies only 8 miles (12 km) from mainland Europe, across the Strait of Gibraltar. The late King Hassan's international prestige gave Morocco status out of proportion to its wealth. The main issues the country faces are the internal threat of Islamic militancy and the unresolved fate of Western Sahara, occupied by Morocco since 1975.

POLITICS

 1997/2002   HM King Mohammed VI   Constitutional monarchy

Morocco is a constitutional monarchy with a bicameral legislature. The new king, Mohammed VI, is seen as a less dominating figure than his late father King Hassan II. His accession has encouraged expectations of change.

AT THE LAST ELECTION

House of Representatives 325 seats

3% MPCD   1% PSD

31% K   31% W   30% C   3% FFD   1% Others

K = Koutla bloc (includes Socialist Union of Popular Forces and Istiqlal) **W** = Wifaq bloc (includes Constitutional Union & Popular Movement) **C** = Center bloc (includes National Rally of Independents and Democratic Popular Movement) **MPCD** = Constitutional & Democratic Popular Movement **FFD** = Democratic Forces Front **PSD** = Democratic Socialist Party

House of Councillors 270 seats

An indirectly elected House of Councillors was formed in December 1997

Under Hassan the government dealt ruthlessly with Islamic militants, but it had begun to take a less repressive stance, and Mohammed VI and the government in office since 1998 have ushered in further liberalizing moves. In May 2000 Abdessalam Yassine, spiritual leader of the banned Islamic movement Justice and Good Deeds, was released after 10 years' imprisonment without trial. Popular support for fundamentalism is fueled by the fear that Morocco is losing its Islamic identity. Pro-Islamist rallies in March 2000 far outnumbered those by supporters of greater rights for women.

Although the majority party in parliament now chooses the government, the king reserved the right to appoint or dismiss the prime minister. Legislative elections in November 1997 left parliament split three ways, with only nine seats going to Islamists. The eventual formation of a socialist-led government was seen as the clearest expression to date of the increasing role of the party system.

WORLD AFFAIRS

 NAM, OIC, AL, AMU, IBRD   1956

International disapproval has focused on Morocco's occupation since 1975 of the former Spanish colony of Western Sahara. Resistance by Polisario Front guerrillas, who are fighting for an independent Western Sahara, commenced in 1983 and has continued, despite a UN-brokered peace plan in 1991. In 1994, the UN approved plans for a voter identification process, to lead to a referendum on self-determination. The whole process was so frequently obstructed that UN representative James Baker proposed in 2001 that Western Sahara should become part of Morocco as an autonomous area for a 10-year trial period.

Relations with the EU have been strengthened with the signing of an association agreement in late 1995, envisaging free trade in industrial goods within 12 years. However, a fisheries dispute with the EU involving Spanish and Portuguese fishing rights off the Moroccan coast remains to be resolved. Morocco's important role in the quest for lasting peace in the Middle East was underlined by Israeli prime minister Yitzhak Rabin's visit to Rabat following the signing in Washington of the 1993 peace accord with the Palestine Liberation Organization. King Hassan's foreign policy was ambiguous, for while he negotiated with Israel he also headed the Jerusalem Committee of the Islamic Conference Organization (OIC). Generally more pro-Western than other Arab states, Morocco has also earned respect by protecting its Jewish minority.

PEOPLE & SOCIETY

 165 people per sq mile

 55% urban
45% rural

 Sunni Muslim 98%
Christian 1%
Jewish 1%

 Death penalty used

Morocco, the westernmost of the Maghreb states, is the main refuge for descendants of the original Berber inhabitants of northwest Africa. About 35% of Moroccans are Berber-speaking. They live mainly in mountain villages, while the Arab majority inhabit the lowlands. Before independence from France, 450,000 Europeans lived in Morocco; numbers have since greatly diminished. Some 45,000 Jews enjoy religious freedom and full civil rights – a position in society unique among Arab countries. Most people speak Arabic, and French is also spoken in urban areas. Sunni Islam is the religion of most of the population. The king is the spiritual leader through his position as Commander of the Faithful. Female emancipation has been slow to take root in Morocco, but women are starting to take a more prominent role in society.

ECONOMIC FOCUS

EXPORTS

USA 5%
Germany 6%
UK 7%
Spain 8%
Other 42%
France 32%

IMPORTS

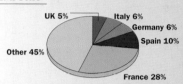

UK 5%
Italy 6%
Germany 6%
Spain 10%
Other 45%
France 28%

STRENGTHS

Morocco's probusiness policies and abundant labor force are helpful in attracting foreign investment. The country has low rates of inflation. The tourist industry (already of importance to the economy), phosphate mining, and agriculture all have great potential for future exploitation.

WEAKNESSES

Morocco suffers from high unemployment rates coupled with a rising population growth. Recent droughts have hit the agricultural sector hard. The illicit production of cannabis (Morocco is Europe's main source of resin) complicates closer links with the EU.

PROFILE

The government's large-scale privatization program, which began in 1992, was designed to attract foreign investment, particularly from Europe. A severe drought in 1995 made austerity measures necessary. The new socialist-led government has given social policy a higher priority. The expected revenue to be gained from the exploitation of Morocco's oil reserves will be channeled into the development of rural areas.

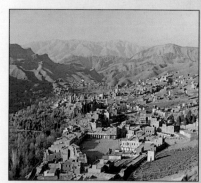

The town of Boumaine-Dadès lies in the southern foothills of the Atlas Mountains. The region's outstanding scenery makes it one of Morocco's major tourist attractions.

Total Land Area : 446 300 sq. km
(172 316 sq. miles)

POPULATION

over 1 000 000
over 500 000
over 100 000
over 50 000
over 10 000
under 10 000

LAND HEIGHT

3000m/9843ft
2000m/6562ft
1000m/3281ft
500m/1640ft
200m/656ft
Sea Level

MAURITANIA

| 1960 | 1960 | Nov 28 | RIM | 0 | +222 | .mr |

OFFICIAL NAME **Islamic Republic of Mauritania** CAPITAL **Nouakchott**
POPULATION **2.7m** CURRENCY **Ouguiya** OFF. LANG. **Arabic & French**

LOCATED IN NORTHWEST AFRICA, Mauritania is a member of both the OAU and the Arab League. Formerly a French colony, the country has taken a strongly Arab direction since 1964; today, it is the Maures who control political life and dominate the minority black population. The Sahara extends across two-thirds of Mauritania's territory; the only productive land is that drained by the Senegal River in the south and southwest.

POLITICS

 L. House 1996/2001
U. House 2000/2002

 President Moaouia ould Sidi Mohammed Taya

Multiparty republic

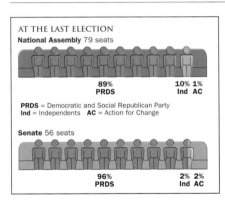

AT THE LAST ELECTION
National Assembly 79 seats

89% PRDS   10% 1%
            Ind AC

PRDS = Democratic and Social Republican Party
Ind = Independents   **AC** = Action for Change

Senate 56 seats

96% PRDS   2%   2%
            Ind AC

Mauritania officially adopted multiparty democracy in 1991. However, the 1992 and 1997 presidential elections simply returned to power the incumbent military ruler, President Moaouia ould Sidi Mohammed Taya, with around 90% of the vote. Legislative elections have been boycotted by the opposition parties, which accuse the government of electoral fraud. The blacks of the south support exiled parties, such as the African Liberation Forces of Mauritania (FLAM).

WORLD AFFAIRS

 OIC, AL, OIF, OAU, CILSS

 1960

Mauritania seeks to maintain a balance between sub-Saharan Africa and the Arab world, but has had political tensions with all its neighbors. It has now effectively withdrawn from the Western Sahara dispute. Relations with Senegal have improved since the conflicts of 1989.

PEOPLE & SOCIETY

 7 people per sq mile

 56% urban
44% rural

Sunni Muslim 100%

 Death penalty used

The politically dominant Maures make up the majority of the population. Ethnic tension centers on the oppression of blacks by Maures. The old black bourgeoisie has now been superseded by a Maurish class; tens of thousands of blacks are estimated to be in slavery.

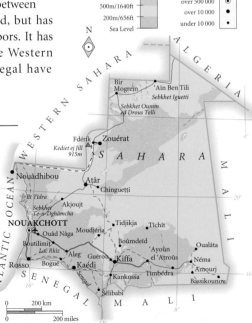

Total Land Area : 1 025 520 sq. km (395 953 sq. miles)

LAND HEIGHT   POPULATION
500m/1640ft   over 500 000 ⊙
200m/656ft   over 10 000 •
Sea Level   under 10 000 ·

 ECONOMICS

 156th

$77m

$390

4.1%

Largest gypsum deposits in the world. Offshore fishing among the best in West Africa. "Debt-distressed", with a debt of nearly $2 billion. Affected by drought, locust attacks, and fluctuating commodity prices.

 RESOURCES

153m kwh

Comb. 82%
Hydro 18%
Nuclear 0%

Sheep 6.2m
Goats 4.1m
Cattle 1.4m

Not an oil producer

Iron continues to be exploited, despite low world prices. There are some gold and diamond deposits. Mining and fisheries represent 99.7% of exports. Phosphates have been found near the Senegal River.

DEFENSE

$24m

Compulsory

None

15,650

The 15,000-strong army is a strain on Mauritania's budget. Troops are used increasingly in public works projects. France is the main arms supplier. Conscription is authorized for 2 years.

 MEDIA

 Censorship

Medium

3 daily
0.5 per 1,000 people

TV:1/0
Radio: 1/0

The press is heavily censored, and the broadcast media are state-owned. *Chaab*, the government newspaper, is also published in French (*Horizons*).

 EDUCATION

 42.3%

8,500

12 years

Primary 57%
Secondary 16%
Tertiary 4%

Despite improvements in education, over half the population continues to be illiterate. Arabic has been compulsory in all schools since 1988.

 **HEALTH**

1 per 10,000 people

51 years

39 per 1,000 people

88 per 1,000 live births

Historic regional inequalities persist and the best facilities are in the capital. The overall level of care is on a par with neighboring states.

 SPENDING

 8 per 1,000 people

2%

 5.1%

 1.4%

The small ruling Maures elite form the richest sector. Wealthy Maures travel to Mecca, Saudi Arabia, to perform the *hajj* (Muslim pilgrimage).

SENEGAL

| 1960 | 1960 | April 4 | SN | 0 | +221 ☎ | .sn |

 115th $-304m

 $500   0.8%

ECONOMICS

OFFICIAL NAME **Republic of Senegal** CAPITAL **Dakar**
POPULATION **9.5m** CURRENCY **CFA franc** OFF. LANG. **French**

Good infrastructure. Relatively strong industrial sector. Few natural resources exploited, other than fish, phosphates, and groundnuts. Access to oil potential hampered by rebellion and poor transportation links.

Senegal's capital, Dakar, lies on the westernmost cape of Africa. The country is mostly low, with open savanna and semidesert in the north and thicker savanna in the south. After independence from France in 1960, Senegal was ruled until 1981 by President Léopold Senghor. He was succeeded by his prime minister, Abdou Diouf, who held power for almost 20 years until his election defeat in March 2000.

 1.2bn kwh   Comb. 100% Hydro 0% Nuclear 0%

 Sheep 4.3m Goats 3.6m Cattle 2.97 m   Not an oil producer

RESOURCES

Senegal's electricity capacity is largely dependent on imported fuel; cheaper supplies are expected to become available soon. Initial explorations suggest that oil reserves may exist off Casamance.

POLITICS

 2001/2006   President Abdoulaye Wade   Presidential democracy

 $81m   Compulsory

 None   9,400

DEFENSE

Senegal has been a multiparty democracy since 1981 when, under the then new president, Abdou Diouf, the constitution was amended to allow more than four political parties. However, the PS held power from the 1950s until 2000, and its influence has been pervasive. Presidential elections in 2000 marked a political watershed. Diouf was defeated by Abdoulaye Wade of the liberal democratic PDS, the dominant party in the "Sopi" (Change) coalition that went on to win a landslide victory in the 2001 legislative elections. A new constitution, approved in 2001 by referendum, abolished the Senate and restricts the president to two terms.

Senegalese troops took part in Operation Desert Storm in 1991, and intervened in conflicts in Liberia, Rwanda, and the Central African Republic. They also helped to quell revolts in Gambia and Guinea-Bissau.

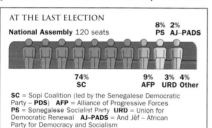

AT THE LAST ELECTION

National Assembly 120 seats   8% 2% PS AJ–PADS

74% SC   9% AFP   3% URD   4% Other

SC = Sopi Coalition (led by the Senegalese Democratic Party – **PDS**) **AFP** = Alliance of Progressive Forces **PS** = Senegalese Socialist Party **URD** = Union for Democratic Renewal **AJ–PADS** = And Jëf – African Party for Democracy and Socialism

 No censorship   Low

 8 daily 5 per 1,000 people   TV: 1/1 Radio: 1/4

MEDIA

The independent media flourished with multipartyism. Senegal had the first satirical journal in Africa with the founding of Le Politicien in 1978.

WORLD AFFAIRS

 OIC, ECOWAS, CILSS OMVG, FZ   UN 1960

Maintaining good relations with its former ruler France, which is also Senegal's main ally and aid donor, is the major foreign affairs concern. Senegal's relations with neighboring Gambia, Mauritania, and Guinea-Bissau continue to be a constant preoccupation.

 37.4%   24,000 students

 13 years   Primary 60% Secondary 16% Tertiary 3%

EDUCATION

Illiteracy is Senegal's major educational challenge, especially for women, of whom only 23% can read. There are universities at Dakar and St.-Louis.

Total Land Area : 192 530 sq. km (74 336 sq. miles)

POPULATION
over 1 000 000
over 100 000
over 50 000
over 10 000
under 10 000

M A U R I T A N I A

Richard Toll
Dagana
Saint-Louis
Lac de Guier
Senegal
Louga
Dara
Linguère
Matam
Mékhé
Pikine
Thiès
Mbaké
Vallée du Ferlo
Vallée du Mbour
DAKAR
Diourbel
Bakel
Mbour
Saloum
Joal-Fadiout
Kaolack
Kaffrine
Koungheul
Nioro du Rip
Tambacounda
GAMBIA
Bignona
Vélingara
Kolda
Médina Gounas
Gambia
581m ▲ Kédougou
Cap Roxo
Ziguinchor
Sédhiou
CASAMANCE
Casamance
GUINEA-BISSAU
G U I N E A

ATLANTIC OCEAN

M A L I

N

0 100 km
0 100 miles

LAND HEIGHT
200m/656ft
Sea Level

 1 per 10,000 people   53 years

 38 per 1,000 people   67 per 1,000 live births

HEALTH

The state health system is very rudimentary. A successful education campaign has helped to contain the incidence of HIV/AIDS.

PEOPLE & SOCIETY

 128 people per sq mile   47% urban 53% rural

 Sunni Muslim 90% Christian 5% Traditional beliefs 5%   Death penalty not used

10 per 1,000 people   1.6%

3.7%   2.6%

SPENDING

Wealth disparities are considerable, and poverty is widespread. Those people who are close to the government are the wealthiest group.

Senegal has a fairly well-developed sense of nationhood, and intermarriage between groups has reduced ethnic tensions. Many groups can still be identified regionally, however. A French-influenced class system, inherited from colonial days, is still prevalent. The 2001 constitution gave women property rights for the first time.

GAMBIA

1965   1965   Feb 18   WAG   0   +220   .gm

OFFICIAL NAME **Republic of the Gambia** CAPITAL **Banjul**
POPULATION **1.3m** CURRENCY **Dalasi** OFF. LANG. **English**

A NARROW COUNTRY on the western coast of Africa, Gambia was renowned as a stable democracy until an army coup in 1994. Agriculture accounts for 65% of GDP, yet many Gambians are leaving rural areas for the towns, where average incomes are four times higher. Its position as a semi-enclave within Senegal seems likely to endure, following the failure of an experiment in federation in the 1980s.

POLITICS

 1997/2001   President Yahya Jammeh   Multiparty republic

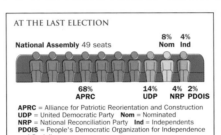

AT THE LAST ELECTION

National Assembly 49 seats

8% Nom   4% Ind

68% APRC   14% UDP   4% NRP   2% PDOIS

APRC = Alliance for Patriotic Reorientation and Construction
UDP = United Democratic Party   **Nom** = Nominated
NRP = National Reconciliation Party   **Ind** = Independents
PDOIS = People's Democratic Organization for Independence and Socialism

The People's Progressive Party (PPP) was in government from 1962 until 1994, for most of which time Gambia was one of Africa's few democracies. Military leader Yahya Jammeh was elected president in controversial elections in September 1996, and the following January his APRC won the majority of seats in a parliamentary election. The government claimed to have foiled a military coup in 2000.

WORLD AFFAIRS

 OIC, OAU, ECOWAS, CILSS, Comm   1965

President Jammeh has vigorously cultivated new partnerships following strong Commonwealth and Western criticism of his coup in 1994. Also, close ties have been forged with Nigeria as a counterweight to Senegal, with which relations have sometimes been strained since the collapse of the 1982–1989 confederation.

PEOPLE & SOCIETY

 337 people per sq mile   32% urban / 68% rural

Sunni Muslim 90% / Christian 9% / Traditional beliefs 1%   Death penalty not used

About 90% of Gambians follow Islam, although there is no official state religion. There is a yearly influx of migrants, who come from Senegal, Guinea, and Mali to trade in groundnuts. Gambia is still a very poor country, with 80% of the labor force engaged in agriculture. Women are active as traders and merchants in an otherwise male-dominated society.

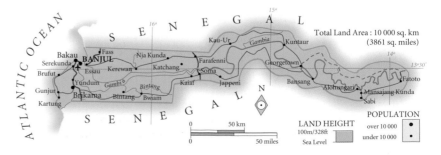

Total Land Area : 10 000 sq. km (3861 sq. miles)

LAND HEIGHT
100m/328ft
Sea Level

POPULATION
over 10 000
under 10 000

ECONOMICS

 171st $-46m

$330   3.8%

Low tariffs make Gambia a focus of regional trade. Its well-managed economy is favorably viewed by donors. Smuggling deprives government of significant revenues. Small size of market can inhibit investment.

RESOURCES

 77m kwh   Comb. 100% / Hydro 0% / Nuclear 0%

Sheep 190,000 / Goats 265,000 / Cattle 360,000   Not an oil producer

The Gambia River is one of Africa's few good waterways, but it is underused owing to its separation from its natural hinterland by the Gambia–Senegal border. Irrigation is provided by a single dam.

DEFENSE

  $16m   Not compulsory

None   800

The Gambia National Army, with two infantry battalions, takes about half of the defense budget; the rest finances the 600-strong gendarmerie. Most arms are bought from the UK.

MEDIA

  Censorship   Low

 2 daily / 2 per 1,000 people   TV: 1/0 / Radio: 1/8

Journalists and newspaper proprietors have suffered low-level harassment since the 1994 coup, and a popular private radio station has been closed down.

EDUCATION

 36.6%   1,590 students

Schooling is not compulsory   Primary 65% / Secondary 25% / Tertiary 2%

The aims are to increase enrollment to 75% in primary and 25% in secondary schools, and to improve teacher quality. A university was established in 1998.

HEALTH

  1 per 20,000 people   46 years

41 per 1,000 people   75 per 1,000 live births

Most people have access to basic medicines, but these are no longer free. Advanced medical care in the public sector is limited. An influx of Cuban doctors has helped extend services.

SPENDING

  8 per 1,000 people   3.5%

 4.9%   1.9%

Public service and the professions have created wealth and some people are comfortably off, but great wealth is not a feature of Gambian life. Unemployed young men in Banjul are regarded as the underclass.

GUINEA

OFFICIAL NAME **Republic of Guinea** CAPITAL **Conakry**
POPULATION **7.4 million** CURRENCY **Guinea franc** OFF. LANG. **French**

GUINEA LIES ON the western coast of Africa. The central, densely forested or savanna highlands slope down to coastal plains and swamps in the west and to the semidesert of the north. Military rule, established in 1984, ended with legislative elections in 1995; however, the results were disputed.

POLITICS

	Postponed indefinitely		President Lansana Conté		Multiparty republic

The death in 1984 of Sekou Touré, who headed the Marxist single-party regime of the Guinea Democratic Party (PDG) from 1958, opened the way for the military to intervene, with promises of multiparty elections. In 1990, a referendum overwhelmingly approved democratic changes, but the military appointed a Transitional Committee to

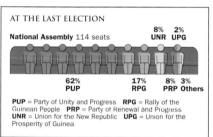

AT THE LAST ELECTION

National Assembly 114 seats

	8% UNR	2% UPG
62% PUP	17% RPG	8% PRP 3% Others

PUP = Party of Unity and Progress **RPG** = Rally of the Guinean People **PRP** = Party of Renewal and Progress **UNR** = Union for the New Republic **UPG** = Union for the Prosperity of Guinea

run the country, delaying elections until the end of 1993, when incumbent leader, General Lansana Conté, won with 52% of the votes. Opposition parties alleged that the elections had been rigged, and serious violence broke out. A disputed victory for Conté's PUP in the 1995 legislative elections was followed by a further win for Conté in the December 1998 presidential election.

WORLD AFFAIRS

	OMVG, OIF, OIC, ECOWAS, OAU		1958

A growing concern is balancing the interests of its two major aid donors, France and the US. Relations with neighboring Liberia deteriorated in 2000 following accusations of playing host to Liberian rebels.

PEOPLE & SOCIETY

 78 people per sq mile

 32% urban 68% rural

Muslim 65% Traditional beliefs 33% Christian 2%

 Death penalty used

The two largest ethnic groups are the Fulani, based in the highland region of Fouta Djallon, and the Malinke, who lost the power they had held under Touré, and have suffered reprisals. Today, the coastal peoples, including the Soussou, are dominant, benefiting from renewed rivalry between the Malinke and Fulani. Women acquired influence within Touré's Marxist party, but a Muslim revival since 1984 has reversed this trend.

[Map]

POPULATION
- over 500 000
- over 50 000
- over 10 000
- under 10 000

LAND HEIGHT
- 1000m/3281ft
- 500m/1640ft
- 200m/656ft
- Sea Level

Total Land Area : 245 860 sq. km (94 926 sq. miles)

SENEGAL

GUINEA-BISSAU

MALI

Koundara, Gaoual, Kalum, Gambia, Niagassola, Doko, Kogon, Tougué, FOUTA Labé, DJALLON, Léouma, Télimélé, Dabola, Séouma, Siguiri, Niger, Niantanina, Boké, Fria, Kamsar, Mamou, Kouroussa, Mandiana, Iles Tristao, Kindia, Faranah, Kankan, Boffa, Coyah, Forécariah, Kissidougou, Kérouané, Koumandou, CONAKRY, Konsankoro, Guékédou, FON, Beyla, Macenta, Nzérékoré, Lola, Monts Nimba 1752m

ATLANTIC OCEAN

SIERRA LEONE

LIBERIA

IVORY COAST (CÔTE D'IVOIRE)

0 100 km
0 100 miles

ALGERIA

| 1962 | 1962 | Nov 1 | DZ | +1 | +213 | .dz |

OFFICIAL NAME **Democratic and Popular Republic of Algeria** CAPITAL **Algiers**
POPULATION **31.5m** CURRENCY **Algerian dinar** OFF. LANG. **Arabic**

AFRICA'S SECOND-LARGEST COUNTRY, Algeria has borders with Morocco, Mauritania, Mali, Niger, Libya, and Tunisia. Algeria won independence from France in 1962. The military blocked Islamist militants from taking power after winning general elections in 1991, setting up a new civilian regime and throughout the 1990s fighting a bloody conflict against terrorists. Algeria has one of the youngest populations, and highest birthrates, in north Africa.

POLITICS

 L.House 1997/2002
U.House 2000/2003

 President Abdelaziz Bouteflika

Military regime

Military rule was imposed in 1992. Elections were held in 1997, but Abdelaziz Bouteflika's presidential election victory in 1999 was marred by the withdrawal of all other candidates.

AT THE LAST ELECTION

National People's Assembly 380 seats

| 41% RND | 18% MSP | 16% FLN | 9% MN | 5% FFS | 5% RCD | 6% Other |

RND = National Democratic Rally **MSP** = Movement for a Peaceful Society **FLN** = National Liberation Front **MN** = en-Nahda Movement **FFS** = Front of Socialist Forces **RCD** = Rally for Culture and Democracy **App** = Appointed **Other** = Workers' Party, Progressive Republican Party, Union for Democracy and Liberty, Social Liberal Party, Independents

Council of the Nation 144 seats

| 53% RND | 33% App | 9% FLN | 2% MSP | 3% FFS |

96 seats are elected, 48 are appointed by the president

Algeria has been scarred by appalling violence since 1992, as Islamist militants struggle to establish a theocracy. Its foremost proponent, the Islamic Salvation Front (FIS) won elections in 1991, but was prevented from taking power by a military clampdown, unleashing violence spearheaded by the extremist Armed Islamic Group (GIA).

The FIS's strong showing in the 1991 polls was in part due to popular reaction against economic reforms first launched in 1988. After a brief suspension following the army takeover in 1992, the liberalization program was revived under pressure from the IMF and the World Bank.

Until 1988, Algeria was a Soviet-style regime. The aging ruling elite adopted privatization policies which were strongly opposed by Islamist militants, who were prevented from taking power by the army. Since 1992 tens of thousands of people have been killed in a terrorist campaign and ruthless state counterterrorist action. Hopes for peace rose when Bouteflika became president in 1999, but some 3,000 people, mainly civilians, were killed in 2000 alone.

WORLD AFFAIRS

 AMU, OPEC, OIC, NAM, AL

 1962

Algeria's struggle for independence from France lasted from 1954 until 1962. Throughout the 1960s and 1970s, Algeria's success in rejecting a colonial power made it a champion for the developing world. It had a leading voice within the UN, the Arab League, and the Organization of African Unity. However, relations with the West remained essentially stable. Algeria was increasingly seen by the diplomatic community as a useful bridge between the West and Iran. In 1981, Algerian diplomats helped to secure the release of US hostages being held in Tehran. Algeria also attempted to act in a mediating role during the 1980–1988 Iran–Iraq War.

ECONOMICS

 52nd

$2,367m

$1,550

2.5%

Oil and gas are major assets. Algeria is moving toward a market economy, though many industries remain under state control. There is a lack of skilled labor and unemployment rates are high.

RESOURCES

 21.5bn kwh

 Comb. 100% Hydro 0% Nuclear 0%

Sheep 18.2m Goats 3.4m Cattle 1.65m

1.6m b/d (reserves 9,200m bbl)

Crude oil and natural gas are Algeria's main resources. Algeria also has diverse minerals, including iron ore, zinc, silver, copper ore, lead, gold, and phosphates. Algeria has a large fishing fleet.

DEFENSE

 $3.1bn

Compulsory

None

124,000

The National Liberation Army (NLA), equipped with Russian weapons, is the dominant power in politics. There have been fears that parts of the army would forge an alliance with Muslim militants.

MEDIA

 Censorship

 Medium

24 daily 38 per 1,000 people

TV: 1/0 Radio: 4/0

Newspapers, TV, and radio are state-controlled and permit no criticism of government actions. TV is broadcast in Arabic, French, and Kabyle (Berber), and received by about two million sets.

EDUCATION

  67.8%

  347,410 students

15 years

Primary 94% Secondary 56% Tertiary 12%

Over three-quarters of the school-age population receive a formal education, and the literacy rate is rising. Since 1973 the curriculum has been Arabicized and the teaching of French has been restricted.

HEALTH

 1 per 1,000 people

 69 years

 25 per 1,000 people

 34 per 1,000 live births

Since 1974 all Algerians have had the right to free health care. Primary health care is rudimentary outside main cities. Because the system is overburdened, many people turn to alternative forms of medicine.

SPENDING

 25 per 1,000 people

6.6%

 5.1%

2.6%

There is great disparity in wealth between the political elite and the rest of the population. Those with connections in the military are the wealthiest group. Prices are soaring for basic necessities.

Algeria's influence overseas has diminished as the country has become increasingly unstable politically. A victory for the fundamentalist FIS in Algeria would greatly encourage Islamist militants in neighboring Morocco and Tunisia, and further undermine Egypt's embattled government.

France fears the spillover of terrorism and has been shocked by the killings, especially those of seven French priests and of the French Roman Catholic bishop of Oran. Many European governments are anxious to help stabilize the regime to avoid refugees seeking entry into France, Spain, and Italy.

PEOPLE & SOCIETY

 34 people per sq mile

 60% urban
40% rural

 Sunni Muslim 99%
Christian & Jewish 1%

 Death penalty used

Algeria's population is predominantly Arab, under 30 years of age, and urban; around a quarter are Berber. More than 85% speak Arabic, the official language, and 99% are Sunni Muslim. Of the million or so French who settled in Algeria before independence, only about 6,000 remain. Most Berbers consider the mountainous Kabylia region their homeland. Demonstrations there have met with violent police crackdowns, particularly in the Berber Spring of 1980, and on its anniversary in 2001. As in the rest of north Africa, the mosque is an important provider of social and medical services.

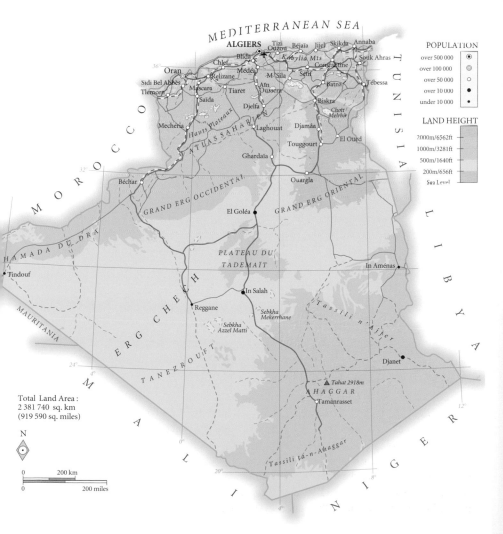

Total Land Area: 2 381 740 sq. km (919 590 sq. miles)

POPULATION
over 500 000
over 100 000
over 50 000
over 10 000
under 10 000

LAND HEIGHT
2000m/6562ft
1000m/3281ft
500m/1640ft
200m/656ft
Sea Level

ECONOMIC FOCUS

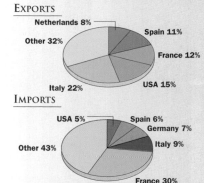

EXPORTS
Netherlands 8%
Other 32%
Spain 11%
France 12%
USA 15%
Italy 22%

IMPORTS
USA 5%
Spain 6%
Germany 7%
Italy 9%
France 30%
Other 43%

STRENGTHS

Oil and gas. Recent collaboration with Western oil companies should see improvements in productivity. Natural gas is supplied to Europe, with plans in hand for a third sub-sea pipeline to be built in 2001–2002.

WEAKNESSES

Political turmoil threatens many new projects and has led to an exodus of European and other expatriate workers important to the economy. Lack of skilled labor coupled with high unemployment. Limited agriculture. Shortages of basic foodstuffs. A thriving black market.

PROFILE

Under the pro-Soviet National Liberation Front, centralized socialist planning dominated the Algerian economy. In the late 1980s, the economic collapse of the Soviet Union led to a change in policy, and Algeria began moving toward a market economy. The majority of the economy's most productive sectors remain under state control, although private investment is encouraged in the oil industry and, since early 2001, in telecommunications. Western investment levels are likely to remain small as long as the political situation is unstable.

Saharan town, *showing the range of Algeria's scenery, from lush, irrigated gardens near water sources to barren sand dunes beyond. 80% of Algeria is desert.*

MALI

1960	1960	Sept 22	RMM	0	+223	.ml

OFFICIAL NAME **Republic of Mali**   CAPITAL **Bamako**
POPULATION **11.2m**   CURRENCY **CFA franc**   OFF. LANG. **French**

 ALI IS LANDLOCKED in the heart of west Africa. Its mostly flat terrain comprises virtually uninhabited Saharan plains in the north and more fertile savanna land in the south. The Niger River irrigates the central and southwestern regions. Mali achieved independence from France in 1960. Multiparty democratic elections under a new constitution, in 1992 and then in 1997, provoked accusations of severe irregularities.

POLITICS

1997/2002	President Alpha Oumar Konaré	Multiparty republic

AT THE LAST ELECTION
National Assembly 147 seats

87% ADEMA   5% PARENA   8% Others

ADEMA = Alliance for Democracy in Mali
PARENA = Party for National Renewal
Others = Democratic and Social Convention, Party for Democracy and Progress, Union for Democracy and Development, Convention for Progress and the People, Democracy and Justice Party, National Democratic Rally

The successful transition to multiparty politics in 1992 followed the overthrow in the previous year of Moussa Traoré, Mali's dictator for 23 years. The army's role was crucial in leading the coup, while Colonel Touré, who acted as interim president, was responsible for the swift return to civilian rule in less than a year. The change marked Mali's first experience of multipartyism. Maintaining good relations with the Tuaregs, after a peace agreement in 1991, is a key issue. However, the main challenge facing President Alpha Oumar Konaré's government is to alleviate poverty while placating the opposition, which accuses his government of fraud in the 1997 general election.

WORLD AFFAIRS

Mali concentrates on maintaining good relations with the ECOWAS countries and its northern neighbors. Relations with Libya, which is suspected of fomenting Tuareg revolt, are tense. There are good relations with the US, and other Western aid providers.

OIF, FZ, OIC, OAU, ECOWAS	UN 1960

PEOPLE & SOCIETY

| 24 people per sq mile | 29% urban
71% rural |
|---|---|
| Muslim 80%
Traditional beliefs 18%
Christian & others 2% | Death penalty not used |

Mali's most significant ethnic group, the Bambara, is also politically dominant. The relationship between the Bambara–Malinke majority and the Tuareg nomads of the Saharan north is tense and sometimes violent. The extended family is a vital social security system and link between the urban and rural poor. There are a few powerful women in Mali but, in general, women have little status.

Total Land Area : 1 220 190 sq. km (471 115 sq. miles)

LAND HEIGHT
500m/1640ft
200m/656ft
over 100m/328ft

0   200 km
0   200 miles

ALGERIA
MAURITANIA
SAHARA
Taoudenni
Tessalit
Adrar des Iforas
Araouane
Tombouctou   Niger
Goundam   L'Nianga   Gao   Ménaka
L. Débo   Hombori
Mopti   Tondo 1155m   Bandiagara
Nioro   Diéma   Ségou   San
Kayes   Kolokani   Bani
Mahina   Kita   Koulikoro   Koutiala
SENEGAL   BAMAKO   Yoroso
Bougouni   Sikasso   BURKINA
GUINEA
IVORY COAST
(CÔTE D'IVOIRE)   N I G E R

POPULATION
over 100 000
over 50 000
over 10 000
under 10 000

NIGER

OFFICIAL NAME **Republic of Niger** CAPITAL **Niamey**
POPULATION **10.7m** CURRENCY **CFA franc** OFF. LANG. **French**

LANDLOCKED IN THE WEST of Africa, Niger is linked to the sea by the Niger River. Saharan conditions prevail in the northern regions, in the area around the Aïr mountains, and, particularly, in the vast uninhabited northeast. Niger was ruled by one-party or military regimes until 1992 when a multiparty constitution was introduced, but a much-troubled democratic process was disrupted by military coups in 1996 and 1999.

POLITICS

 1999/2004   President Mamadou Tandja   Multiparty republic

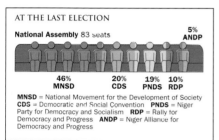

AT THE LAST ELECTION

National Assembly 83 seats

5% **ANDP**

46% **MNSD**   20% **CDS**   19% **PNDS**   10% **RDP**

MNSD = National Movement for the Development of Society **CDS** = Democratic and Social Convention **PNDS** = Niger Party for Democracy and Socialism **RDP** = Rally for Democracy and Progress **ANDP** = Niger Alliance for Democracy and Progress

The death in 1987 of the military dictator, President Seyni Kountché, paved the way for prodemocracy demonstrations and eventually led to multiparty elections in 1993. An ensuing power struggle between President Mahamane Ousmane and his political opponents provoked a military coup in 1996. General Ibrahim Barre Mainassara promulgated a new constitution and won a presidential election condemned as fraudulent by the opposition. Mainassara was assassinated by his presidential guard in early 1999. The new military leadership drew up yet another constitution. MNSD leader Mamadou Tandja won the presidential poll later that year.

WORLD AFFAIRS

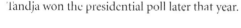

 OIC, CILSS, OAU, ECOWAS, FZ   UN 1960

Relations have improved with Libya and Algeria since the end of the Tuareg rebellion in 1995. ECOWAS members and the OAU condemned the 1999 coup, as did all key donors.

PEOPLE & SOCIETY

 22 people per sq mile   20% urban 80% rural

 Muslim 84% Traditional beliefs 14% Christian & others 2%   Death penalty not used

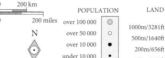

Total Land Area : 1 266 700 sq. km (489 073 sq. miles)

POPULATION
over 100 000
over 50 000
over 10 000
under 10 000

LAND HEIGHT
1000m/3281ft
500m/1640ft
200m/656ft
150m/492ft

Considerable tensions exist in Niger between the Tuaregs in the north and the southern groups. A five-year rebellion by northern Tuaregs ended in 1995 with a peace agreement. In eastern Niger, Toubou and Arab groups have also been in revolt. A more subtle antagonism exists between the Djerma and Hausa groups. The Djerma elite dominated politics for many years, until 1993 when control passed to the Hausa majority. Niger is an overwhelmingly Islamic society. Women have only limited rights and restricted access to education.

 139th $-174m

 $190   -2.3%

ECONOMICS

Niger has vast uranium deposits. Discoveries of gold and oil in the late 1990s revived hopes for economic viability. The collapse of uranium prices in the 1980s created a large debt burden.

 177m kwh   Comb. 100% Hydro 0% Nuclear 0%

 Sheep 4.3m Goats 6.6m Cattle 2.2m   Not an oil producer

RESOURCES

During the 1970s, Niger's uranium mines boomed. Other mining is small-scale and oil reserves, discovered in the Lake Chad area, are not yet commercially viable. Salt is a traditionally exploited resource.

 $28   Compulsory

 None   5,300

DEFENSE

Niger's armed forces and paramilitary elements total 5,300 personnel. Niger politics have been dominated by the military since 1974.

 Censorship   Low

 1 daily 0.2 per 1,000 people   TV: 2/1 Radio: 1/2

MEDIA

The government controls most broadcasting, though the BBC World Service's Hausa based programming is an influential medium.

 15.9%   4,500 students

 15 years   Primary 25% Secondary 6% Tertiary 1%

EDUCATION

The various local languages are emphasized more strongly than in most francophone states. School attendance only accounts for 30% of children.

 1 per 20,000 people   45 years

 51 per 1,000 people   116 per 1,000 live births

HEALTH

In spite of the progress made in rural health care, immunization, malaria control, and child nutrition are still unavailable to much of the population.

4 per 1,000 people   1.7%

2.3%   1.2%

SPENDING

A small circle of secretive trading families controls much of Niger's wealth. These families are very successful in evading taxation.

NIGERIA

ECONOMICS

 57th $506m

$260   6.6%

One of world's top oil producers. Vast reserves of natural gas, only partly exploited. Almost self-sufficient in food. Strong entrepreneurial class. Large domestic market. Overdependence since the 1970s on oil.

RESOURCES

 14.6bn kwh   Comb. 60% Hydro 40% Nuclear 0%

 Sheep 1.94m Goats 24.3m Cattle 19.8m   2.1m b/d (reserves of 22,500m bbl)

Oil has been Nigeria's main resource since the 1970s. The state retains 60% control of the oil and gas industry. There are plans for establishing an aluminum industry. Nigeria also has deposits of coal and tin.

DEFENSE

 $2,237m   Not compulsory

None   76,500

The military in Nigeria suffers the consequences of corruption. Soldiers' salaries have been steadily declining in real terms in recent years, barrack conditions have deteriorated, and morale is low.

MEDIA

 Some censorship   Medium

 25 daily 27 per 1,000 people   TV: 21/60 Radio: 2/2

Nigerians are avid newspaper readers and the press is one of Africa's liveliest. Media freedom has improved under the civilian government. There are about 60 TV stations; the Nigerian Television Authority runs 21.

EDUCATION

63.9%   207,982 students

12 years   Primary 98% Secondary 33% Tertiary 4%

Education has suffered from the government's massive debt repayment burden. During the oil-boom years, about 90% of children attend primary school, but only about 30% receive secondary education.

HEALTH

 1 per 5,000 people   52 years

 40 per 1,000 people   83 per 1,000 live births

The health service is mainly concentrated in urban areas, and only 49% of the population had access to water and health services. By 2000, more than 2.7 million Nigerians were HIV/AIDS carriers.

SPENDING

 8 per 1,000 people   4.4%

 0.7%   0.8%

Nigerians with access to the rich pickings of political office spent on a massive scale during the country's oil boom. Habits have not changed with the fall in oil revenues: borrowing has simply grown.

1960   1961   Oct 1   NGR   +1   +234   .ng

OFFICIAL NAME **Federal Republic of Nigeria**   CAPITAL **Abuja**
POPULATION **112m**   CURRENCY **Naira**   OFF. LANG. **English**

AFRICA'S MOST POPULOUS STATE, Nigeria gained its independence from Britain in 1960. Its terrain varies from tropical rain forest and swamps in the south to savanna in the north. Nigeria has been dominated by military governments since 1966. After many delays, a promised return to civilian rule came about in 1999, with the election as president of Olusegun Obasanjo, a former general who had been head of state from 1976 to 1979.

POLITICS

L. House 1999/2003
U. House 1999/2003   President Olusegun Obasanjo   Multiparty republic

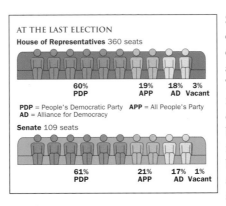

AT THE LAST ELECTION
House of Representatives 360 seats

60% PDP   19% APP   18% AD   3% Vacant

PDP = People's Democratic Party   APP = All People's Party
AD = Alliance for Democracy

Senate 109 seats

61% PDP   21% APP   17% AD   1% Vacant

Since May 1999 Nigeria has had a civilian constitution, after 16 years of military dictatorships. President Olusegun Obasanjo and his PDP promise national reconciliation. The Obasanjo regime faces difficulties in reversing ethnic rivalries. The situation deteriorated in early 2000 with rioting between Christians and the majority Muslims in the north so severe that state governments backed off from proposals on implementing sharia law. However, by 2001 ten northern states had introduced the Islamic code.

WORLD AFFAIRS

 OPEC, ECOWAS, OAU, Comm, OIC   1960

Nigeria is a strong sponsor of ECOWAS and of the OAU, and has been the main contributor to ECOWAS intervention forces. An implacable opponent of apartheid, its relations with South Africa were restored after democratic elections there in 1994.

Total Land Area : 910 770 sq. km (351 648 sq. miles)

LAND HEIGHT
2000m/6562ft
1000m/3281ft
500m/1640ft
200m/656ft
Sea Level

POPULATION
over 1 000 000
over 500 000
over 100 000
over 50 000
over 10 000
under 10 000

PEOPLE & SOCIETY

230 people per sq mile   43% urban 57% rural

Muslim 50% Christian 40% Traditional beliefs 10%   Death penalty used

Until fighting erupted in the southwest in mid-1999, Nigeria had enjoyed some success in containing tensions caused by ethnic, religious, and linguistic diversity. Traditionally, except in the Islamic north, women have possessed independent economic status. In recent years they have, however, been subjected to some prejudice in professional circles.

CHAD

| 1960 | 1960 | Aug 11 | TCH | +1 | +235 | .td |

OFFICIAL NAME: **Republic of Chad**   CAPITAL   **N'Djamena**
POPULATION **7.7m**   CURRENCY   **CFA franc**   OFF. LANG.   **Arabic and French**

LANDLOCKED IN NORTH CENTRAL Africa, Chad has had a turbulent history since independence from France in 1960. Intermittent periods of civil war, involving French and Libyan troops, followed a military coup in 1975. Following a coup in 1990, an interim government commenced the transition to multipartyism, now enshrined in a new constitution. The discovery of large oil reserves could eventually have a dramatic impact on the economy. The tropical, cotton-producing south is the most populous region.

POLITICS

 1997/2002   President Idriss Déby   Presidential democracy

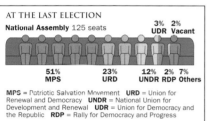

AT THE LAST ELECTION
National Assembly 125 seats

51% MPS   **23% URD**   **12% UNDR**   **2% RDP**   **7% Others**   **3% UDR**   **2% Vacant**

MPS = Patriotic Salvation Movement   **URD** = Union for Renewal and Democracy   **UNDR** = National Union for Development and Renewal   **UDR** = Union for Democracy and the Republic   **RDP** = Rally for Democracy and Progress

Idriss Déby overthrew President Hissène Habré in 1990 after an armed invasion from Sudan. He promised multipartyism, and in 1992 legalized political parties for the first time since the early 1960s. After many delays, the transitional process led to a successful referendum in 1996 on a new constitution based on the French model. President Déby was confirmed in office in elections in 1996 and again in 2001. His ruling MPS won 63 seats in parliament in the 1997 elections, just achieving an overall majority. Despite the government's attempts to restore peace, a new rebellion broke out in the north in early 1999, among the nomadic Toubou people.

WORLD AFFAIRS

 OIC, CILSS, FZ, LCBC, OAU   1960

Chad's most important relationship is with France. Libya occupied the uranium-rich Aozou strip in 1973–1994.

PEOPLE & SOCIETY

 16 people per sq mile   23% urban 77% rural

 Muslim 50% Traditional beliefs 43% Christian 7%   Death penalty used

About half the population, mainly the Sara-speaking and related peoples, is concentrated in the south in one-fifth of the national territory. Most of the rest are located in the central sultanates. The northern third of Chad has a population of only 100,000 people, mainly nomadic Muslim Toubou.

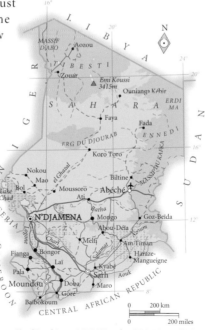

Total Land Area : 1 259 200 sq. km (486 177 sq. miles)

POPULATION
- over 500 000
- over 100 000
- over 50 000
- over 10 000
- under 10 000

LAND HEIGHT
- 3000m/9843ft
- 2000m/6562ft
- 1000m/3281ft
- 500m/1640ft
- 200m/656ft
- 100m/328ft

 145th $-161m

 $210   -6.8%

Recent discovery of large oil deposits could transform Chad's poor financial situation. Cotton industry; potential for other agriculture in south. Lack of transportation infrastructure. Political instability.

RESOURCES

 90m kwh   Comb. 100% Hydro 0% Nuclear 0%

 Sheep 2.43m Goats 4.97m Cattle 5.58m   No production Reserves unexploited

A consortium of ESSO, Shell, and ELF has discovered large oil reserves in the south. Natron, found north of Lake Chad, is the only mineral currently exploited. There is uranium in the Aozou strip.

DEFENSE

 $47m   Compulsory

 None   25,350

On seizing power, Déby swelled the existing army with irregulars. The policy has now been reversed and the army reduced to 25,000, including former rebels. France provides military aid and personnel.

MEDIA

 Censorship   Low

 2 daily 0.2 per 1,000 people   TV: 1/0 Radio: 1/0

Broadcasting is controlled by the government, which sometimes allows the airing of opposition views. There are a few independent publications, of which the best known is the weekly *N'Djamena-Hebdo*.

EDUCATION

 42.6%   3,446 students

 12 years   Primary 46% Secondary 6% Tertiary 1%

Education is based on the French model, though there are Koranic schools in the north. Primary school is compulsory, but enrollment is only 46%. World Bank aid has been directed at elementary schooling.

HEALTH

 1 per 20,000 people   46 years

 45 per 1,000 people   101 per 1,000 live births

Chad has very few city hospitals and under 300 smaller health centers in rural areas; over half are funded by religious groups or charities.

SPENDING

 2 per 1,000 people   2.9%

 1.7%   2.3%

Poverty is almost universal in Chad; the middle class is very small. There are very few wealthy individuals. Habré looted the treasury when he was overthrown in 1990.

TUNISIA

ECONOMICS

67th $-503m

$2,090   2.7%

A healthy economy is sustained with the help of Tunisia's main trading partners, the member states of the EU. Tourism from Europe is also high. The agricultural sector is hampered by droughts.

RESOURCES

8.4bn kwh

Comb. 99%
Hydro 1%
Nuclear 0%

Sheep 6.6m
Goats 1.4m
Cattle 790,000

80,000 b/d
(reserves of 300m bbl)

Tunisia is one of the world's leading producers of phosphates for fertilizers. Oil and gas are important exports, but growing domestic energy demands mean that Tunisia is now a net energy importer.

DEFENSE

$384m   Compulsory

None   35,000

Despite its small size, the military is an important political force, armed mainly with US weapons. Officer training is carried out in the US and France, as well as in Tunisia.

MEDIA

Some censorship   Medium

8 daily
31 per 1,000 people

TV: 2/0
Radio: 1/0

Reforms since the late 1980s have in theory increased press freedom in Tunisia, traditionally considered a source of liberal ideas in the Arab world. In practice, government restrictions remain.

EDUCATION

71%   121,800 students

16 years

Primary 98%
Secondary 64%
Tertiary 14%

Education is compulsory for nine years between the ages of six and 16. Arabic is the first language in schools, but French is also taught, and is used almost exclusively in higher education.

HEALTH

1 per 1,429 people   70 years

17 per 1,000 people

24 per 1,000 live births

Well-developed family planning facilities have almost halved Tunisia's birthrate over the past 30 years. Primary care facilities cover all but the most isolated rural communities.

SPENDING

30 per 1,000 people   1.7%

7.7%   2.2%

Today 6% of Tunisians are estimated to live in absolute poverty. In 1970, the figure was 30%. Special projects are being set up in the most deprived urban areas to offset the worst effects of poverty.

     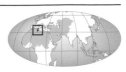

| 1956 | 1956 | March 20 | TN | +1 | +216 | .tn |

OFFICIAL NAME Republic of Tunisia   **CAPITAL** Tunis
POPULATION 9.6m   **CURRENCY** Tunisian dinar   **OFF. LANG.** Arabic

NORTH AFRICA'S SMALLEST COUNTRY, Tunisia lies sandwiched between Libya and Algeria. The populous north is mountainous, fertile in places, and has a long Mediterranean coastline. The south is largely desert. Habib Bourguiba ruled the country from independence in 1956 until a bloodless coup in 1987. Under President Ben Ali, the government has slowly moved toward multiparty democracy, but faces a challenge from Islamic fundamentalists. Closer ties with the EU, Tunisia's main trading partner, were strengthened through the first Euro-Mediterranean conference held in 1995. Manufacturing and tourism are expanding.

POLITICS

 1999/2004   President Zine al-Abidine Ben Ali   Presidential democracy

Formally a multiparty democracy since 1988, Tunisia is still dominated by the RCD and President Ben Ali. The RCD has clamped down on Islamic fundamentalists, particularly the outlawed Al-Nahda, or Renewal Party. In 1991, 500 Al-Nahda members were arrested following a failed coup, thought to be inspired by fundamentalists. Its leader, Rachid Ghannouchi, is in exile.

The RCD has been under increasing attack over its human rights record. The Tunisia League of Human Rights was suspended in January 2001. The RCD is committed to promoting women's rights.

President Ben Ali has made some effort to liberalize the political system. The life presidency has been abolished, and political parties and press freedom are encouraged. While allowing for a degree of political plurality, a complex proportional representation system ensured that there was an overwhelming victory for the RCD in the 1994 general election. This situation was confirmed in 1999 by the result of the next elections. Since 1994, there has been evidence of a renewed crackdown against the left-wing opposition. In 2000, more measures were announced with the aim of furthering democratization and promoting human rights.

AT THE LAST ELECTION

Chamber of Deputies 182 seats

4% PUP   3% MR

81% RCD

7% MDS   4% UDU   1% SLP

RCD = Constitutional Democratic Rally   **MDS** = Movement of Social Democrats   **PUP** = Popular Unity Party   **UDU** = Unionist Democratic Union   **MR** = Movement for Renewal   **SLP** = Social Liberal Party

WORLD AFFAIRS

 AL, OIC, NAM, OIF, AMU   1956

A foreign policy priority is to strengthen contacts with the West, which have generally been good because of Tunisia's liberal economic and social policies. Attention is focused on the EU, Tunisia's main export market, with Tunisia playing an important role in the run-up to the first Euro-Mediterranean conference, which was held in 1995.

Tunis was host to the PLO after that organization was expelled from Lebanon. Relations with other Arab states, particularly Kuwait and Saudi Arabia, were soured by Tunisia's support for Iraq in the Gulf War. The government regards the political success of Islamic fundamentalism in neighboring Algeria with concern. Relations with Libya are improving, helped by the fact that Tunisia turned a blind eye to sanctions-busters operating through its territory.

PEOPLE & SOCIETY

 160 people per sq mile

 65% urban
35% rural

Sunni Muslim 98%
Christian 1%
Jewish 1%

Death penalty used

The population of Tunisia is almost entirely Muslim, of Arab and Berber descent, although there are Jewish and Christian minorities. Many Tunisians still live in extended family groups, in which three or four generations are represented.

Tunisia has traditionally been one of the most liberal Arab states. The 1956 Personal Statutes Code of President Bourguiba gave women fuller rights than in any other Arab country. Further legislation has since given women the right to custody of children in divorce cases, made family violence against women punishable by law, and helped divorced women to get alimony. Family planning and contraception have been freely available since the early 1960s. Tunisia's population growth rate has halved since the 1980s. Women make up 31% of the total workforce and 35% of the industrial workforce. Company ownership by women is steadily increasing; politics, however, remains an exclusively male preserve.

These freedoms are threatened by the growth in recent years of Islamic fundamentalism, which also worries the mainly French-speaking political and business elite who wish to strengthen links with Europe.

The Ben Ali regime, although not as repressive as its predecessor, has been criticized for its actions against Islamic activists, in particular the banned Al-Nahda party. Amnesty International has detailed a number of human rights abuses, mainly against female members of Al-Nahda.

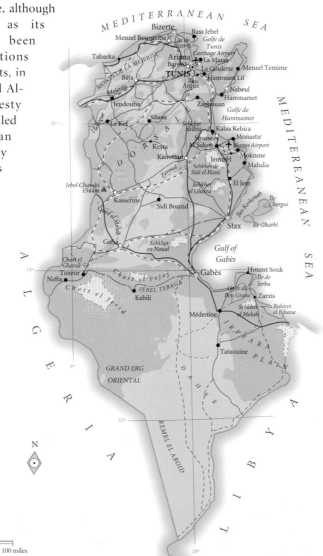

Total Land Area :
155 360 sq. km
(59 984 sq. miles)

POPULATION

⊙ over 500 000
◉ over 100 000
○ over 50 000
● over 10 000
· under 10 000

LAND HEIGHT

1000m/3281ft
500m/1640ft
200m/656ft
Sea Level

ECONOMIC FOCUS

EXPORTS

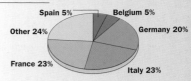

Spain 5%
Belgium 5%
Other 24%
Germany 20%
France 23%
Italy 23%

IMPORTS

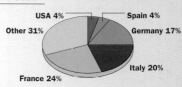

USA 4%
Spain 4%
Other 31%
Germany 17%
Italy 20%
France 24%

STRENGTHS

A well-diversified economy, despite limited resources. Oil and gas exports, also agricultural exports: olive oil, olives, citrus fruit, dates. Expanding manufacturing sector; important sectors are textiles, construction materials, machinery, chemicals. European investment. Ranked as the most competitive economy in Africa by the World Economic Forum in 2000.

WEAKNESSES

Dependence on growth of drought-prone agricultural sector. Growing domestic energy demand on oil and gas resources.

PROFILE

Since Tunisia began a process of structural adjustment in 1988, supported by the IMF and the World Bank, it has had an increasingly open, market-oriented economy. Annual inflation remained stable, despite higher food and energy prices. Prices have been freed, most state companies privatized, and import barriers reduced. The balance of payments relies on fluctuating tourism receipts to offset a trade deficit. The government must also balance growth with better social provisions. Members of the EU are Tunisia's main trading partners; trade has increased significantly since 1999.

Roman remains in the western Tozeur region. Diverse archaeological remains can be found throughout Tunisia.

LIBYA

1951	1951	Sept 1	LAR	+1	+218	.ly

OFFICIAL NAME **Great Socialist People's Libyan Arab Jamahiruyah**
CAPITAL **Tripoli** POPULATION **5.6m** CURRENCY **Libyan dinar** OFF. LANG. **Arabic**

L IBYA IS SITUATED between Egypt and Algeria on the Mediterranean coast of north Africa, with Chad and Niger on its southern borders. Apart from the coastal strip and the mountains in the south, it is desert or semidesert. Libya's strategic position in north Africa and its abundant oil and gas resources made it an important trading partner for the European states. It has for many years been politically marginalized by the West for its links with terrorist groups, but UN sanctions were suspended in 1999, when it handed over the two men suspected of the 1988 Lockerbie bombing.

ECONOMICS

58th		$1,476m	
$5,220		18%	

Reliance on production of oil, gas, aluminum, and petrochemicals. Sanctions in protest to the harboring of terrorists have recently been lifted. The Great Man-Made River project has proved unsuccessful.

RESOURCES

18.3bn kwh		Comb. 100% Hydro 0% Nuclear 0%
Sheep 6.45m Goats 2.25m Cattle 143,000		1.5m b/d (reserves of 29,500m bbl)

Libya's economy depends almost entirely on petroleum and natural gas resources. Libya also has reserves of iron ore, potassium, sulfur, magnesium, and gypsum. Animal husbandry is the basis of farming.

DEFENSE

$1,311m		Compulsory
None		76,000

In 1989 the armed forces were replaced by "the Armed People." Conscription is selective, and can last up to two years. In addition, there is a People's Militia numbering 40,000.

MEDIA

Censorship		Medium
4 daily 14 per 1,000 people		TV: 1/0 Radio: 1/1

Libya's press and TV are a mouthpiece for the leadership. Satellite TV and the internet are heavily censored. The main daily newspaper is published in Arabic and has a circulation of 40,000 readers. The TV station broadcasts mostly in Arabic.

EDUCATION

80.1%		72,900 students
15 years		Primary 100% Secondary 100% Tertiary 18%

Some one million Libyans are in formal education. It is compulsory between the ages of six and 15, and rates of attendance are very high. There are 13 universities, and institutes for vocational training.

HEALTH

1 per 769 people		70 years
28 per 1,000 people		22 per 1,000 live births

An adequate system of free primary health care exists except in remote areas, and there are two big hospitals. However, hospitals lack equipment, and there is a shortage of medical supplies.

SPENDING

159 per 1,000 people		4.7%
7.1%		3.4%

There is widespread poverty after years of import constraints; UN sanctions worsened the situation. Gaddafi refuses to use oil revenues for basic expenses, such as salaries – teachers earn about $1,200 a year.

POLITICS

Not applicable	Colonel Muammar al-Gaddafi	One-party state

Executive power is exercised by the General People's Committee. The General People's Congress elects the head of state, the Leader of the Revolution. Political dissidents, including Islamist militants, are violently suppressed. Libyan dissidents have been murdered abroad, allegedly by government agents. Political parties were banned in 1971, but opposition groups are active in Egypt and Sudan. In the past few years, the regime has made an effort to improve its image. Measures have included the freeing of some political prisoners and permitting foreign travel.

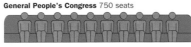

AT THE LAST ELECTION

General People's Congress 750 seats

The constitution makes no provision for direct elections. Last renewal May 2000

In 1977, a new form of direct democracy was promulgated, through which some 2000 People's Congresses sought to involve every adult in policy-making. In theory, their wishes are carried out by popular committees. In practice, ultimate control rests with Colonel Gaddafi and his collaborators, many of whom date from the 1969 revolution. In recent years some are thought to have been alienated from Gaddafi, including his deputy, Major Abdessalem Jalloud, who in 1994 was reportedly marginalized after expressing differences with him. In 1995, another of Gaddafi's close associates, Khoueldi Hamidi, a defense commander, was also said to have become disillusioned with Gaddafi. In 2000, Gaddafi embraced African unity – an unpopular concept among most Libyans, increasing Gaddafi's alienation from his fomer associates. He is now believed to rely on members of his own clan, particularly his five sons.

WORLD AFFAIRS

AL, NAM, OIC, OPEC, AMU	1955

Gaddafi's regime was by 2001 indicating a less confrontational stance than that which had left it isolated for decades, in particular its support for various terrorist groups and its strong opposition to the ongoing Middle East peace process. UN sanctions imposed in 1992 were eased in 1999, after Libya finally handed over two men accused of involvement in the 1988 bombing of a US airliner over Lockerbie, Scotland. The conviction of one of them in January 2001, by a Scottish court sitting at The Hague, prompted calls for the complete removal of sanctions. The UK resumed relations in 1999, when Libya admitted responsibility for the London shooting of a policewoman in 1984. Relations also improved with other EU countries and even the US.

PEOPLE & SOCIETY

8 people per sq mile	87% urban 13% rural	Sunni Muslim 97% Others 3%	Death penalty used

Arabs and Berbers, split into many tribal groupings, form 95% of the population. They were artificially brought together when Libya was created in 1951 by the unification of three historic Ottoman provinces. The pro-Western monarchy then set up perpetuated the dominance of Cyrenaican tribes and the Sanusi religious order.

The 1969 revolution brought to the fore Arab nationalist Colonel Gaddafi, who embodied the character and aspirations of the rural Sirtica tribes from Fazzan: fierce independence, deep Islamic convictions, belief in a communal lifestyle, and hatred for the urban rich. His revolution wiped out private enterprise and the middle class, banished European settlers and Jews, undermined the religious Muslim establishment, and imposed a form of popular democracy through the *jamahiriyah* (state of the masses). However, resentment of the regime grew as it became clear that power now lay mainly with the Sirtica tribes, especially Gaddafi's own clan, the Qadhadhfa.

Since the revolution, Libya has become a society where most are city-dwellers. Jews have been invited to return as investors, and immigrants from sub-Saharan Africa have been drawn in to provide low-cost labor. However, clashes in 2000, in which 100 died, highlighted unresolved social issues.

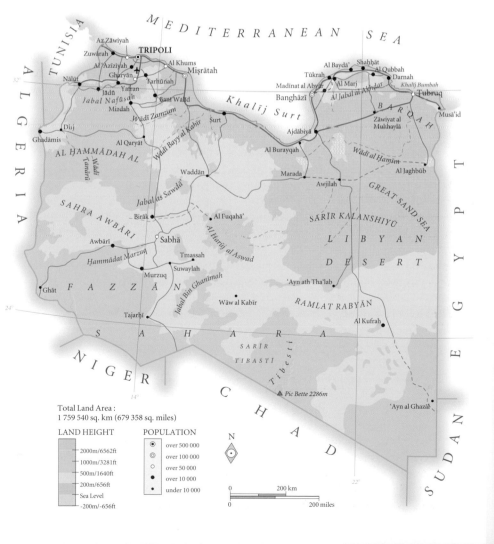

Total Land Area :
1 759 540 sq. km (679 358 sq. miles)

LAND HEIGHT

2000m/6562ft
1000m/3281ft
500m/1640ft
200m/656ft
Sea Level
-200m/-656ft

POPULATION
- ◉ over 500 000
- ◎ over 100 000
- ○ over 50 000
- ● over 10 000
- • under 10 000

0   200 km
0   200 miles

ECONOMIC FOCUS

EXPORTS

France 5%
Turkey 6%
Spain 12%
Italy 38%
Other 17%
Germany 22%

IMPORTS

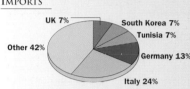

UK 7%
South Korea 7%
Tunisia 7%
Other 42%
Germany 13%
Italy 24%

STRENGTHS

Oil and gas production. High investment in downstream industries – petrochemicals, refineries, fertilizers, and aluminum smelting.

WEAKNESSES

Single-resource economy subject to oil-market fluctuations. Most food is imported. Reliance on foreign labor. Lack of water for agriculture. History of international unreliability.

PROFILE

Western oil companies had close business ties with Libya until the imposition in 1992 of UN sanctions over the Lockerbie affair. In 1993, Colonel Gaddafi called for the program of privatization, authorized by the General People's Congress in late 1992, to be revived, but there have been few tangible results. An ambitious program of industrialization was launched in the 1970s. Gaddafi's most controversial economic project has been the Great Man-Made River. Started in 1984 and engineered jointly by European and Korean companies, this program was designed to bring underground water from the deserts of the Sahara to the coast, but the pipes are already corroding, with thousands of gallons of water leaking into the sand.

Roman amphitheater, Sabratah. *Libya's impressive classical heritage testifies to its importance in ancient times.*

EGYPT

1936 | 1982 | July 23 | ET | +2 | +20 | .eg

OFFICIAL NAME **Arab Republic of Egypt** CAPITAL **Cairo**
POPULATION **68.5m** CURRENCY **Egyptian pound** OFF. LANG. **Arabic**

OCCUPYING THE NORTHEAST CORNER of Africa, Egypt is bisected by the highly fertile Nile valley separating the arid western desert from the smaller semiarid eastern desert. Egypt's 1979 peace treaty with Israel brought security, the return of the Sinai, and large injections of US aid. Its essentially pro-Western military-backed regime is now being challenged by an increasingly influential Islamic fundamentalist movement.

POLITICS

 2000/2005   President Mohammed Hosni Mubarak   Presidential democracy

Egypt is a multiparty system in theory. In practice, the ruling NDP, backed by the military, runs a one-party state. The NDP government is engaged in a struggle against Islamist terrorist groups seeking to turn Egypt into a Muslim theocracy along Iranian lines. Extremists have been responsible for numerous attacks on police and tourists. The fundamentalist message, with promises of improved conditions, has proved attractive to both urban and rural poor. Although the government uses draconian measures to counter the terrorist threat, and banned the only legal Islamic party, the Labor Party, in May 2000, it continues to allow religious organizations to pursue their social programs.

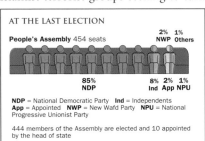

AT THE LAST ELECTION

People's Assembly 454 seats

2% NWP 1% Others

85% NDP 8% Ind 2% App 1% NPU

NDP = National Democratic Party Ind = Independents
App = Appointed NWP = New Wafd Party NPU = National Progressive Unionist Party

444 members of the Assembly are elected and 10 appointed by the head of state

The ruling NDP in 1994 extended the national state of emergency in force since the assassination of President Sadat by Islamic terrorists in 1981. Emergency laws have been invoked to justify the ban on religious parties, especially the Muslim Brotherhood. Opposition parties accused the NDP of using existing laws to ensure its electoral success in general elections held in 1995. Human rights groups claim that emergency powers are routinely applied to silence the NDP's political opponents.

Egypt has been politically stable since World War II, with just three leaders since 1954 when Nasser came to power. Anwar Sadat was assassinated in 1981, but was immediately replaced by Hosni Mubarak, a man in the same mold. The NDP retains its grip on the political process by means of the state of emergency, and has close links with the military. Elections in 2000 were more transparent, and the Islamic opposition fared slightly better than before, but many candidates elected as independents then joined the NDP.

WORLD AFFAIRS

 Damas, OIC, OU, OAPEC, AL   1945

Following the 1979 peace treaty with Israel, Egypt developed closer relations with the US. Its political and military support for the US-led response to Iraq's invasion of Kuwait in 1990 was critical to the success of Operation Desert Storm in 1991. Egypt received a massive economic reward from Saudi Arabia for its participation.

Relations with Iran are tense. Iran actively supports the Islamist groups operating against the NDP government, and characterizes Egypt as a corrupt state under US influence. Egypt is concerned that the international boycott and air exclusion zones

ECONOMICS

 39th $-1,635m
 $1,380   3.1%

High revenues from tourism and the Suez Canal. Light industry and manufacturing, but both in need of development. New awareness of poverty has led to measures to narrow the gap between rich and poor.

RESOURCES

 54.9bn kwh   Comb. 79% Hydro 21% Nuclear 0%
 Sheep 4.3m Goats 3.3m Cattle 3.2m   795,000 b/d (reserves 2,900m bbl)

Oil and gas are Egypt's most valuable resources. 55% of Egypt's oil production is consumed locally. Most electricity is derived from coal and hydroelectric power. The Aswan Dam provides the bulk of hydroelectricity.

DEFENSE

 $2,988m   Compulsory
 None   368,500

Egypt's armed forces, the largest in the Arab world, are battle-hardened from successive wars with Israel and from participation in Operation Desert Storm. More than 500,000 reservists augment the regular troops.

MEDIA

 Censorship   Medium
 17 daily 38 per 1,000 people   TV: 1/0 Radio 1:1

Severe restrictions were imposed in 1998, after criticism of the government's security clampdown. The first Arab state to have its own satellite, Egypt is now the center of a flourishing satellite TV industry.

EDUCATION

 55.4%   850,000 students
 14 years   Primary 93% Secondary 68% Tertiary 20%

Most Egyptians attend elementary school until the age of 11, but not many complete secondary education. The quality of the education given by Egyptian universities is widely respected in the Arab world.

HEALTH

 1 per 625 people   67 years
 26 per 1,000 people   47 per 1,000 live births

Health care remains basic – there is only one hospital bed for every 500 people. Islamic medical centers based on the mosque organization are spreading, and are replacing the state system.

SPENDING

 23 per 1,000 people   3.4%
 4.8%   1.8%

Wealth disparities are highly marked in Egypt. The largely urban Coptic Christian community has the country's highest standard of living. Most Egyptians remain subsistence farmers wih low incomes.

imposed on Iraq are simply allowing Iran to extend its influence in the Middle East. President Mubarak now advocates a diplomatic solution, and has opposed recent US-led air strikes against Iraq and against supposed terrorist targets elsewhere.

Egypt's diplomatic service is the Arab world's largest, and many Egyptians, such as former UN Secretary-General Boutros Boutros Ghali, have served on international bodies. The headquarters of the Arab League is in Cairo.

PEOPLE & SOCIETY

178 people per sq mile	45% urban 55% rural	Sunni Muslim 94% Coptic Christian and others 6%	Death penalty used

Egypt has a long tradition of ethnic and religious tolerance, though the rise in Islamic fundamentalism has sparked sectarian clashes between Muslims and Coptic Christians. Most Egyptians speak Arabic, though many also have French or English as a second language. There are Berber-speaking communities in the western oases. Small colonies of Greeks and Armenians live in the larger towns. Islam is the dominant religion, followed by Coptic Christianity. Although many Jews left Egypt for Israel after 1948, a small community remains in Cairo.

Cairo is the second-most populous city in Africa, and a key social question in Egypt is the high birthrate. In 1985 the government set up the National Population Council, which made birth control readily available. Since then, the birthrate has dropped from 39 to fewer than 25 per 1,000 people, but population growth is still high. The population is predicted to reach almost 100 million by 2025. The growing influence of Islamic fundamentalists, who oppose contraception, could see the rate accelerate once more.

Egyptian women have been among the most liberated in the Arab world, and under a law passed in 2000 they now have the right to initiate divorce proceedings. The steady rise of Islamic fundamentalism, however, threatens their position, particularly in rural areas.

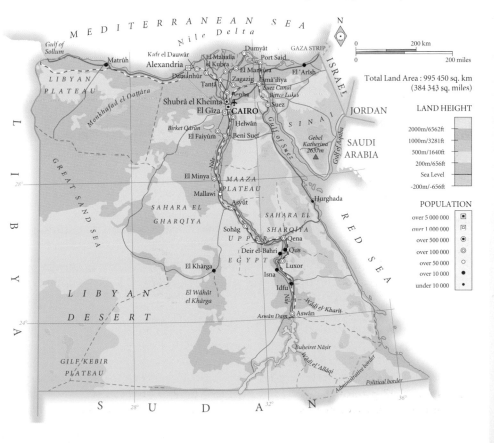

ECONOMIC FOCUS

EXPORTS

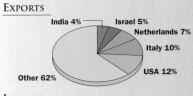

India 4%
Israel 5%
Netherlands 7%
Italy 10%
USA 12%
Other 62%

IMPORTS

Saudi Arabia 4%
France 5%
Italy 7%
Germany 9%
Other 61%
USA 14%

STRENGTHS

Oil and gas revenues. Tourist industry is still buoyant. Remittances from Egyptians working overseas. Suez Canal tolls. Agricultural produce, especially cotton. Light industry and manufacturing.

WEAKNESSES

Remittances from Egyptians working overseas vulnerable to regional recession. Dependence on imported technology. High birthrate.

PROFILE

Under President Nasser, Egypt followed an economic policy inspired by the Soviet model. Rigid and highly centralized, it gave Egypt one of the largest public sectors of all developing countries. Economic restrictions were first relaxed in 1974. President Sadat's open-door policy allowed joint ventures with foreign partners for the first time, although the business classes were the only ones to profit. Most Egyptians suffered from new austerity measures. Under President Mubarak, economic reform has quickened and there is more awareness of poverty and high unemployment. Priorities now are to encourage manufacturing, sustain economic growth, and reduce the gap between rich and poor.

18th-Dynasty Temple of Queen Hatshepsut *dating from the Middle Kingdom, c.1480 BCE. It is at Deir el-Bahri on the west bank of the Nile opposite Thebes, the capital at the time.*

Total Land Area : 995 450 sq. km (384 343 sq. miles)

LAND HEIGHT

2000m/6562ft
1000m/3281ft
500m/1640ft
200m/656ft
Sea Level
-200m/-656ft

POPULATION

over 5 000 000
over 1 000 000
over 500 000
over 100 000
over 50 000
over 10 000
under 10 000

SUDAN

 1956 1956 Jan 1 SUD +2 +249 .sd

OFFICIAL NAME **Republic of Sudan** CAPITAL **Khartoum**
POPULATION **29.5m** CURRENCY **Sudanese pound or dinar** OFF. LANG. **Arabic**

BORDERED BY THE RED SEA, Sudan is the largest country in Africa. Its landscape changes from desert in the north to lush tropical in the south, with grassy plains and swamps in the center. Tensions between the Arab north and African south have led to two civil wars since independence in 1956. The second of these conflicts remains unresolved. In 1989, an army coup installed a military Islamic fundamentalist regime.

POLITICS

 2000/2004   President Omar Hassan Ahmad al-Bashir President Omar Hassan Ahmad al-Bashir Presidential regime

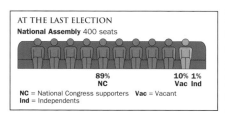

AT THE LAST ELECTION
National Assembly 400 seats

89% NC 10% Vac 1% Ind

NC = National Congress supporters **Vac** = Vacant
Ind = Independents

Having sidelined his main Islamist political rival, former NC leader Hassan al-Turabi, General Omar Bashir called a national reconciliation conference in mid-2000. Elections in December, under the 1999 constitution allowing "political associations," were boycotted by the opposition, and returned Bashir and his NC bloc to power. The willingness of the Sudanese People's Liberation Army (SPLA) to enter peace talks raised the possibility of an end to nearly 20 years of civil conflict between Muslim north and Christian south.

WORLD AFFAIRS

 OAU, OIC, AL, IGAD, COMESA   1956

Sudan's support for Iraq in the Gulf War and suspicion that it sponsors terrorism have led to its increasing isolation from the West and the Arab world. Only Iran, Yemen, and Libya maintain friendly relations.

PEOPLE & SOCIETY

 32 people per sq mile   35% urban 65% rural

 Sunni Muslim 70% Traditional beliefs 20% Christian & other 10%   Death penalty used

Sudan has a large number of ethnic and linguistic groups. About two million Sudanese are nomads. The major social division, however, is between the Arabized Muslims in the north and the mostly African, largely animist or Christian population in the south. Attempts to impose Arab and Islamic values throughout Sudan have been the root cause of the civil war that has ravaged the south since 1983.

Total Land Area : 2 376 000 sq. km (917 374 sq. miles)

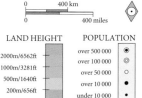

LAND HEIGHT
2000m/6562ft
1000m/3281ft
500m/1640ft
200m/656ft
Sea Level

POPULATION
over 500 000
over 100 000
over 50 000
over 10 000
under 10 000

 86th $-465m

 $330   16%

Sudan produces oil, gas, cotton, gum arabic, sesame, and sugar. Low levels of industrialization. Lack of foreign exchange for importing energy and spare parts for industry. Drought. Huge distances between towns.

RESOURCES

 1.3bn kwh   Comb. 29% Hydro 71% Nuclear 0%

 Sheep 42.8m Goats 37.8m Cattle 35.3m No production (reserves of 300m bbl)

Large oil and gas reserves were found in the south in the 1980s; oil exports started in 1999. The half-thermal, half-hydroelectric generating capacity is insufficient, and week-long power cuts are frequent.

DEFENSE

 $424m   Compulsory

 None   104,500

The NC controls the military and police and has its own paramilitary militia. Sudan's 100,000-strong army is engaged in fighting the two factions of the southern SPLA, which number a similar size.

MEDIA

 Censorship   Medium

 7 daily 27 per 1,000 people   TV: 1/0 Radio: 1/1

The press and broadcasting industries were relatively free from 1985 to 1989, but are now fully under the control of either the government or the army, and are heavily censored.

EDUCATION

 58%   59,800 students

13 years Primary 51% Secondary 21% Tertiary 3%

Primary school children must have two years of Islamic religious instruction, and men wishing to enter university must first serve for a year in the People's Militia.

HEALTH

 1 per 10,000 people   56 years

33 per 1,000 people 67 per 1,000 live births

As most health funds are tied to urban hospitals, health service standards in rural areas are basic. The civil war has led to an increase in communicable diseases, especially the parasitic infection leishmaniasis.

SPENDING

 10 per 1,000 people   4.9%

0.9%   0.7%

Wealth is limited to the NC and southern rebel elites, while the rest of the population struggles to survive from day to day.

SOMALIA

| 1960 | 1960 | Oct 21 | SO | +3 | +252 | | .so |

OFFICIAL NAME **Somali Democratic Republic** CAPITAL **Mogadishu**
POPULATION **10.1m** CURRENCY **Somali shilling** OFF. LANG. **Somali & Arabic**

OCCUPYING THE HORN OF AFRICA, Italian Somaliland and British Somaliland were united in 1960 to form an independent Somalia. Except in the more fertile south, the land is semiarid. Years of clan-based civil war have resulted in the collapse of central government, the frustration of US and UN intervention initiatives aimed at easing a huge refugee crisis, and mass starvation.

POLITICS

 1984/Uncertain   No internationally recognized head of state   Transitional regime

Somalia has remained in anarchy since the former dictator President Siad Barre fled in 1991. The unified state dissolved amid conflict in the south and separatism in the north.

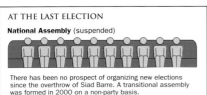

AT THE LAST ELECTION

National Assembly (suspended)

There has been no prospect of organizing new elections since the overthrow of Siad Barre. A transitional assembly was formed in 2000 on a non-party basis.

The US led a UN peacekeeping force to the south in 1992, but failed to loosen the grip of the warring factions. Throughout the 1990s rival warlords contended for supreme power.

A conference of businessmen and influential figures, held in neighboring Djibouti in 2000, established a transitional assembly and appointed former Barre minister Abdulkassim Salat Hassan as president. The new government, although warmly received in Mogadishu, was immediately rejected by most of the warlords and by the northern separatist authorities in "Somaliland" and "Puntland".

WORLD AFFAIRS

OIC, IGAD, AL, NAM, OAU   1960

After the withdrawal in 1995 of the UN force, the international community appeared to abandon Somalia, although the formation of a transitional parliament in mid-2000 did receive international support. The self-declared Somaliland Republic is pressing for international recognition.

PEOPLE & SOCIETY

 42 people per sq mile   26% urban 74% rural

Sunni Muslim 98% Others 2%   Death penalty used

The clan system is fundamental to Somalia. Shifting allegiances characterize its structure – a tendency stifled by Siad Barre's dictatorship but revived after his fall in 1991. His undermining of the traditional brokers of justice, the elders, contributed to the power vacuum that resulted in civil war, and his persecution of the Issaqs led to Somaliland's declaration of secession in 1991. However, national identity remains strong, shown by widespread opposition to the UN peacekeeping force.

(Map of Somalia showing Gulf of Aden, Indian Ocean, Ethiopia, Kenya, Djibouti, with cities including Berbera, Hargeysa, Garoowe, MOGADISHU, Kismaayo)

Total Land Area :
627 340 sq. km
(242 216 sq. miles)

POPULATION

over 1 000 000
over 100 000
over 50 000
over 10 000
under 10 000

LAND HEIGHT

2000m/6562ft
1000m/3281ft
500m/1640ft
200m/656ft
Sea Level

0 200 km
0 200 miles

ECONOMICS

 158th $-157m

$100 81.9%

Every commodity, except arms, is in extremely short supply, with a growing market in stolen food aid. The south has little economic potential. Export of livestock to the Arabian peninsula has resumed in the north.

RESOURCES

276m kwh   Comb. 100% Hydro 0% Nuclear 0%

Sheep 12m Goats 11m Cattle 4.5m Not an oil producer

Commercially exploitable minerals remain untapped. An oil exploration agreement was signed with a French oil group in February 2001.

DEFENSE

 $40m Not compulsory

None No formal data, estimated to be 75,000 militia

Former soldiers have been urged to reenlist. Efforts to demobilize Somalia's estimated 75,000 militia began in 2000.

MEDIA

 Censorship Low

5 daily 1 per 1,000 people   TV: 2/0 Radio: 11/0

In Mogadishu there are three faction-run radio stations. Somali Television Network, an independent service, began broadcasting in 1999. There are few newspapers, paper being in very short supply.

EDUCATION

24.1% 15,670 students

14 years Primary 10% Secondary 3% Tertiary 2%

The system collapsed during the civil war. There were reports of improvised open-air schools starting up again in urban areas in 1993. Somali has been a written language only since 1972.

HEALTH

 1 per 25,000 people   48 years

 52 per 1,000 people 121 per 1,000 live births

The state-run health system has collapsed entirely. A few very rudimentary facilities are run by foreign relief workers.

SPENDING

 1 per 1,000 people   4.6%

 0.4%   0.6%

Bandits and warlords gained rich pickings in the aid-stealing racket. Money sent by relatives living overseas is the main income for some people.

DJIBOUTI

 1977   1977   June 27   DJI   +3   +253   .dj

OFFICIAL NAME Republic of Djibouti   **CAPITAL Djibouti**
POPULATION 630,000   **CURRENCY Djibouti franc**   **OFF. LANG. Arabic & French**

A CITY-STATE WITH a desert hinterland, Djibouti lies in northeast Africa on the strait linking the Red Sea and the Indian Ocean. Known from 1967 as the French Territory of the Afars and Issas, Djibouti became independent in 1977. Its economy relies on the main port, the railroad to Addis Ababa, and French aid. A guerrilla war which erupted in 1991 as a result of tension between the Issas in the south and the Afars in the north has largely been resolved.

ECONOMICS

 170th $-23m

 $790   3%

Free port in key Red Sea location. Continuing development of Djibouti and Tadjoura port facilities. Dependence on French aid and garrison. Other ports on Red Sea now providing stiff competition.

RESOURCES

 187m kwh   Comb. 100% Hydro 0% Nuclear 0%

 Sheep 465,000 Goats 513,000 Cattle 269,000   Not an oil producer

The few mineral resources are scarcely exploited. Geothermal energy is being developed and natural gas has been found. The guerrilla war delayed attempts to develop underground water supplies for agriculture.

DEFENSE

 $22m   Not compulsory

 None   8,400

The size of the armed forces is a state secret, but is estimated at 8,400 personnel; former FRUD guerrillas were integrated into the army. There is a 3,200-strong French garrison.

MEDIA

 Censorship   Low

No daily papers   TV: 1/0 Radio: 1/0

Djibouti is a member of the Arab Satellite Communications Organization. The media are largely state-controlled, but there is one opposition newspaper.

EDUCATION

 64.6%   161 students

12 years   Primary 32% Secondary 20% Tertiary 0%

Schooling is mostly in French, although there has been a growing emphasis on Islamic teaching, particularly as Saudi Arabia has declared an interest in providing aid for education.

HEALTH

 1 per 5,000 people   44 years

39 per 1,000 people   109 per 1,000 live births

AIDS is a growing problem in Djibouti port, with its large prostitute population. 1999 estimates suggested that there were some 37,000 AIDS and HIV sufferers. French-financed hospitals cater for the urban elite.

SPENDING

 15 per 1,000 people   5%

 3.8%   2.8%

The wealth in Djibouti tends to be concentrated among those closest to government. Djiboutians working in the ports also do well. The nomads of the interior are the poorest group.

POLITICS

 1997/2002   President Ismael Omar Guelleh   Presidential democracy

AT THE LAST ELECTION

National Assembly 65 seats

100% RPP–FRUD

RPP–FRUD = Alliance of the Popular Rally for Progress (RPP) and the Front for the Restoration of Unity and Democracy (FRUD)

President Hassan Gouled Aptidon, an Issa, backed by France, dominated politics from independence in 1977 until his retirement in 1999. Afar fears of Issa domination erupted in 1991, when the Afar guerrilla group FRUD took control of much of the country. The French intervened militarily to keep Gouled in power, but forced him to hold elections in 1992, won by the RPP. The FRUD became a legal political party following a 1996 peace agreement. An alliance of the RPP and FRUD won the elections in 1997. Presidential elections in April 1999 were won by Ismael Omar Guelleh, a former close aide of Gouled, amid opposition claims of electoral fraud.

WORLD AFFAIRS

 OIC, OIF, IGAD, OAU, AL   1977

France, with a key military presence, presses for greater democratization. Djibouti and its neighbors Ethiopia and Eritrea all seek to contain Afar secessionism. In 2000 the southern town of Arta hosted the Somali reconciliation conference.

PEOPLE & SOCIETY

 71 people per sq mile   83% urban 17% rural

Sunni Muslim 94% Christian 6%   Death penalty not used

Total Land Area : 23 180 sq. km (8950 sq. miles)

POPULATION
over 100 000
under 10 000

LAND HEIGHT
1000m/3281ft
500m/1640ft
200m/656ft
Sea Level
-200m/656ft

0   30 km
0   30 miles

The main ethnic groups are the Afars and Issas, who make up 35% and 60% of the population respectively. Tensions between these groups developed into a guerrilla war in 1991. The population was swelled in 1992 by 20,000 Somali refugees fleeing civil war in their own country. The rural people are mostly nomadic.

AZERBAIJAN

| 1991 | 1991 | May 28 | AZ | +4 | +994 | .az |

OFFICIAL NAME: **Republic of Azerbaijan** CAPITAL: **Baku**
POPULATION: **7.7 million** CURRENCY: **Manat** OFFICIAL LANGUAGE: **Azerbaijani**

SITUATED ON THE WESTERN coast of the Caspian Sea, Azerbaijan was the first Soviet republic to declare independence. The issue of the disputed enclave of Nagorno Karabakh, which Armenia seeks to annex, led to full-scale war until 1994 and is still a dominant concern. Over 200,000 refugees and more than twice as many internally displaced added to the problems of the troubled economy. Azerbaijan's oil wealth, however, gives it long-term potential.

POLITICS

 2000/2005 | President Heydar Aliyev | Multiparty republic

The determination of the Nagorno Karabakh enclave to unite with Armenia led to a protracted war lasting until 1994, with Armenia gaining control over 20% of Azeri territory. Peace talks have yet to reach an accord.

New Azerbaijan (NA) replaced the Communists in power in 1995, and again dominated elections in 2000, which observers criticized as seriously flawed. NA supports the septuagenarian President Heydar Aliyev, first elected in 1993 and reelected in 1998.

AT THE LAST ELECTION

National Assembly 125 seats

2% CSP   1% Vacant

61% NA   21% Ind   5% APF   10% Others

NA = New Azerbaijan Ind = Independents APF = Azerbaijan Popular Front CSP = Civic Solidarity Party Vacant = Seat reserved for member from Nagorno Karabakh

WORLD AFFAIRS

 EAPC, OIC, CIS, CE, OSCE | 1992

The West, as well as neighboring Iran (with its large Azeri population) and Russia, are interested in Azeri oilfields in the Caspian Sea. Relations with Russia under President Putin have improved. Turkey – with its common history and culture – is a natural ally. Azerbaijan joined the Council of Europe in 2001.

PEOPLE & SOCIETY

 230 people per sq mile | 57% urban 43% rural

Shi'aithna Muslim 61% Sunni Muslim 26% Other 13% | Death penalty not used

Thousands of Armenians, Jews, and Russians have left as a result of rising Azeri nationalism. Racial hostility against those who remain is increasing. Women, once prominent in the ruling party, have lost their political status. The once effective social security system is under great strain.

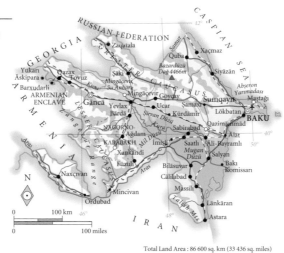

Total Land Area : 86 600 sq. km (33 436 sq. miles)

POPULATION

over 1 000 000
over 100 000
over 50 000
over 10 000
under 10 000

LAND HEIGHT

4000m/13 124ft
3000m/9843ft
2000m/6562ft
1000m/3281ft
500m/1640ft
200m/656ft
Sea Level

ECONOMICS

 121st | $-600m

 $460 | -8.6%

Extensive oil and natural gas reserves. Antiquated Soviet-era industry. Poor infrastructure and corruption threaten development. Fallout from war in Nagorno Karabakh still drains state resources.

RESOURCES

 17bn kwh | Comb. 90% Hydro 10% Nuclear 0%

Sheep 5.39m Goats 400,000 Cattle 1.95m | 300,000 b/d (reserves of 6,900m bbl)

Azerbaijan's Caspian Sea oilfields have attracted international interest. The shallow-water Guneshli field alone has over four million barrels of reserves. Offshore natural gas is plentiful.

DEFENSE

 $203m | Compulsory

None | 72,100

Azerbaijan has been a member of NATO's Partnership for Peace program since 1994. Its naval forces operate under CIS control.

MEDIA

 Some censorship | High

6 daily 28 per 1,000 people | TV: 1/1 Radio: 1/0

A 1998 decree abolished censorship, but media freedom is limited by newsprint controls, license restrictions, and intimidation.

EDUCATION

 96% | 115,116 students

17 years | Primary 100% Secondary 77% Tertiary 17%

When it came to power in the mid-1990s NA began to reverse communist control over education policy, especially history teaching. Baku, the main university, specializes in Oriental studies.

HEALTH

 1 per 263 people | 71 years

15 per 1,000 people | 16 per 1,000 live births

The already poor health care system effectively collapsed as a result of war and the transition to a market economy.

SPENDING

 38 per 1,000 people | 4.4%

 3% | 1.2%

New oil revenues are threatening to create a nouveau riche elite without reaching the 60% of Azerbaijan's population currently living in poverty.

TURKEY

| 1923 | 1939 | Oct 29 | TR | +2 | +99 | .tr |

ECONOMICS

23rd		$1871m	
$2,900		64.9%	

Advanced market economy, but with persistently high inflation. Self-sufficient in agriculture. Government bureaucracy hampers growth, but structural reforms are underway.

RESOURCES

 105bn kwh

 Sheep 30.24m Goats 8.38m Cattle 11.18m

 Comb. 62% Hydro 38% Nuclear 0%

 69,150 b/d (reserves of 252.5m bbl)

Under the controversial Southeastern Anatolian Project, Turkey is building 22 dams on the Euphrates and Tigris rivers. East provinces are rich in chromium, of which Turkey is the world's largest producer.

DEFENSE

 $10,180m

 None

 Compulsory

 609,700

Turkey's armed forces are the second-largest in NATO. The great majority of its personnel are conscripts; 18 months' service is compulsory for all males at the age of 20.

MEDIA

Censorship

High

 57 daily 110 per 1,000 people

TV: 1/5 Radio: 1/>50

The press is diverse and largely privately owned. Censorship laws were amended to ease restrictions on the propagation of Kurdish rights. A high number of journalists are, however, imprisoned in Turkey.

EDUCATION

 85.1%

 14 years

1,434,000 students

Primary 99% Secondary 51% Tertiary 21%

In 1997, compulsory education was extended from five to eight years. State schools are coeducational and free. Engineering is usually the strongest faculty in Turkey's many universities.

HEALTH

 1 per 833 people

21 per 1,000 people

70 years

36 per 1,000 live births

Turkey possesses an adequate national system of primary health care. By Western standards, however, hospitals are underequipped. There are fewer doctors per head than in any western European country.

SPENDING

 63 per 1,000 people

 2.2%

5.5%

2.9%

The economic expansion of the 1980s has created a new class of wealthy entrepreneurs. Many Turks take jobs as *Gastarbeiter* (guest workers) in Germany and the Netherlands.

OFFICIAL NAME **Kingdom of Turkey** CAPITAL **Ankara**
POPULATION **66.6m** CURRENCY **Turkish lira** OFF. LANG. **Turkish**

TURKEY, MAINLY IN WESTERN ASIA, also includes the region of Eastern Thrace in Europe. It thus controls the entrance to the Black Sea, which is straddled by Turkey's largest city, Istanbul. Most Turks live in the western half of the country. The eastern and southeastern reaches of the Anatolia Plateau are Kurdish regions. Turkey's strategic location gives it great influence in the Black Sea, the Mediterranean, and the Middle East. Lying on a major earthquake fault line, many Turkish towns are vulnerable to earthquakes such as the one which devastated Izmit in 1999.

POLITICS

1999/2004	President Ahmet Necdet Sezer	Parliamentary democracy

Under its 1982 constitution, Turkey is a multiparty republic with a national assembly elected every five years. The president, who serves a seven-year term, appoints the prime minister. Modern Turkey's identity as a secular state was profoundly challenged in the mid-1990s by the Islamist agenda of the Welfare Party (RP) – the largest parliamentary party after the 1995 election. A secular coalition to keep the RP out of power disintegrated in mid-1996, when RP leader Necmettin Erbakan formed a coalition with the True Path Party. Ousted in mid-1997, the RP was banned in 1998.

AT THE LAST ELECTION

Turkish Grand National Assembly 550 seats

| 25% DSP | 23% MHP | 20% Virtue | 16% ANAP | 15% DYP | 1% Ind |

DSP = Democratic Left Party **MHP** = Nationalist Action Party
Virtue = Virtue Party **ANAP** = Motherland Party **DYP** = True Path Party **Ind** = Independents

Thousands have been killed since 1984 in a bitter civil war in southeast Turkey. The secessionist Kurdistan Workers' Party (PKK) has proclaimed three cease-fires since 1992 and now professes simply to favor recognition of Kurdish rights within Turkey. In 1999 its leader Abdullah Ocalan was captured, tried, and sentenced to death. He has not yet been executed and, from prison, has urged his supporters to abandon armed struggle.

Turkey's human rights record has been subject to intense international criticism. Reforms in 1995 lifted a number of civil liberty restrictions written into the 1982 constitution, but concerns remain over illegal executions and the treatment of Kurds. A hunger strike campaign against conditions in high-security prisons gained worldwide attention in early 2001.

Bulent Ecevit became prime minister in 1999 after the strong showing of the DSP in the election. Ecevit formed a new coalition with the far-right MHP, and with ANAP (backed by Istanbul's metropolitan interests). He staked his government's future on the reelection of President Süleyman Demirel, but the Assembly failed to vote through the required constitutional changes in April 2000. The coalition remained in power, however, and Demirel was replaced in May by a non-party candidate, Ahmet Necdet Sezer.

WORLD AFFAIRS

 OIC, OSCE, CE, NATO, OECD   1945

Turkey had great strategic significance as NATO's first line of defense during the Cold War. It now has closer ties with former Communist neighbors, particularly Bulgaria and Georgia, and with Turkic-speaking central Asian states. It has joined the Black Sea Economic Cooperation Project, and has tried to mediate in the war between Armenia and Azerbaijan. In 2000 Turkey agreed to send arms to Uzbekistan to contain Islamic rebels – its first such military involvement in central Asia since the collapse of the Soviet Union in 1991. Turkey's pro-Islamic government in 1996–1997 sought briefly to strengthen ties with Arab states.

Negotiations on joining the EU opened in 1999, and are aided by a recent improvement in Turkey's relations with Greece, although the Turkish-backed *de facto* partition of Cyprus remains an obstacle, as are the EU's concerns over human rights.

PEOPLE & SOCIETY

 224 people per sq mile   74% urban 26% rural   Sunni Muslim 99% Other 1%   Death penalty not used

The Turks are racially diverse. Many are the descendants of refugees, often from the Balkans, but a strong sense of national identity is rooted in a shared language and religion. Most are Sunni Muslim, although a Shi'a community is growing fast, including the heterodox Alawite sect. The largest minority are the Kurds, while there are some 500,000 Arabic speakers. While women have equal rights in law, men dominate political and even family life. There is controversy over the right of women to wear Islamic headscarves, which are banned in state universities. Tansu Çiller was Turkey's first woman prime minister, in 1993–1996.

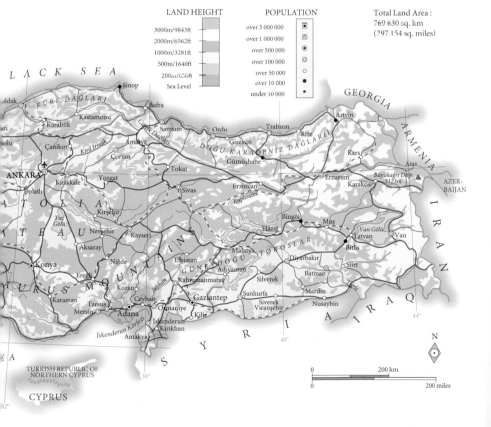

LAND HEIGHT		POPULATION	
3000m/9843ft		over 5 000 000	
2000m/6562ft		over 1 000 000	
1000m/3281ft		over 500 000	
500m/1640ft		over 100 000	
200m/656ft		over 50 000	
Sea Level		over 10 000	
		under 10 000	

Total Land Area : 769 630 sq. km (297 154 sq. miles)

ECONOMIC FOCUS

EXPORTS

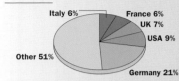

Italy 6% | France 6% | UK 7% | USA 9% | Germany 21% | Other 51%

IMPORTS

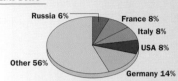

Russia 6% | France 8% | Italy 8% | USA 8% | Germany 14% | Other 56%

STRENGTHS

Liberalized economy resulted in strong growth in the 1990s. Self-sufficient in agriculture. Textiles, manufacturing, and construction sectors competitive on world markets. Tourism industry. Dynamic private sector economy. Skilled labor force. Customs union with EU since 1995.

WEAKNESSES

Persistently high inflation. Unsound public finances. Large government bureaucracy. Uneven privatization program. Ailing banking sector. Influence of organized crime. High cost of military action against Kurds.

PROFILE

Turkey has one of the oldest and most advanced emerging market economies. In the 1990s it grew strongly, but continued to suffer from persistently high inflation. In 1997–1998, the government introduced new tax laws to improve tax collection, and embarked on structural reforms. These were threatened by a serious financial crisis in 2000–2001, which necessitated rescue packages by the IMF in February and May 2001, in return for radical laws reforming the banking sector and privatizing debt-laden state companies.

The Church of the Holy Cross, *on Akdamar Island in Lake Van, was built in the 10th-century when Christianity was dominant.*

SYRIA

 1941 1967 April 17 SYR +2 +963 .sy

OFFICIAL NAME **Syrian Arab Republic**   CAPITAL **Damacus**
POPULATION **16.1m**   CURRENCY **Syrian pound**   OFF. LANG. **Arabic**

ECONOMICS

 77th $59m

 $970   -0.5%

Rapid growth after Gulf War. Healthy oil production rates are increasing. Despite international cash injections, Syria lacks foreign investment. Agriculture is improved, but the water supply is vulnerable.

RESOURCES

 18.3bn kwh   Comb. 86% Hydro 14% Nuclear 0%

 Sheep 14.5m Goats 1.1m Cattle 920,000   540,000 b/d (reserves of 2,500m bbl)

Syria has large supplies of oil and gas. Syria's other important minerals are phosphates and iron ore. Hydroelectric power satisfies most other energy requirements. Cotton is the main cash crop.

DEFENSE

 $989m   Compulsory

 None   261,000

Syria sees its extensive military capability as a significant deterrent to Israel's territorial expansion. It has fought four wars against Israel since 1948, and is the Arab world's strongest military power after Egypt.

MEDIA

 Censorship   Medium

10 daily 20 per 1,000 people   TV: 1/0 Radio 1/0

Virtually all media outlets are controlled by the regime. Information is becoming freer after Jordanian papers were again allowed into Syria in 1999, and with the advent of satellite TV, which is widely watched.

EDUCATION

 74.5%   215,800 students

 12 years   Primary 91% Secondary 38% Tertiary 16%

The development of a modern and universally accessible system of education remains an important objective. Higher education is provided by seven state universities, notably at Damascus, Aleppo, and Tishrin.

HEALTH

 1 per 769 people   71 years

 29 per 1,000 people   26 per 1,000 live births

An adequate system of primary health care has been set up since the Ba'ath Party came to power. Hospitals often lack modern equipment and medical services are in need of further investment.

SPENDING

 9 per 1,000 people   5.6%

 3.1%   0.8%

The gulf between Syria's rich and poor is widening. The political elite is more numerous and richer than ever before. Palestinian refugees and the urban unemployed make up the poorest groups.

SYRIA SHARES BORDERS WITH Lebanon, Israel, Jordan, Iraq, and Turkey. Many Syrians regard their country as an artificial creation of French mandated rule, which lasted from 1920 to independence. They identify instead with a Greater Syria encompassing Lebanon, Jordan, and Palestine. Since independence, Syria's foreign relations have been turbulent, although President Hafez al-Assad's authoritarian Ba'athist regime brought a measure of internal stability.

POLITICS

 1998/2002   President Bashar al-Assad   One-party state

Syria is in effect a single-party state. Its military-backed leader from 1970 to 2000 was Hafez al-Assad, a lifelong Ba'ath Party militant. His personal dominance ensured the succession of his son Bashar after his death in June 2000.

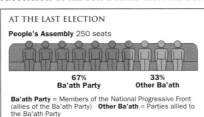

AT THE LAST ELECTION

People's Assembly 250 seats

67% Ba'ath Party   33% Other Ba'ath

Ba'ath Party = Members of the National Progressive Front (allies of the Ba'ath Party)   **Other Ba'ath** = Parties allied to the Ba'ath Party

Martial law has not been rescinded since 1963, but the regime has improved its human rights record in recent years. Political prisoners are released under frequent amnesties, and in 1994 all members of the Jewish minority were granted exit visas to travel abroad.

President Assad dominated Syrian politics for 30 years. His military-backed regime, drawn mainly from his own Alawi minority grouping, kept a tight hold on power, although in his last decade Sunnis gained high political posts. Despite promises made under heavy international pressure Assad never permitted genuine multipartyism. Shortly before Assad's death the long-serving prime minister, Mahmoud az-Zoubi, was forced from office and replaced by the modernizing Mohammed Miro. However, Assad's death was immediately followed by his son's election to the party leadership, which was overwhelmingly approved by referendum.

The Ba'athist military swept to power in 1963 with a vision of uniting all Arab nations under a single Syrian-dominated socialist system. The coup ended the power of city elites and promoted citizens from rural areas. The state became the main employer.

When Assad came to power in 1970, he consolidated the Ba'ath Party as the major political force. Unrest among Islamic militants was crushed, and Assad focused on foreign affairs in a bid to make Syria a major power. Plans in 1978 to unite with fellow Ba'athist Iraq fell apart, however, amid mutual recriminations.

WORLD AFFAIRS

Damas, NAM, G24 OIC, AL   1945

Following Egypt's 1979 accord with Israel, Syria sees itself as the major barrier to Israel's regional dominance. Syria has extended its influence over Lebanon (where it has achieved a high degree of control) and radical Palestinian factions, as well as seeking alliances with north African states. The biggest issue between Syria and Israel remains the strategically vital Golan Heights, seized by Israel during the Six Day War in 1967. Peace negotiations foundered in the wake of Ariel Sharon becoming prime minister of Israel.

There are enduring tensions with Turkey over attitudes to Israel and to Turkish Kurdish guerrillas, access to water, and Syria's desire for the return of its Alexandretta Province. Syria, alone among Arab states, backed Iran in the Iran–Iraq War in the 1980s. Facing international isolation because of its alleged backing of terrorists, Syria regained a measure of respect by securing the release of Western hostages in Lebanon by Shi'a militants. Assad backed the US-led Western allies in the 1990–1991 Gulf War, and by contributing troops legitimized the action in the eyes of the Arab world. In 2000, however, Syria sent humanitarian aid to Iraq, in defiance of the UN blockade.

PEOPLE & SOCIETY

 227 people per sq mile

 54% urban
46% rural

 Sunni Muslim 74%
Other Muslim 16%
Christian 10%

Death penalty used

Most Syrians live near the coast, where the largest cities are sited. About 90% are Muslim. They include the politically dominant Alawis, a heterodox offshoot of Shi'a, representing 12% of the population, based in Latakia and Tartous provinces. There is also a sizable Christian minority. In the west and north a mosaic of groups exists, including Kurds, Turkic-speakers, and Armenians, the latter based in cities. Damascus, Al Qamishli, and Aleppo have small Jewish communities, and there are three villages where Aramaic is spoken. In addition, some 300,000 Palestinian refugees have settled in Syria. Minorities were initially attracted to the ruling Ba'ath Party because of its emphasis on the state over sectarian interests. However, disputes between factions led to the Alawis taking control, fostering resentment among the Sunni Muslim majority.

The emancipation of women, promoted initially in the late 1960s, was carried forward under President Hafez al-Assad. His first woman cabinet minister was appointed in 1976.

Total Land Area : 184 060 sq. km
(71 066 sq. miles)

LAND HEIGHT

2000m/6562ft
1000m/3281ft
500m/1640ft
200m/656ft
Sea Level

POPULATION

over 500 000
over 100 000
over 50 000
over 10 000
under 10 000

ECONOMIC FOCUS

EXPORTS

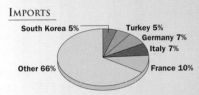

Turkey 8%
Saudi Arabia 9%
France 10%
Italy 12%
Germany 21%
Other 40%

IMPORTS

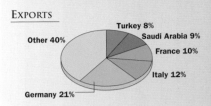

South Korea 5%
Turkey 5%
Germany 7%
Italy 7%
France 10%
Other 66%

STRENGTHS

Exporter of crude oil – production increasing as a result of new oil strikes. Manufacturing base has grown. Thriving agricultural sector.

WEAKNESSES

Defense spending is a major drain on economy. Large black market. Domination of inefficient state-run companies. Lack of foreign investment; foreign currency accounts banned. High population growth. Vulnerable water supply.

PROFILE

Billions of dollars flowed into the economy from the US, Japan, the EU, and Saudi Arabia and other Gulf states after the 1990–1991 Gulf War. This cash injection, along with increased oil revenue, led to rapid growth. Diversion of water from the Euphrates River toward fertile plains, rather than poorer land, led to a rise in agricultural output. However, long-term economic prospects remain uncertain. The public sector employs 20% of the workforce, and state controls inhibit private enterprise and investment, and have created a booming black market. Businessmen often channel funds through the freer Lebanese economy. An economic reform package in 2000 created a stock exchange and permitted private banks.

The ancient city of Palmyra, *in Syria's central region, was once the capital of the kingdom of Queen Zenobia.*

JORDAN

| 1946 | 1967 | May 25 | HJK | +2 | +962 | .jo |

ECONOMICS

 96th $14m

 $1,630 0.6%

Major exporter of phosphates. Skilled workforce. Recovery of tourist industry after 1991 Gulf War. Unemployment, exacerbated by influx of refugees from Kuwait after Gulf crisis. Little arable land.

RESOURCES

 6.4bn kwh   Comb 100% Hydro 0% Nuclear 0%

 Sheep 1.6m Goats 630,000 Cattle 55,000 Production low (reserves of 4,000,000 bbl)

Oil deposits have been discovered. Phosphates, livestock and crops such as tomatoes, wheat, olives, and vegetables are the main resources.

DEFENSE

 $588m   Not compulsory

 None 103,880

The armed forces are loyal to the monarchy. They have a reputation for professionalism and thorough training. The forces are dependent on Western support for credit in purchasing arms and equipment.

MEDIA

 Censorship   Medium

 8 daily 42 per 1,000 people TV: 1/0 Radio 1/0

A restrictive press and publications law was enacted by the government in 1998. All radio stations and TV channels are controlled by the state.

EDUCATION

 89.8%   112,959 students

 15 years   Primary 68% Secondary 41% Tertiary 18%

Female students fare better than in some states in the area; men and women receive the same education. Jordanian teachers work all over the Middle East.

HEALTH

 1 per 588 people   70 years

 30 per 1,000 people 26 per 1,000 live births

Primary health care is subsidized by the government. There are numerous hospitals, all well distributed throughout the country.

SPENDING

 49 per 1,000 people   7.7%

 6.8% 5.3%

Poverty is relatively rare, though refugee camps still exist and 25% unemployment damaged many family incomes in the late 1990s.

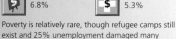

OFFICIAL NAME: **Hashemite Kingdom of Jordan** CAPITAL: **Amman**
POPULATION **6.7m** CURRENCY **Jordanian dinar** OFF. LANG. **Arabic**

SHARING BORDERS WITH Iraq, Syria, Israel, and Saudi Arabia, Jordan has just 16 miles (26 km) of coastline on the Gulf of Aqaba. Jordan formally includes the West Bank of the Jordan River and East Jerusalem in its territory, but Israel has occupied these areas since 1967. Jordan ceded its claim to the West Bank to the PLO in 1988. Phosphates, and tourism associated with important historical sites such as Petra, are the mainstays of the economy.

POLITICS

 L. House 1997/2001 U. House 1997/2001   HM King Abdullah II Constitutional monarchy

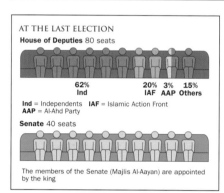

AT THE LAST ELECTION
House of Deputies 80 seats

62% Ind 20% IAF 3% AAP 15% Others

Ind = Independents IAF = Islamic Action Front
AAP = Al-Ahd Party

Senate 40 seats

The members of the Senate (Majlis Al-Aayan) are appointed by the king

King Abdullah II acceded to the throne in February 1999 upon the death of his father, King Hussein. Although lacking in political experience, he is respected by the army and enjoys the support of Jordan's tribal leaders. Multiparty elections, initiated in 1993, have benefited pro-government parties, despite a strong Islamist opposition lobby. The appointment in 2000 of Prime Minister Ali Abu al-Ragheb marked a shift toward a modernizing and pro-business government.

WORLD AFFAIRS

 NAM, OIC, AMF, AL, WTO   1955

Jordan's position as a key player in Middle East politics is under question since the death of King Hussein. Policy toward the emerging Palestinian state is uncertain since its relations with Israel remain much less aggressive than those of other Arab countries. The US signed a free trade agreement in 2000.

PEOPLE & SOCIETY

 195 people per sq mile   74% urban 26% rural

 Sunni Muslim 92% Christian & others 8% Death penalty used

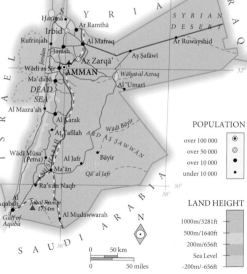

POPULATION
over 100 000
over 50 000
over 10 000
under 10 000

LAND HEIGHT
1000m/3281ft
500m/1640ft
200m/656ft
Sea Level
-200m/-656ft

Total Land Area : 88 930 sq. km (34 336 sq. miles)

Jordan is a predominantly Muslim country drawn from Bedouin roots, with a Christian minority. About half the population are Palestinian in origin. The monarchy's power base lies among the rural tribes, which also provide the backbone of the military. National identity is strong.

LEBANON

1941 | 1941 | Nov 22 | RL | +2 | +961 | .lb

OFFICIAL NAME **Republic of Lebanon** CAPITAL **Beirut**
POPULATION **3.3m** CURRENCY **Lebanese pound** OFF. LANG. **Arabic**

LEBANON IS DWARFED by its two powerful neighbors, Syria and Israel. The country's coastal strip is fertile and the hinterland mountainous. Maronite Christians have traditionally ruled Lebanon. A civil war between Muslim and Christian factional groups which began in 1975 threatened to lead to the breakup of the state. However, Saudi Arabia brokered a peace agreement in 1989; politics became more stable and reconstruction began.

POLITICS

 2000/2004 | President Émile Lahoud | Multiparty republic

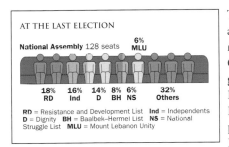

AT THE LAST ELECTION

National Assembly 128 seats

6% MLU

18% RD | 16% Ind | 14% D | 8% BH | 6% NS | 32% Others

RD = Resistance and Development List Ind = Independents
D = Dignity BH = Baalbek–Hermel List NS = National
Struggle List MLU = Mount Lebanon Unity

The Arab-brokered 1989 Taif peace agreement ending the civil war in Lebanon redressed the constitutional balance between Christian and Muslim groups and guaranteed a power-sharing structure. Relative stability has been maintained under President Rafiq al-Hariri, who won the first postwar legislative elections in 1992. General Émile Lahoud was elected president in 1998. After a brief term as premier by Salim al-Hoss, Hariri was elected to a third term in 2000. Syria remains the main power-broker in Lebanon, especially following the withdrawal of Israeli troops in 2000.

WORLD AFFAIRS

 AL, G24, OIF, NAM, OIC | 1945

The agreement ending the civil war has left Syria with enormous influence in domestic politics. Until mid-2000, when Israeli troops withdrew, clashes in the south between Israeli occupying forces (and their proxy militias) and the Hezbollah militia were frequent and bloody.

PEOPLE & SOCIETY

 836 people per sq mile | 89% urban 11% rural

 Muslim 70% Christian 30% | Death penalty used

The Lebanese population is fragmented into subsects of Christians and Muslims, but retains a strong sense of national identity. There has been a large Palestinian refugee population in the country since 1948. Islamic fundamentalism is influential among poorer Shi'a Muslims, who constitute the largest single group.

Map

LAND HEIGHT

3000m/9843ft
2000m/6562ft
1000m/3281ft
500m/1640ft
200m/656ft
Sea Level

POPULATION

over 1 000 000
over 100 000
over 10 000
under 10 000

El Mina
Tripoli
Zgharta
Qoubaïyat
Amioûn
Hermel
Batroûn
Bcharré
3087m
Jbaïl
Qartaba
Orontes
Joûnié
Baalbek
BEIRUT
Baabda
Zahlé
Aaley
Rayak
Bhamdoun
Aanjar
Damoûr
Saïda
Baroûk
Lac de Qaraaoun
Jezzîne
Rachaïya
Nabatiyé
Litani
Marjayoun
Soûr
El Khiyam
Tibnîne
GOLAN HEIGHTS
Ed Nâqoûra
Bent Jbaïl
ISRAEL

MEDITERRANEAN SEA
SYRIA
LEBANON MTS
QORNET ES-SAOUDA
ANTI-LEBANON MTS

Total Land Area :
10 230 sq. km
(3950 sq. miles)

N
0   20 km
0   20 miles

SAUDI ARABIA

ECONOMICS

 27th $-1701m

 $6,900   -1.4%

Rise of oil prices in 2000 signaled recovery from 1986 collapse, though the country continues to reduce its dependency on oil exports. Large income from pilgrims traveling to Mecca.

RESOURCES

107bn kwh   Comb. 100%
Hydro 0%
Nuclear 0%

Sheep 8.3m
Goats 4.7m
Cattle 265,000   9.1m b/d
(reserves of
261,700m bbl)

With the world's biggest oil and gas reserves, Saudi Arabia plays a key role in the global economy and is among the top 10 traders of all the world's major industrialized nations.

DEFENSE

 $21,876m   Not compulsory

 None   110,500

Saudi Arabia's substantial military contribution to the 1991 Gulf War, at a cost of $55 billion, enhanced its image as a major regional power. Military equipment is purchased mostly from the US, the UK, and France.

MEDIA

 Censorship   High

13 daily
59 per 1,000
people   TV: 2/0
Radio: 1/1

The government imposes total press censorship. The international *Sharq Al Awsat* is a leading Arabic daily. In 2001 the government announced strict rules regarding state and religion on the internet.

EDUCATION

 77%   274,000 students

Schooling is free but not compulsory   Primary 61%
Secondary 43%
Tertiary 16%

Growing numbers of Western-educated Saudis have intensified pressure for social and political change. Much government money has gone into higher education and Islamic universities.

HEALTH

 1 per 588 people   71 years

34 per 1,000 people   19 per 1,000 live births

Infant mortality has dropped and endemic disease has been nearly eradicated. Health care outside major centers still remains relatively undeveloped, given Saudi Arabia's huge economic resources.

SPENDING

 93 per 1,000 people   15.5%

 7.5%   6.4%

Saudi citizens are among the most prosperous in the world. The al-Sa'uds have used their wealth to create a cradle-to-grave welfare system. Ownership of TVs, telephones, and VCRs is among the region's highest.

 1932   1932   Sept 23   SA   +3   +966   .sa

OFFICIAL NAME **Kingdom of Saudi Arabia**   CAPITAL **Riyadh**
POPULATION **21.6m**   CURRENCY **Saudi riyal**   OFF. LANG. **Arabic**

OCCUPYING MOST OF THE Arabian peninsula, Saudi Arabia covers an area as large as western Europe. Over 95% of its land is desert, with the most arid part, known as the "Empty Quarter" or Rub al Khali, being in the southeast. Saudi Arabia has the world's largest oil and gas reserves and major refining and petrochemicals industries. It includes Islam's holiest cities, Medina and Mecca, visited each year by two million Muslims performing the pilgrimage known as the *hajj*. The al-Sa'ud family have been Saudi Arabia's absolutist rulers since 1932.

POLITICS

 Not applicable   HM King Fahd ibn Abd al-Aziz   Monarchy

Since 1993 a Consultative Council (*Majlis ash-Shoura*) has been appointed by the king. Following the 1991 Gulf War, a civil rights campaign emerged to challenge the authority of the ruling family, demanding closer adherence to Islamic values. The

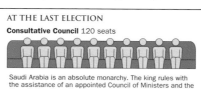

AT THE LAST ELECTION
Consultative Council 120 seats
Saudi Arabia is an absolute monarchy. The king rules with the assistance of an appointed Council of Ministers and the Consultative Council

movement objected to the presence of US troops on Saudi territory and the consequent exposure to "corrupt" Western culture. The al-Sa'uds moved swiftly to quash the protest but exiled opponents have continued their activities using fax machines and email.

The question of succession and the possibility of a future power struggle, rooted in rivalries endemic to the House of Sa'ud, emerged as major issues in early 1996, when King Fahd – suffering the effects of a stroke – formally ceded the management of day-to-day affairs to his half-brother, Crown Prince Abdullah. A few weeks later, Fahd resumed control.

The royal family rules by carefully manipulating appointments in all sectors of government. Frequent changes of personnel within the armed forces ensure that officers do not build personal followings. All influential cabinet portfolios, apart from those of oil and religious affairs, are held by members of the royal family.

Absolutist rule means that domestic politics are virtually nonexistent. The regime retains feudal elements: weekly *majlis*, or councils, are held where citizens can present petitions or grievances to leading members of the royal family. Large cash sums are often dispensed at these meetings.

The legitimacy of the regime is built on its adherence to Islamic values, and the backing of the *ulema* (scholars). It is the stress on Islam that colors Saudi life most. The 5,000-strong *mutawa* (religious police) enforce the five-times-a-day call to prayer, when businesses must close. During Ramadan the *mutawa* are especially active.

WORLD AFFAIRS

AL, Dam Dec, GCC, OIC, OPEC   UN 1945

Saudi Arabia's strategic importance is derived largely from its oil reserves and worldwide investments. Relations with the US are particularly close, and the Saudis remain important institutional investors in the West. After Iraq's invasion of Kuwait in 1990, it took a leading role in consolidating the Arab coalition against Iraq and sheltered the Kuwaiti royal family. It also provided military bases to the Western allies and supplied more troops than any other Arab country. However, the continued presence of foreign forces has provoked some hostility; in mid-1996 a bomb attack at a US military complex near Az Zahran killed 19 US personnel. Increasing rapprochement with Iran has also led to tensions with the US.

Saudi Arabia has been an influential power broker in the civil war in Afghanistan, where its support ensured the success of the taliban. A pact signed with Yemen in June 2000 ended a simmering border dispute. As the guardian of Mecca, Saudi Arabia has immense importance as the spiritual center for more than a billion Muslims all over the world.

PEOPLE & SOCIETY

	26 people per sq mile		85% urban 15% rural		Sunni Muslim 85% Shi'a Muslim 15%		Death penalty used

The Saudis, who take their name from the ruling al-Sa'ud family, were united by conquest between 1902 and 1932 by King Abd al-Aziz al-Sa'ud, who expelled the Turks. The vast majority of Saudis are Sunni Muslims who follow the *wahhabi* (puritan) interpretation of Islam and embrace *sharia* (Islamic law). The politically dominant Nejadi tribes from the central plateau around Riyadh are Bedouin in origin. The Hejazi tribes, from the south and west, have a more cosmopolitan, mercantile background, but are largely displaced from politics. In the eastern province there is a Shi'a minority of some 300,000, many of whom are employed in the oilfields. Women have to wear the veil, cannot hold a driver's license, and have no role in public life. They are effectively barred from the workplace except as teachers and nurses. However, in 2000 Saudi Arabia decided to sign the UN convention on women's rights – provided it did not contradict *sharia*.

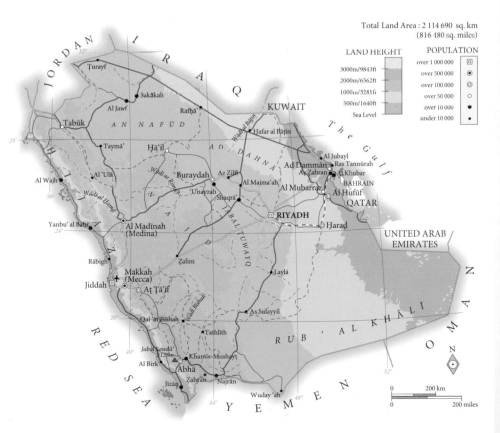

Total Land Area : 2 114 690 sq. km (816 480 sq. miles)

LAND HEIGHT

3000m/9843ft
2000m/6562ft
1000m/3281ft
500m/1640ft
Sea Level

POPULATION

over 1 000 000
over 500 000
over 100 000
over 50 000
over 10 000
under 10 000

ECONOMIC FOCUS

EXPORTS

France 4% / Singapore 6% / South Korea 11% / Japan 16% / USA 17% / Other 46%

IMPORTS

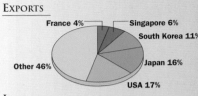

Italy 4% / Germany 7% / UK 8% / Japan 9% / USA 19% / Other 53%

STRENGTHS

Vast oil and gas reserves. Soaring world oil prices in 2000 signified recovery from 1986 collapse. World-class associated industries. Accumulated surpluses and steady current income. Large income from two million pilgrims to Mecca annually.

WEAKNESSES

Lack of indigenous skilled workers. Food production requires heavy subsidy. Most consumer items and industrial raw materials imported. Up to 20% youth unemployment.

PROFILE

Since the 1970s, great efforts have been made to reduce dependence on oil exports and to provide employment for young Saudis. By the latter part of 2000, Saudi influence within OPEC was directed toward controlling a surge in oil prices to avoid recession in the industrialized countries or spurring a drive to develop alternative energy. Since 2000, foreigners have been allowed complete ownership of Saudi businesses and rights to property. Large sums have been spent on achieving a US-standard infrastructure, to provide the basis for a manufacturing economy. The economy, however, remains dependent on foreign workers.

Network of modern road junctions *spread out across the desert landscape near the* hajj *pilgrimage destination of Mecca.*

IRAQ

1932   1991   July 17   IRQ   +3   +964   .iq

OFFICIAL NAME **Republic of Iraq** CAPITAL **Baghdad**
POPULATION **23.1m** CURRENCY **Iraqi dinar** OFF. LANG. **Arabic**

O IL-RICH IRAQ is divided by the Euphrates and Tigris rivers. The Euphrates valley is fertile, but most of the country is desert or mountains. Iraq was the site of the ancient civilization of Babylon. Today, it encompasses Shi'a Muslim holy shrines. After the removal of the monarchy in 1958, it experienced domestic political turmoil. Despite Iraq's defeat in the 1991 Gulf War, the regime in place since 1979 retains power – through repression.

POLITICS

 2000/2004   President Saddam Hussein   One-party state

President Saddam Hussein has dominated Iraqi politics since overthrowing his predecessor in 1979. In theory, the highest state authority rests with the nine-member Revolutionary Command Council, of which Saddam Hussein is the chairman.

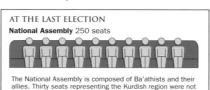

AT THE LAST ELECTION
National Assembly 250 seats

The National Assembly is composed of Ba'athists and their allies. Thirty seats representing the Kurdish region were not elected.

Iraq's invasion of Kuwait in 1990 and its defeat in the 1991 Gulf War resulted in the imposition of UN sanctions. These remain in force pending Iraq's full compliance with UN Gulf War resolutions. In 1994, Iraq recognized Kuwait but continued to defy UN weapons inspection programs. Campaigns for the lifting of sanctions, which gained momentum in 2000, focus on the impact they have on innocent civilians, particularly children. Since 1996 Iraq has been authorized by the UN to sell limited quantities of oil to purchase humanitarian supplies. Despite the sanctions, Iraq pursues a program of reconstruction. From 2000 limited oil revenue was permitted to be reinvested in the oil industry.

There is little unity among opposition groups. The most significant are the Tehran-based Supreme Council for the Islamic Revolution in Iraq and the Iraqi National Congress operating from London. The murder in 1996 of one of Saddam Hussein's senior ministers, a close relative who had defected, was a blow to the opposition, as well as a further demonstration of the regime's ruthlessness.

Iraq's repressive regime is dominated by Saddam Hussein and trusted members of his Takriti tribe. The defection to Jordan in 1995 of Saddam Hussein's relative, senior government minister General Hussein Kamil, suggested dissent within the ruling circle, but his assassination in 1996 effectively neutralized a potential threat.

Saddam Hussein has promoted a massive personality cult. His regime relies on terror and a ruthless intelligence network. Legislative elections, held most recently in 2000, allow voters only to choose between approved candidates, and produce results such as the 99.99% vote for Saddam Hussein's son Uday. The formation of a new Communist Party was announced in 2000, but it forms a section of the Ba'ath party.

WORLD AFFAIRS

 AL, OAPEC, OPEC, OIC, NAM   1945

The legacy of the Iran–Iraq war in the 1980s, the invasion of Kuwait in 1990, and the Gulf War in 1991 still dominate foreign relations. A US-led military force, assisted by several Arab states, inflicted a crushing defeat on Iraq in 1991. Since then the UN has

imposed a severe sanctions regime. Continued tensions still lead to punitive air strikes by US and UK forces. Russia, France, and several Arab states led the way in late 2000 in undermining sanctions on humanitarian grounds. Flights from Saddam International Airport were resumed. No major Western state has yet restored diplomatic relations, as the regime still refuses entry to UN weapons inspectors, but limited economic links have been resumed with some countries. Though there have been some signs of improvement, relations with Iran remain tense. Iranian opposition groups continue to use Iraq as a base for their operations.

PEOPLE & SOCIETY

 137 people per sq mile

 76% urban 24% rural

 Shi'a Muslim 63% Sunni Muslim 33% Other 4%

 Death penalty used

In addition to the Arab and Kurdish populations, Iraq has a small number of minority groups, such as Turks and Persians. Over 90% of the population are Muslim, while the rest comprise a variety of Christian sects. Since the creation of Israel, most Iraqi Jews have emigrated. The Arab Muslims are divided into Sunni and Shi'a sects. The Shi'a form the largest single religious group; however, Shi'a divines do not have as intimate a connection with the people as they do in Iran and their influence on government is limited. Since the mid-1970s, many Iraqis have moved, or been forced to move, to the cities, where some three-quarters of the population now live.

In the marshes of the extreme south, communities of Marsh Arabs survive. In the wake of the 1991 Gulf War, some of these attempted a rebellion against the state, which continues to drain the marshes in order to destroy both the people and their culture.

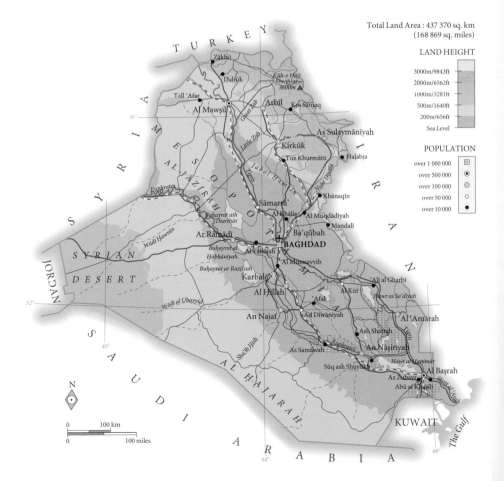

ECONOMIC FOCUS

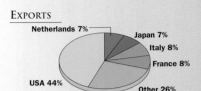

EXPORTS

Netherlands 7%, Japan 7%, Italy 8%, France 8%, Other 26%, USA 44%

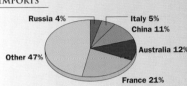

IMPORTS

Russia 4%, Italy 5%, China 11%, Australia 12%, France 21%, Other 47%

STRENGTHS

Second-largest crude oil and natural gas reserves in OPEC. Large labor force.

WEAKNESSES

Inability to sell oil on the international market; Iraq's gross national product halved by UN sanctions. Once-thriving agricultural sector devastated by war.

PROFILE

Before 1990, Iraq was the world's third-largest oil supplier. Under sanctions, oil was produced only for domestic consumption. Limited oil exports under strict UN supervision were resumed for the first time in December 1996, and in 2000 the UN Security Council approved a resolution permitting Iraq to buy parts and equipment for the oil industry. The denial of Western assistance following the 1991 Gulf War has stifled Iraq's economy, although the recent resumption of informal economic links with France and Russia may lead to improvement. The once thriving agricultural sector was badly affected by the war. The manufacturing industry is at a standstill. The introduction of draconian penalties, including the death sentence, have failed to curb the black market or halt the sharp depreciation in the value of the dinar.

Golden Mosque *at Sāmarrā' on the Tigris. Among the extensive remains of its ancient city are those of the Great Mosque built in 847CE.*

KUWAIT

1961 | 1961 | Feb 25 | KWT | +3 | +965 | .kw

OFFICIAL NAME **State of Kuwait** CAPITAL **Kuwait City**
POPULATION **2m** CURRENCY **Kuwaiti dinar** OFF. LANG. **Arabic**

AT THE NORTHWEST EXTREME of the Gulf, Kuwait is dwarfed by its neighbors. The flat, almost featureless landscape conceals huge oil and gas reserves, which put Kuwait among the world's first oil-rich states. In 1990 Iraq invaded, claiming Kuwait as its 19th province. A US-led alliance, under the aegis of the UN, expelled Iraqi forces following a short war in 1991. Since its liberation, Kuwait has built a wall separating its territory from Iraq.

POLITICS

 1999/2003   Amir Shaikh Jabir al-Ahmad al-Jabir al-Sabah   Constitutional monarchy

AT THE LAST ELECTION

National Assembly 50 seats

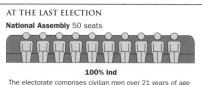

100% Ind

The electorate comprises civilian men over 21 years of age whose families have been resident in Kuwait since before 1921. Elections on July 3, 1999, were contested by independents. The 50 seats were split evenly between Islamists, liberals, and government supporters.

In 1992 Amir Shaikh Jabir restored the National Assembly. There was then a government of "national unity" until 1999, when elections strengthened the amir's Islamist and liberal opponents. The Council of Ministers resigned in 2001 in the face of Assembly criticism. In the new cabinet the ruling al-Sabah family still holds the top posts.

WORLD AFFAIRS

 AL, Dam Dec, GCC, OIC, OPEC   1963

Kuwait's strategic importance is as a major exporter of crude oil and natural gas. As such, it has always maintained very close links with the West, which have deepened since the war with Iraq, and on which it depends for its future security. Kuwait still awaits the return of POWs from Iraq.

Total Land Area :
17 820 sq. km
(6880 sq. miles)

POPULATION
◎ over 100 000
○ over 50 000
● over 10 000
• under 10 000

LAND HEIGHT
200m/656ft
Sea Level

0 ___ 25 km
0 ___ 25 miles

PEOPLE & SOCIETY

 291 people per sq mile   97% urban 3% rural

 Muslim 85% Christian, Hindu & others 15%   Death penalty used

Kuwait is a conservative Sunni Muslim society (27% of the population are Shi'ite). Women have considerable freedom, although the amir's decree providing for female enfranchisement is repeatedly rejected by the National Assembly.

Kuwait's oil wealth has drawn in thousands of workers from south Asia and other Arab countries. The PLO's support for the Iraqi invasion led to most Palestinians, hitherto more numerous in Kuwait than elsewhere in the Arabian peninsula, being driven out. Now native Kuwaitis are outnumbered by resident foreign nationals.

ECONOMICS

 54th $5,062m

 $22,110   2%

Recovery of oil and gas production. Benefits from return of high oil prices after the collapse of 1986. Stable banking system. Adverse consequences of Iraqi invasion. Strategic vulnerability deters investment.

RESOURCES

27.2bn kwh   Comb. 100% Hydro 0% Nuclear 0%

Sheep 450,000 Goats 155,000 Cattle 20,400   2.2m b/d (reserves of 96,500m bbl)

The oil industry is Kuwait's most profitable sector, accounting for over 80% of export earnings. Although badly hit by the Gulf War, when a number of wells were deliberately fired, it was quickly rehabilitated.

DEFENSE

$3,275m   Compulsory

None   15,300

In August 1990 Kuwait's 11,000-strong, partly volunteer army was easily overrun by vastly superior Iraqi forces. Since its liberation, defense pacts have been signed with the US, the UK, France, and Russia.

MEDIA

Some censorship   High

7 daily 377 per 1,000 people   TV: 1/0 Radio 1/0

All radio and terrestrial TV transmissions are controlled by the state, but satellite TV is freely available. Freedom of the press exists in theory.

EDUCATION

82.6%   29,509 students

14 years   Primary 62% Secondary 61% Tertiary 19%

Kuwaiti citizens receive free education from nursery to university. Since the liberation, more emphasis has been placed on technology in the curriculum.

HEALTH

1 per 526 people   76 years

22 per 1,000 people   11 per 1,000 live births

Despite theft of equipment during the Iraqi invasion, Kuwait has restored its Western-standard health care service. Nationals receive free treatment.

SPENDING

 317 per 1,000 people   11.1%

 5%   2.9%

As well as the oil-rich elite, most Kuwaitis enjoy high incomes, and the government has repeatedly rescued citizens who have suffered stock market or other financial losses.

BAHRAIN

1971 | 1971 | Dec 16 | BRN | +3 | +973 | .bh

OFFICIAL NAME **State of Bahrain** CAPITAL **Manama**
POPULATION **617,000** CURRENCY **Bahrain dinar** OFF. LANG. **Arabic**

BAHRAIN IS AN ARCHIPELAGO of 33 islands situated between the Qatar peninsula and the Saudi Arabian mainland. Only three of the islands are inhabited. Bahrain Island is connected to Saudi Arabia's eastern province by a causeway opened in 1986. Bahrain was the first Gulf emirate to export oil; its reserves are now almost depleted. Services such as offshore banking, insurance, and tourism are major employment sectors for skilled Bahrainis.

POLITICS

Not applicable	Amir Shaikh Hamad bin Isa al-Khalifa	Monarchy

AT THE LAST ELECTION

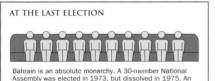

Bahrain is an absolute monarchy. A 30-member National Assembly was elected in 1973, but dissolved in 1975. An advisory Consultative Council was formed in 1993. Its 40 members are to be elected from 2001. A referendum in 2001 approved the resurrection of a legislative body.

The al-Khalifa family has dominated politics since 1783 by means of an effectively autocratic system, although the amir has been advised since 1993 by an appointed Consultative Council. In 2000 the council approved a national charter proposing a transition to a democratic kingdom, with the amir as king and a partially elected assembly.

Shaikh Hamad bin Isa al-Khalifa, who succeeded as amir in 1999, supports the policy of economic liberalization initiated by his late father. The repeal of the State Security Law in 2001 promised an end to the detention of political dissidents. Many were Shi'a opponents of the regime, traditionally backed by Iran.

WORLD AFFAIRS

AL, Dam Dec, GCC, OIC, OAPEC	1971

Bahrain has good relations with the UK and the US, but is eager to restore relations with Iraq. There is tension with Iran, but a dispute with Qatar over the Hawar islands was resolved in Bahrain's favor in 2001.

PEOPLE & SOCIETY

2,354 people per sq mile	92% urban 8% rural
Shi'a Muslim 70% Sunni Muslim 30%	Death penalty used

Bahrain is the smallest and most densely populated Arab state. The key division is between Sunni and Shi'a Muslims. Sunnis hold the best jobs in business and government. Shi'a Muslims tend to do menial work and have a lower standard of living. The most impoverished Shi'a Muslims tend to be of Iranian descent.

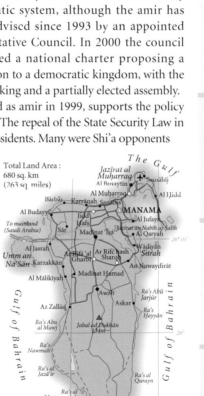

Total Land Area : 680 sq. km (263 sq. miles)

The Gulf

Jazirat al Muharraq
Al Busaytin
Al Muharraq
Al Hidd
Barbar
Karranah Samahij
Al Budayyi
Jidd Hafs
Al Jufayr
To mainland (Saudi Arabia)
Sar
Madinat 'Isa
Jazirat an Nabih as Salih
Al Qaryah
Al Jasrah
Ar Rifa' al Gharbi
Ar Rifa ash Sharqi
Wadiyan Sitrah
Umm an Na'san
Karzakkan
An Nuwaydirat
Al Malikiyah
Madinat Hamad
Awali
Ra's Abu Jarjur
Az Zallaq
Askar
Ra's Hayyan
Ra's Abu al Mawj
Jabal ad Dukhan 134m
Ra's Nawmah
Ra's al Jaza'ir
Ra's al Qurayn
Ra's al Mumma alah
Hadd al Jamal
Ra's al Barr

MANAMA

Gulf of Bahrain

LAND HEIGHT
100m/328ft
Sea Level

Hawar Islands

N

POPULATION
◎ over 100 000
○ over 50 000
● over 10 000
• under 10 000

0   5 km
0   5 miles

110th	$-420m
$7,640	-0.4%

Bahrain is the Arab world's major offshore banking sector following conflict within Lebanon. Depleted oil reserves and insufficient diversification. High unemployment. High levels of government borrowing.

5bn kwh	Comb. 100% Hydro 0% Nuclear 0%
Sheep 17,500 Goats 16,300 Cattle 13,350	34,927 b/d (reserves of 165.8m bbl)

Bahrain remains dependent on its oil and gas production. As oil has declined, so gas has assumed greater importance. Most is used to supply local industries, particularly the aluminum plant.

$441m	Not compulsory
None	11,000

The emirate's strong defense force includes a small but well-equipped air force. US air bases on Bahrain were used in the 1990–1991 Gulf War. The small navy is hard-pressed to patrol the 33-island archipelago.

Some censorship	High
5 daily 117 per 1,000 people	TV: 1/0 Radio: 1/1

Bahrain has a less authoritarian media regime than most of the Gulf states. CNN and BBC satellite TV are freely available.

87.6%	7,676 students
15 years	Primary 98% Secondary 87% Tertiary 20%

Female literacy rates are well above the Gulf average. Lack of funding has held up plans for Bahrain's first university.

1 per 1,000 people	73 years
21 per 1,000 people	8 per 1,000 live births

The high-quality health service is free to Bahraini nationals. Some go abroad for advanced care. The Muharraq Health Center was upgraded in 2001.

243 per 1,000 people	7.7%
4.4%	2.6%

Beneficiaries of the amir's extensive patronage form the wealthiest group in society. The country's largest religious community, the Shi'a Muslims, is also the poorest.

OMAN

1951	1951	Nov 18	OM	+4	+968	.om

OFFICIAL NAME Sultanate of Oman   **CAPITAL Muscat**
POPULATION 2.5m   **CURRENCY Omani rial**   **OFF. LANG. Arabic**

S HARING BORDERS WITH Yemen, the United Arab Emirates, and Saudi Arabia, Oman occupies a strategic position at the entrance to the Gulf. It is the least developed of the Gulf states. The most densely populated areas are the northern coast and the southern Salalah plain. Oil exports have given Oman modest prosperity under a paternalistic sultan, who defeated a Marxist-led insurgency in the 1970s.

POLITICS

 2000/2003   Sultan Qaboos bin Said   Monarchy

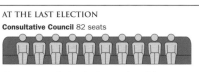

AT THE LAST ELECTION

Consultative Council 82 seats

There are no political parties. The members of the Consultative Council (Majlis ash-shoura) were directly elected for the first time in 2000 by electoral committees in each province, and included two women.

Sultan Qaboos is an authoritarian but paternalistic monarch, whose dynasty traces its roots to the 18th century. As well as being head of state, the sultan is prime minister and minister for foreign affairs, defense, and finance. The regime faces no serious challenge, although Qaboos keeps a careful eye on the religious right wing. In 1991, he created the Consultative Council (*Majlis ash-shoura*), which gives a semblance of democracy. From 2000 its members were directly elected by provincial committees, rather than being appointed. Major political issues include the planned privatization of medium-sized government projects, and improving Oman's self-defense capability.

WORLD AFFAIRS

 Damas, GCC, AMF, OIC, AL   1971

Relations with Israel are maintained. Oman is firmly pro-Western, but has ties with Iran and calls for an easing of sanctions against Iraq. A founding member of the GCC, Oman clarified the demarcation of its border with Saudi Arabia in 1992, and Yemen in 1997.

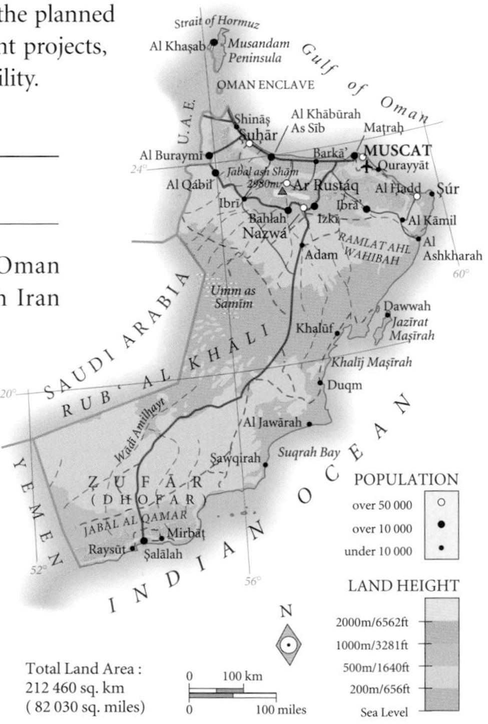

PEOPLE & SOCIETY

 30 people per sq mile   82% urban 18% rural

Ibadi Muslim 75% Other Muslim & Hindu 25%   Death penalty used

Native Omanis, who include Arab refugees who fled Zanzibar in the 1960s, make up three-quarters of the population. Expatriates pose no threat to the regime and Westerners enjoy considerable freedom. Urban drift has taken place, and most Omanis now live in cities. Most Omanis are Ibadi Muslims who follow an appointed leader, the Imam.

Total Land Area : 212 460 sq. km (82 030 sq. miles)

POPULATION
over 50 000 ○
over 10 000 ●
under 10 000 ·

LAND HEIGHT
2000m/6562ft
1000m/3281ft
500m/1640ft
200m/656ft
Sea Level

QATAR

1971 1971 Sept 3 Q +3 +974 .qa

OFFICIAL NAME State of Qatar **CAPITAL** Doha
POPULATION 699,000 **CURRENCY** Qatar riyal **OFF. LANG.** Arabic

PROJECTING NORTH FROM the Arabian peninsula into the Gulf, Qatar has land borders with Saudi Arabia and the United Arab Emirates, and a sea border with Bahrain. Most of the country is flat, semiarid desert. Qatar is a founding member of OPEC, and its plentiful oil and natural gas reserves make it one of the wealthiest states in the region. The country enjoys political stability under the rule of the al-Thani clan.

POLITICS

 Not applicable

 Amir Shaikh Hamad bin Khalifa al-Thani

 Monarchy

Qatar is a traditional emirate. The government and religious establishment is dominated by the amir, Shaikh Hamad, who took power from his father, Shaikh Khalifa, in 1995. A failed coup against Hamad in early 1996 was linked with efforts to regain power by Khalifa, now based in the United Arab Emirates. The prodemocracy movement has called for reform of the 35-member Advisory Council. Shaikh Hamad responded by authorizing Qatar's first elections, to a new municipal council, in 1999, in which all adults, including women, were able to vote and stand as candidates.

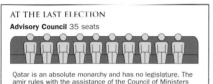

AT THE LAST ELECTION
Advisory Council 35 seats

Qatar is an absolute monarchy and has no legislature. The amir rules with the assistance of the Council of Ministers and the Advisory Council.

WORLD AFFAIRS

 AL, GCC, OIC, OPEC

 1971

Qatar is a founding member of the GCC. In the late 1990s Qatar agreed to supply liquefied natural gas (LNG) to Israel. Although eager to retain strong links with the West, the amir criticized the US and the UK in early 1999 for their bombing of Iraq to force compliance with UN Gulf War resolutions. Qatar has supported a moderate oil price.

PEOPLE & SOCIETY

 165 people per sq mile

 92% urban 8% rural

 Sunni Muslim 95% Other 5%

 Death penalty used

Since the advent of oil wealth, the Qataris, who were formerly nomadic Bedouins, have become a nation of city-dwellers. Almost 90% of the population now inhabit the capital Doha and its suburbs. As a result, northern Qatar is dotted with depopulated and abandoned villages.

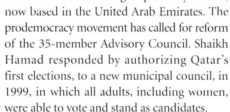

Total Land Area : 11 000 sq. km (4247 sq. miles)

POPULATION
over 100 000
under 10 000

LAND HEIGHT
200m/1640ft
Sea Level

0   30 km
0   30 miles

 98th $-1,658m

 $11,570   2.8%

ECONOMICS

A steady supply of crude oil and huge gas reserves, plus related industries. Dependence on foreign workforce. Potential threat to security from Iraq and Iran makes some multinationals wary of investment.

 6.9bn kwh   Comb. 100% Hydro 0% Nuclear 0%

Sheep 207,000 Goats 179,000 Cattle 14,200   795,000 b/d (reserves of 13,200m bbl)

RESOURCES

Qatar has the smallest reserves of crude oil within OPEC but abundant reserves of gas (the third-largest in the world), including the world's largest field of gas unassociated with oil.

 $1,468m   Not compulsory

 None   12,330

DEFENSE

The estimated 12,000-strong armed forces are too small to play a significant role in Qatari affairs, even in the event of political turmoil. The country has a 10-year defense agreement with the US.

 Some censorship   High

6 daily 161 per 1,000 people   TV. 1/1 Radio: 1/0

MEDIA

Shaikh Hamad has relaxed press censorship. Qatari TV is the most independent in the region. Al Jazeera is a major news channel for the whole area.

 81.2%   8,475 students

Schooling free but not compulsory   Primary 83% Secondary 73% Tertiary 27%

EDUCATION

Education is free, all the way from primary to university level. The government finances students to study overseas.

 1 per 699 people   69 years

 18 per 1,000 people   16 per 1,000 live births

HEALTH

Primary health care is free to Qataris. Hospitals operate to Western standards of care and the government also funds treatment abroad.

 205 per 1,000 people   15.4%

 3.4%   2.9%

SPENDING

Qataris have a high income per capita. There is no income tax, public services are free, and the government guarantees jobs for school graduates. There are no exchange controls.

UAE (UNITED ARAB EMIRATES)

1971 1972 Dec 2 UAE +4 +971 .ae

ECONOMICS

 49th

 $24,300m

 $17,870

 1.6%

Oil and gas reserves are the fourth-biggest in OPEC. Development of service industries and manufacturing sector. Lack of skilled manpower. Most raw materials and foodstuffs have to be imported.

RESOURCES

20.6bn kwh

Comb. 100%
Hydro 0%
Nuclear 0%

Sheep 440,000
Goats 1.05m
Cattle 85,000

2.5m b/d
(reserves of
97,800m bbl)

The UAE is a major exporter of crude oil and natural gas. Mina Jabal Ali in Dubai is the world's largest man-made port. Saadiyat Island off Abu Dhabi is being developed as a financial resort.

DEFENSE

$3,187m

Not compulsory

None

65,000

Training of UAE forces is limited, and personnel are mainly drawn from other Arab states and the Indian subcontinent. During the Gulf War, UAE air bases were used by Western forces for strikes against Iraq.

MEDIA

No censorship

High

7daily
170 per 1,000
people

TV: 4/0
Radio: 7/0

Satellite TV programming is unrestricted in the UAE. Dubai Media City, opened in 2001, promotes greater press freedoms.

EDUCATION

75.6%

16,213 students

12 years

Primary 78%
Secondary 71%
Tertiary 12%

UAE citizens enjoy completely free education from primary to tertiary level. Zayed University was set up in three emirates in 1998.

HEALTH

1 per 556 people

75 years

18 per 1,000 people

8 per 1,000 live births

A high-quality system of primary health care is in place for all UAE citizens, with hospitals able to carry out most operations.

SPENDING

82 per 1000 people

6.2%

1.8%

0.8%

UAE nationals have one of the highest per capita incomes in the Arab world. There is no income tax and oil revenues subsidize public services. Government policies encourage entrepreneurs.

OFFICIAL NAME **United Arab Emirates** CAPITAL **Abu Dhabi**
POPULATION **2.4m** CURRENCY **UAE Dirham** OFF. LANG. **Arabic**

THE ARAB WORLD'S only working federation, the United Arab Emirates (UAE) shares borders with Oman, Saudi Arabia, and Qatar, as well as a disputed maritime boundary with Iran. The UAE is mostly semiarid desert relieved by occasional oases. The cities, watered by extensive irrigation systems, have lavish greenery. The UAE's economic prosperity once relied on pearls, but it is now a sizable gas and oil exporter, and has a growing services sector.

POLITICS

 Not applicable

 President Shaikh Zayed bin Sultan al-Nahyan

 Monarchy

The UAE's seven emirates – Abu Dhabi, Dubai, Sharjah, Ras al Khaimah, Ajman, Umm al Qaiwain, and Fujairah – are dominated by their ruling families. The main personalities are the ruler of Abu Dhabi, Shaikh Zayed, who holds the UAE presidency, and the four al-Maktoum brothers who control Dubai. The eldest, Shaikh Maktoum al-Maktoum, is ruler of Dubai and vice president and prime minister of the UAE.

AT THE LAST ELECTION

Federal National Council 40 seats

There are no political parties. The method of appointment of members of the Federal National Council is determined individually by each of the seven members of the Federation.

President Zayed has relaunched the advisory Federal National Council in response to criticism of the lack of democracy. The growth of Islamic fundamentalism is also a concern. The freedoms granted to Westerners have aroused some anger but, for economic reasons, they are unlikely to be withdrawn.

WORLD AFFAIRS

 AL, OPEC, GCC, OAPEC, OIC

 1971

The UAE is an advocate of moderation within the Arab world. It maintains close links with most OECD states. In 1992, conflict flared when Iran seized control of three islands in the Strait of Hormuz. Attempts are being made to settle the dispute through diplomacy.

Total Land Area : 83 600 sq. km (32 278 sq. miles)

POPULATION
over 100 000
under 10 000

LAND HEIGHT
1000m/3281ft
500m/1640ft
Sea Level

PEOPLE & SOCIETY

 74 people per sq mile

 85% urban
15% rural

Sunni Muslim 96%
Christian, Hindu &
others 4%

Death penalty used

UAE nationals are largely city dwellers, with Abu Dhabi and Dubai the dominant centers. They are mostly conservative Sunni Muslims of Bedouin descent. They are greatly outnumbered by expatriates who arrived in the 1970s during the oil boom. Poverty is rare in the UAE. Women in theory enjoy equal rights with men.

YEMEN

 1990 | 1990 | May 22 | ADN | +3 | +967 | .ye

OFFICIAL NAME **Republic of Yemen** CAPITAL **Sana**
POPULATION **18.1m** CURRENCY **Rial** OFF. LANG. **Arabic**

YEMEN IS LOCATED in southern Arabia. The north is mountainous, with a fertile strip along the Red Sea. The south is largely arid mountains and desert. Until 1990 Yemen was two countries, the Yemen Arab Republic in the north and the People's Democratic Republic of Yemen in the south. The north was run by successive military regimes; the poorer south was the Arab world's only Marxist state. Postunification conflict between the two ruling hierarchies, nominally in coalition, led to full-scale civil war in 1994 and the ousting of the southern-based former Marxists.

POLITICS

 1997/2003 | President Ali Abdullah Saleh | Multiparty republic

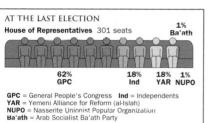

AT THE LAST ELECTION
House of Representatives 301 seats
1% Ba'ath

62% GPC | 18% Ind | 18% YAR | 1% NUPO

GPC = General People's Congress **Ind** = Independents
YAR = Yemeni Alliance for Reform (al-Islah)
NUPO = Nasserite Unionist Popular Organization
Ba'ath = Arab Socialist Ba'ath Party

The merger of North and South Yemen in 1990 united Yemenis under one ruler for the first time since 1735. At first, President Ali Saleh skillfully maintained unity. Then, in 1994, a bloody civil war erupted, fueling a secessionist movement in the south. By mid-1994, the fighting had subsided and the southerners were crushed. In 1999 President Saleh won the region's first ever direct election of a head of state. However, Saleh's regime still faces threats from disgruntled southern tribesmen angry at levels of poverty in their oil-rich country. Since 1992, tribesmen have kidnapped more than 100 foreigners, including diplomats and tourists.

WORLD AFFAIRS

NAM, OIC, AMF, AL, IBRD | UN 1947

Agreement in 2000 with Saudi Arabia over their disputed border resolved what had been the main foreign policy issue. Yemen remains relatively isolated after supporting Iraq in the 1991 Gulf War.

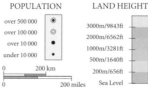

PEOPLE & SOCIETY

 83 people per sq mile | 24% urban 76% rural

Sunni Muslim 55% Shi'a Muslim 42% Others 3% | Death penalty used

N

POPULATION
over 500 000
over 100 000
over 10 000
under 10 000

Total Land Area :
562 970 sq. km
(217 362 sq. miles)

0   200 km
0   200 miles

LAND HEIGHT
3000m/9843ft
2000m/6562ft
1000m/3281ft
500m/1640ft
200m/656ft
Sea Level

Yemenis are almost entirely of Arab and Bedouin descent, though there is a small, dwindling, Jewish minority and people of mixed African and Arab descent along the south coast. In rural areas and in the north, Islamic orthodoxy is strong and most women wear the veil. In the south, however, women still claim the freedoms they had under the Marxist regime.

IRAN

 1502   1990   Feb 11   IR   +3.5   +98   .lr

OFFICIAL NAME **Islamic Republic of Iran**   CAPITAL **Tehran**
POPULATION **67.7m**   CURRENCY **Iranian rial**   OFF. LANG. **Farsi (Persian)**

IRAN IS SURROUNDED by turbulent neighbors, with republics of the former Soviet Union to the north, Afghanistan and Pakistan to the east, and Iraq and Turkey to the west. The south faces the Persian Gulf and the Gulf of Oman. Since 1979, when a revolution led by Ayatollah Khomeini deposed the shah, Iran has become the world's largest theocracy and the leading center for militant Shi'a Islam. Iran's active support for Islamic fundamentalist movements has led to strained relations with central Asian, Middle Eastern, and north African states, as well as the US and western Europe.

POLITICS

 2000/2004   President Mohammad Khatami   Islamic theocracy

A power struggle between the clergy and the secular state has arisen from the ill-defined division of power between the two. The conservative faction in parliament lost its overall majority in 1996 and has been steadily displaced by reformists, who in 2000 made sweeping gains in parliamentary elections. In 2001 reformist president Mohammad Khatami was reelected, this time with an overwhelming 77% of the vote.

AT THE LAST ELECTION

Consultative Council (Majlis) 290 seats

65% IIPF   17% C   11% Ind   5% Vacant   2% Rel

IIPF = Islamic Iran Participation Front (reformists)
C = Coalition of Followers of the Line of Imam (conservatives)
Ind = Independents   **Rel** = Religious Minorities

Khatami is committed to modernizing the economy, but is strongly opposed by the mullahs, for whom adherence to religious values is more important than material welfare. Student proreform protests were heavily suppressed by hardliners, who remain a force, despite the 2000 elections, through the powerful Council of Guardians.

Iran's religious revolution of 1979 was fueled by popular outrage at the corruption, repression, and inequalities of the shah's regime. Since the time of Ayatollah Khomeini, successive Iranian governments have maintained that the clergy have a religious duty to establish a just social system. Accordingly, the legislature, the executive, and the judiciary may, in theory, be overruled by the religious leadership; former president Hashemi Rafsanjani's moderate policies were questioned by radical clergymen advocating "permanent revolution." However, the mullahs' failure to address Iran's economic problems has eroded their political standing. Reformists were encouraged by the election of President Khatami in 1997, but the clergy remains powerful. Huge student demonstrations in 1999 and 2000 in favor of reform were offset by crackdowns on reformist politicians and newspapers. The mullahs, so far unbowed by reformist election victories, have continued to confront the modernizers.

WORLD AFFAIRS

 OPEC, OIC, G24, ECO, NAM   UN 1945

Following the 1979 revolution, Iran assumed international significance as the voice of militant Shi'a Islam. Iran is accused of backing terrorist activity by Muslim extremists and fostering unrest throughout the Middle East and central Asia. In 1995 the US took action by imposing sanctions against Iran.

ECONOMICS

 33rd $-1,897m

 $1,810   21%

OPEC's second-biggest oil-producer. Traditional exports include carpets, pistachio nuts, and caviar. Theocratic authorities restrict contact with the West and access to technology.

RESOURCES

97.7bn kwh   Comb. 93% Hydro 7% Nuclear 0%

 Sheep 55m Goats 26m Cattle 8.1m   3.8m b/d (reserves of 89,700m bbl)

Iran has substantial oil reserves. It also has metal, coal, and salt deposits, but these are relatively undeveloped. Principal crops are wheat, barley, rice, sugar beet, tobacco, and pistachio nuts.

DEFENSE

 $5,711m   Compulsory

None   388,000

Iran has almost 400,000 men under arms, including the 125,000-strong Revolutionary Guard Corps (*Pasdaran Inquilab*), and is regarded by neighboring states as a serious military threat.

MEDIA

 Censorship   Medium

 32 daily 26 per 1,000   TV: 1/0 Radio: 1/0

Radio and TV are state-controlled. Satellite dishes are banned. Closures of reformist newspapers by the conservative Council of Guardians, and prosecutions of their editors, peaked in 2000.

EDUCATION

 76.8%   579,070 students

 11 years   Primary 90% Secondary 71% Tertiary 18%

Most of the population is literate. Primary education, which lasts for five years from the age of six, is free, as are universities, but a small fee is charged for secondary education. Most schools are single-sex.

HEALTH

1 per 1,250 people   69 years

21 per 1,000 people   26 per 1,000 live births

Although an adequate system of primary health care exists in the cities, conditions in rural areas are basic. Growing drug addiction has resulted in rehabilitation programs and anti-drug propaganda.

SPENDING

 30 per 1,000 people   6.2%

4%   1.7%

After the 1979 revolution, living standards in Iran declined markedly. A shortage of foreign exchange has stifled imports of consumer goods. Rationing, brought in during the war with Iraq, is still partly in force.

Under President Khatami, Iran has tried to convey a less confrontational image. Improved relations with Saudi Arabia, troubled since Iran's seizure of the islands of Abu Musa and the Tumbs in 1970, resulted in the signing of a pact in 2001. Relations with the West have also improved. In 1999 Khatami visited Italy, the first Iranian leader since the fall of the shah to be officially welcomed by a Western government.

PEOPLE & SOCIETY

	107 people per sq mile		61% urban 39% rural		Shi'a Muslim 95% Sunni Muslim 4% other 1%		Death penalty used

The population comprises several ethnic groups. The people of the north and center – about half of all Iranians – speak Farsi (Persian), while about a quarter speak related languages, including Kurdish in the west and Baluchi in the southeast. Another quarter of the population speaks Turkic languages, primarily the Azeris and the Turkmen in the northwest. Smaller groups, such as the Circassians and Georgians, are found in the northern provinces.

Until the 16th century, much of Iran followed the Sunni interpretation of Islam, but since then the Shi'a sect has been dominant. Religious minorities, accounting for just 1% of the population, include followers of the Bahai faith, who suffer discrimination, Zoroastrians, Christians, and Jews. The regime has a remarkably liberal attitude to refugees of the Muslim faith. Nearly three million Afghan refugees were received during the height of the Afghan civil war, although many have since been repatriated. In Khorosan province in the east, refugees account for nearly a quarter of the population; near the Turkish border they constitute half the total population. Many are young, resulting in intense competition with Iranians for jobs and consequent ethnic tensions.

Total Land Area :
1 636 000 sq. km
(631 660 sq. miles)

LAND HEIGHT

- 3000m/9843ft
- 2000m/6562ft
- 1000m/3281ft
- 500m/1640ft
- 200m/656ft
- Sea Level

POPULATION
- over 1 000 000
- over 500 000
- over 100 000
- over 50 000

ECONOMIC FOCUS

EXPORTS
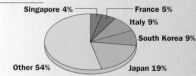
Singapore 4%
France 5%
Italy 9%
South Korea 9%
Japan 19%
Other 54%

IMPORTS
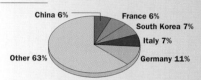
China 6%
France 6%
South Korea 7%
Italy 7%
Germany 11%
Other 63%

STRENGTHS

OPEC's second-biggest oil producer; soaring world oil prices in 2000. There is potential for related industries and the increased production of traditional exports: carpets, pistachio nuts, and caviar.

WEAKNESSES

Theocratic authorities restrict contact with Western countries and access to technology. High unemployment and inflation. Excessive foreign debts.

PROFILE

With few industries other than oil, US sanctions and fluctuations in oil prices made foreign earnings volatile; higher prices in 2000 held out the prospect of being able to invest in diversification.

The Reshteh-ye Kuhhā-ye Alborz
(Elburz Mountains) in northern Iran. Their Caspian Sea slopes are rainy and forested; the south-facing slopes are dry.

TURKMENISTAN

 | 1991 | 1991 | Oct 27 | TM | +5 | +993 | .tm |

ECONOMICS

 130th
$-571m
$670
13.5%

Decision to abolish collective farms is gradually encouraging private initiative and enterprise. Cotton monoculture has forced rising food imports. Thriving black market all but wiped out value of manat.

RESOURCES

9.4bn kwh
Comb. 100%
Hydro 0%
Nuclear 0%
Sheep 5.6m
Goats 368,000
Cattle 850,000
150,000 b/d
(reserves of 500m bbl)

During the Soviet administration most Turkmen agriculture was turned over to cotton – seen by Moscow as a strategic crop.

DEFENSE

$112m
Compulsory
None
17,500

Turkmenistan is totally dependent on Russia for defense. The military is under the joint control of both countries.

MEDIA

Censorship
Medium
2 daily
No data for circulation
TV: 1/0
Radio: 1/0

Iranian and Afghan radio stations, beaming in Islamic programs, are popular. TV channels are only available in urban areas.

EDUCATION

98%
76,000 students
17 years
Primary 94%
Secondary ?
Tertiary 22%

The Turkmen language and literature (banned until 1987) are now on the syllabus. However, Russian schools continue to have higher standards.

HEALTH

 1 per 5,000 people
66 years
21 per 1,000 people
33 per 1,000 live births

Highly polluted water is a major health hazard; less than 40% of the population have a treated water mains supply.

SPENDING

No data
3.3%
3.9%
4.1%

The ex-communist bureaucrats are still the richest group in the country. They favor Japanese and Korean luxury goods.

OFFICIAL NAME **Turkmenistan** CAPITAL **Ashgabat**
POPULATION: **4.5m** CURRENCY **Manat** OFF. LANG. **Turkmen**

ORIGINALLY THE POOREST state among the former Soviet republics, Turkmenistan has adjusted better than most to independence, exploiting the market value of its abundant natural gas supplies. A largely Sunni Muslim area, Turkmenistan is part of the former Turkestan, the last expanse of central Asia incorporated into czarist Russia. Much of life is still based on tribal relationships.

POLITICS

 L. House 1999/2004
U. House 1998/2003
 President Saparmurad Niyazov
 One-party state

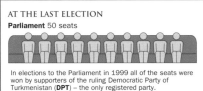

AT THE LAST ELECTION
Parliament 50 seats

In elections to the Parliament in 1999 all of the seats were won by supporters of the ruling Democratic Party of Turkmenistan (**DPT**) – the only registered party.

People's Council 110 seats

The People's Council has 50 directly elected members, the 50 members of the Parliament, 10 appointed regional members and a varying number of ex-officio members.

Officially, Turkmenistan became a multiparty democracy at independence, although President Niyazov has banned the formation of new parties. As in other ex-Soviet states, former communists, regrouped as the Democratic Party of Turkmenistan, still dominate the political process. The DPT harbors the traditional communist suspicion of Islamic fundamentalism. Turkmenistan's main concern is to prevent the social and nationalistic conflicts that have blighted other CIS republics. Russian remains the bureaucratic language.

WORLD AFFAIRS

 EAPC, OIC, ECO, OSCE, CIS
 1992

Turkmenistan is concentrating on establishing good relations with Iran and Turkey, but is wary of Islamic fundamentalism. President Niyazov opposes economic union with the CIS, and has also expressed caution about closer political union with other Turkic-speaking Asian states.

PEOPLE & SOCIETY

 24 people per sq mile
 45% urban
55% rural
Sunni Muslim 87%
Eastern Orthodox 11%
Other 2%
Death penalty not used

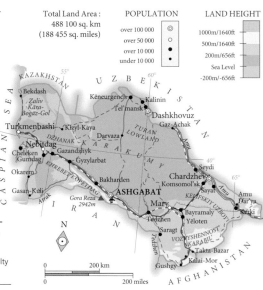

Total Land Area : 488 100 sq. km (188 455 sq. miles)

POPULATION
over 100 000
over 50 000
over 10 000
under 10 000

LAND HEIGHT
1000m/1640ft
500m/1640ft
200m/656ft
Sea Level
-200m/-656ft

Before czarist Russia annexed Turkmenistan in 1884, the Turkmen were a largely nomadic tribal people, and the tribal unit remains strong. Tribal conflicts among the Turkmen, rather than tensions with the two main minorities – Russians and Uzbeks – are a source of strife. Since 1989, Turkmenistan has been rehabilitating its traditional language and culture, as well as reassessing its history. Islam is again central to the Turkmen.

OFFICIAL NAME Republic of Uzbekistan **CAPITAL** Tashkent
POPULATION 24.3m **CURRENCY** Som **OFF. LANG.** Uzbek

SHARING THE ARAL SEA COASTLINE with its northern neighbor, Kazakhstan, Uzbekistan has common borders with five countries, including Afghanistan to the south. It is the most populous central Asian republic and has considerable natural resources. Uzbekistan contains the ancient cities of Samarqand, Bukhara (Bukhoro), Khiva, and Tashkent. The dictatorship of President Karimov has prevented the spread of Islamic fundamentalism.

POLITICS

 1999/2004   President Islam Karimov   Presidential democracy

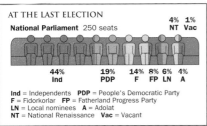

AT THE LAST ELECTION
National Parliament 250 seats

4% NT 1% Vac
44% Ind 19% PDP 14% F 8% FP 6% LN 4% A

Ind = Independents **PDP** = People's Democratic Party
F = Fidorkorlar **FP** = Fatherland Progress Party
LN = Local nominees **A** = Adolat
NT = National Renaissance **Vac** = Vacant

President Karimov's PDP has not been willing to devolve or share power. A constitution adopted in December 1992 appeared to endorse multiparty politics along Western lines. However, Karimov took advantage of greater powers granted to his office by banning a number of opposition parties, including the nationalist Birlik (Unity) movement and the Islamic Renaissance Party. The only legal opposition party, Erk (Will), was proscribed in 1993, and in 1995 incurred the wrath of the government when a group of activists received stiff prison sentences after being found guilty of political subversion.

WORLD AFFAIRS

 SCO, CIS, NAM, OSCE, OIC   1992

Uzbekistan has established itself as the CIS regional power base, and was a key player in the formation of a central Asian common market in 1994. The crucial relationship remains that with Russia, which has 100,000 troops stationed in the country.

Total Land Area : 447 400 sq. km
(172 741 sq. miles)

POPULATION
over 1 000 000
over 100 000
over 50 000
over 10 000

LAND HEIGHT
3000m/9843ft
2000m/6562ft
1000m/3281ft
500m/1640ft
200m/656ft
Sea Level

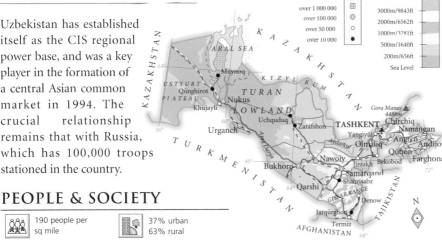

PEOPLE & SOCIETY

190 people per sq mile 37% urban 63% rural

Sunni Muslim 88% Eastern Orthodox 9% Other 3% Death penalty used

Among the former Soviet republics, Uzbekistan has a relatively complex makeup. In addition to the Uzbeks, Russians, Tajiks, and Kazakhs, there are small minorities of Tatars and Karakalpaks. The proportion of Russians has been declining since the 1970s. Tensions among ethnic groups have the potential to create regional and racial conflict.

 72nd $-39m
 $720   -24.6%

Well-developed cotton market. Current production of natural gas makes significant contribution to electricity generation. Dependent on grain imports, as domestic production meets only 25% of needs.

 46.1bn kwh   Comb. 88% Hydro 12% Nuclear 0%
 Sheep 8.9m Goats 640,000 Cattle 5.3m   175,00 b/d (reserves of 600m bbl)

Uzbekistan has the world's largest gold mine, and also large deposits of natural gas, petroleum, coal, and uranium. An important oilfield was discovered in 1992 and production will rise with further investment.

 $615m   Compulsory
 None   59,100

Uzbekistan has a 1,000-strong National Guard, which generally acts as the personal army of Karimov. Russian troops are still based on Uzbek territory to protect the Russian minority.

 Censorship   High
3 daily 3 per 1,000 people TV: 2/0 Radio: 1/0

Restrictions on independent publications, designed to encourage the promotion of the personality cult and policies of Karimov, were eased in mid-1998 with the publication of the first private newspaper.

 88.9% 638,200 students
17 years Primary 78% Secondary 94% Tertiary 33%

The state system still follows the Soviet model, though some instruction is in Uzbek. In the late 1980s, there were a few ethnic Tajik schools and a university in Samarkand. These were closed down in 1992.

 1 per 303 people   69 years
 23 per 1,000 people   22 per 1,000 live births

The health service has been in decline since the dissolution of the USSR. Some rural areas are not served at all. Serious respiratory diseases among cotton growers are increasing.

 No data   3.9%
 7.7%   3.4%

Former Communists are still the wealthiest group, since they retain control of the economy. Many rural poor live below the poverty line.

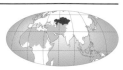

KAZAKHSTAN

ECONOMICS

68th

$-171m

$1,250

8.2%

First of the former Soviet states to establish a free market economy. Energy and consumer goods must be imported. A mass privatization program was launched in 1994.

RESOURCES

52bn kwh

Comb. 88%
Hydro 12%
Nuclear 0%

Sheep 9.8m
Goats 705,400
Cattle 4m

745,000 b/d
(reserves
8,000m bbl)

Mining is the single most important industry in Kazakhstan. Joint ventures to exploit substantial oil and gas reserves in the Caspian Sea were agreed with Russia in 1995, and the US and Japan in 1998.

DEFENSE

$504m

Compulsory

None

64,000

In 1993, the US agreed to grant Kazakhstan $84 million to dismantle its nuclear weapons. In 1995, Kazakhstan announced that all its nuclear weapons had been transferred to Russia or destroyed.

MEDIA

Some censorship

Medium

5 daily
30 per 1,000
people

TV: 1/2
Radio: 1/several

The state-owned media compete with independent publications and privately owned radio and television stations, many of which are controlled by members of President Nazarbayev's family.

EDUCATION

 99%

 419,460 students

17 years

Primary 98%
Secondary 87%
Tertiary 33%

Education remains based on the Soviet model. Since the adoption of Kazakh as the state language in 1995, Russian is gradually being replaced by Kazakh as the main medium of instruction in schools.

HEALTH

1 per 286 people

64 years

14 per 1,000 people

22 per 1,000 live births

The health system is limited in terms of facilities and coverage. Rural people have minimal access to clinics. The country's size means that extending coverage and improving the quality of care will be costly.

SPENDING

 66 per 1,000 people

3.5%

4.4%

3.5%

Life for the majority of Kazakhs has always been hard, and has grown even more difficult since 1989. Living standards have deteriorated and unemployment has risen as a result of market-oriented reforms.

OFFICIAL NAME **Republic of Kazakhstan** CAPITAL **Astana**
POPULATION **16.2m** CURRENCY **Tenge** OFF. LANG. **Kazakh**

THE SECOND-LARGEST of the former Soviet republics, Kazakhstan extends almost 1,240 miles (2,000 km) from the Caspian Sea in the west to the Altai Mountains in the east, and 806 miles (1,300 km) north to south. It borders Russia to the north and China to the east. Kazakhstan was the last Soviet republic to declare its independence, in 1991. In 1999, elections confirmed the former communist Nursultan Nazarbayev and his supporters in power. Kazakhstan has considerable economic potential, and many Western companies seek to exploit its mineral resources.

POLITICS

L. House 1999/2004
U. House 1999/2002

President Nursultan
Nazarbayev

Presidential
democracy

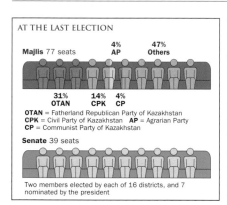

AT THE LAST ELECTION

Majlis 77 seats

4% AP

47% Others

31% OTAN

14% CPK

4% CP

OTAN = Fatherland Republican Party of Kazakhstan
CPK = Civil Party of Kazakhstan   AP = Agrarian Party
CP = Communist Party of Kazakhstan

Senate 39 seats

Two members elected by each of 16 districts, and 7 nominated by the president

The increased powers of President Nazarbayev are the focus of political controversy, prompting his critics to accuse him of developing a personality cult. The 1995 constitution strengthened presidential powers, conferring a veto over the decisions of the Constitutional Council. Nazarbayev, who was due to face reelection in 1996, also won a referendum which extended his term of office until 2000. However, in 1998 the legislature approved constitutional amendments forcing him to hold a presidential election in 1999.

Despite a democratic government, the president enjoys political dominance, and the patronage of the Kazakh clans is still important. Since coming to power in 1989, Nazarbayev has concentrated on market reforms. His political credibility was badly shaken in 1994, when allegations of widespread fraud led to the annulment of legislative elections. Nazarbayev faces mounting domestic and international criticism of his attempts to expand the scope of his powers. In June 2000 the Assembly granted him special powers to advise future presidents after his term expires in 2006.

WORLD AFFAIRS

CIS, EAPC, SCO,
OIC, OSCE

 1992

Maintaining close ties with other former Soviet republics is a priority. Sandwiched between the massive states of Russia and China, President Nazarbaev has signed major treaties with both countries in the hope of improving relations with both.

Total Land Area :
2 717 300 sq. km
(1 049 150 sq. miles)

POPULATION

over 500 000
over 100 000
over 50 000
over 10 000
under 10 000

LAND HEIGHT

3000m/9843ft
2000m/6562ft
1000m/3281ft
500m/1640ft
200m/656ft
Sea Level
-200m/-656ft

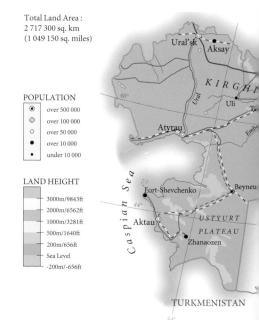

Relations with Russia, although strained at times by Moscow's concern over Kazakhstan's ethnic Russians, have been cemented by a 25-year cooperation treaty, which includes currency convertability between the rouble and the tenge.

The largest of the former Soviet central Asian republics, Kazakhstan has recently assumed a broader role in the region, offering military assistance to both Kyrgyzstan and Uzbekistan in 2000 as a "guarantor of peace." President Nazarbayev was the first chairman of the Eurasian Economic Community, set up in October 2000.

Kazakhstan's rich mineral resources have attracted investors from Europe, the US, and Asia, particularly South Korea. Relations with China have improved, with agreements in 1998 and 1999 on border issues.

PEOPLE & SOCIETY

 15 people per sq mile

 56% urban 44% rural

 Muslim 50% Russian Orthodox 13% Others 37%

 Death penalty not used

Kazakhstan's ethnic diversity arose from the forced settlement during the Soviet era of Germans, Tatars, and Russians. By 1959, Kazakhs were outnumbered by ethnic Russians. This balance has been redressed by the immigration of ethnic Kazakhs from neighboring states and the departure in the 1990s of some 1.5 million ethnic Russians. In addition, a majority of ethnic Germans have opted to live in Germany, although in 2000 the government announced a campaign to try to lure some of them back.

In 1995, ethnic Russians criticized the country's new constitution for preventing dual citizenship with Russia and refusing to recognize Russian as an official language. Central control over ethnic Russians has been reinforced by shifting the capital to Astana (formerly Akmola) in the north, where the majority of ethnic Russians reside.

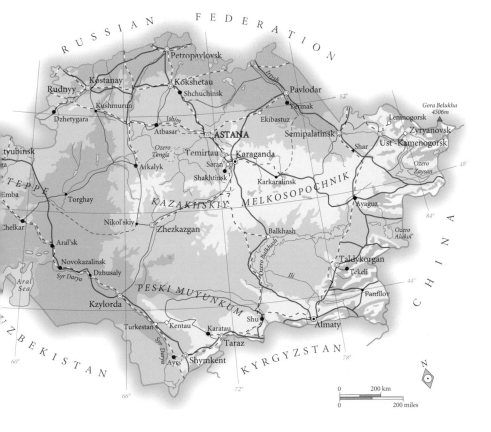

ECONOMIC FOCUS

EXPORTS

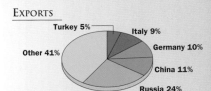

Turkey 5%
Italy 9%
Germany 10%
China 11%
Russia 24%
Other 41%

IMPORTS

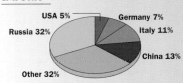

USA 5%
Germany 7%
Russia 32%
Italy 11%
China 13%
Other 32%

STRENGTHS

Mineral resources, notably oil, gas, and bismuth and cadmium, used in electronics industry. Joint oil and gas ventures with Western companies. Mass privatization program launched in 1994.

WEAKNESSES

Collapse of former Soviet economic and trading system. Reliance on imported consumer goods. Rapid introduction of the tenge in 1993 increased instability and fueled sharp price rises.

PROFILE

Kazakhstan has moved faster than other former Soviet republics to establish a market economy. Prices have been freed, foreign trade deregulated, and the tax system reformed. Growth has still been elusive. Unemployment and inflation have risen sharply, due in large part to the collapse of the wider Soviet economy. Foreign direct investment is mainly in the energy sector. Outdated equipment and inadequate distribution networks mean that energy has to be imported, although Kazakhstan exports fossil fuel. An oil price boom set the tone for the country's first "five-year plan" in 2000, part of Nazarbayev's "Kazakhstan 2030" program. It promised long-term land leases, although not full private ownership, from 2001.

The Altai Mountains, *eastern Kazakhstan. Subject to harsh continental winters, the Altai range is a cold, inhospitable place. Rivers carry meltwater down onto the vast steppe.*

KYRGYZSTAN

| 1991 | 1991 | Aug 31 | KS | +6 | +996 | .kg |

OFFICIAL NAME **Kyrgyz Republic**   CAPITAL **Bishkek**
POPULATION **4.7m**   CURRENCY **Som**   OFF. LANG. **Kyrgyz & Russian**

KYRGYZSTAN IS A SMALL and very mountainous state in central Asia. It is the least urbanized of the former Soviet republics and was among the last to develop its own cultural nationalism. Its moderate government is treading uncertainly between Kyrgyz nationalist pressures and ensuring that the minority Russians are not alienated, since they tend to possess the skills necessary to run a market-based economy.

POLITICS

 L. House 2000/2005
U. House 2000/2005

 President
Askar Akayev

 Presidential democracy

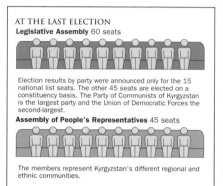

AT THE LAST ELECTION
Legislative Assembly 60 seats

Election results by party were announced only for the 15 national list seats. The other 45 seats are elected on a constituency basis. The Party of Communists of Kyrgyzstan is the largest party and the Union of Democratic Forces the second-largest.

Assembly of People's Representatives 45 seats

The members represent Kyrgyzstan's different regional and ethnic communities.

In 1991 Kyrgyzstan was the first former Soviet republic to ban the Communist Party. It was revived in 1992 as the Party of Communists of Kyrgyzstan. Relations with the large Uzbek minority have remained calm since serious clashes in 1990.

President Akayev has been accused of fostering a personality cult. Already in power under the Soviet regime before independence, he was reelected in 1995 and in 2000, after objections to a third term were overruled by the Constitutional Court.

WORLD AFFAIRS

 SCO, CIS, OSCE, OIC, EAPC

 1992

Kyrgyzstan is working to reduce its dependence on Russia. Turkey is developing close links aimed at restraining the fundamentalist influence in the region. Relations with Uzbekistan, which allegedly supports some of the antigovernment forces in Kyrgyzstan, are tense.

Total Land Area : 198 500 sq. km (76 640 sq. miles)

PEOPLE & SOCIETY

 61 people per sq mile

 34% urban
66% rural

 Sunni Muslim 70%
Russian Orthodox 30%

 Death penalty not used

POPULATION

over 500 000
over 100 000
over 50 000
over 10 000
under 10 000

LAND HEIGHT

4000m/13 124ft
3000m/9843ft
2000m/6562ft
1000m/3281ft
500m/1640ft

Like other former Soviet republics, Kyrgyzstan has witnessed the rise of militant nationalism. Relations are most strained with the large Uzbek minority. The preference given to Kyrgyz in the political system has aggravated ethnic tensions. The trend in politics is toward greater Islamization, which is linking religion and race issues more closely.

ECONOMICS

 148th

 $300

 $-371m

35.9%

Agricultural self-sufficiency. Gold and mercury exports. Hydropower potential. Dominant state and collective farming mentality. Sharp decline since breakup of USSR, on which it depended for trade and supplies.

RESOURCES

12.6bn kwh

Comb. 11%
Hydro 89%
Nuclear 0%

 Sheep 4.4m
Goats 234,000
Cattle 955,000

1,704 b/d (reserves of 36.7m bbl)

Kyrgyzstan has small quantities of coal, oil, and gas, and hydroelectric power potential. Energy policy is primarily aimed at developing these further and eventually to achieve self-sufficiency.

DEFENSE

 $51m

 Compulsory

None

9,000

In 1992, a national army was set up and a defense treaty was signed with five other CIS states. The army is weak and not influential in politics.

MEDIA

 Little censorship

Low

4 daily
15 per 1,000 people

TV: 1/0
Radio: 1/3

Television programming relies mainly on Russian transmissions. The Kyrgyz press has the most liberal rules in central Asia.

EDUCATION

 97%

 49,744 students

16 years

Primary 95%
Secondary 79%
Tertiary 12%

Replacing Russian as the main teaching language is proving an enormous task. Russian is likely to survive at tertiary level, as the Kyrgyz language lacks key technical and scientific terms.

HEALTH

 1 per 323 people

67 years

21 per 1,000 people

26 per 1,000 live births

Kyrgyzstan has one of the least developed public health systems in central Asia, and the country's infant mortality rate is high.

SPENDING

 39 per 1,000 population

4.5%

 5.3%

2.9%

In 2000, almost 90% of the population were estimated as living in poverty. The old Communist Party *nomenklatura* are the main beneficiaries of privatization.

TAJIKISTAN

OFFICIAL NAME **Republic of Tajikistan**   CAPITAL **Dushanbe**
POPULATION **6.2m**   CURRENCY **Somoni**   OFF. LANG. **Tajik**

TAJIKISTAN LIES ON the western slopes of the Pamirs in central Asia. Language and traditions are similar to those of Iran rather than those of Turkic Uzbekistan. Tajikistan decided on independence only when neighboring Soviet republics declared theirs in late 1991. Fighting between Communist government forces and Islamist rebels, which erupted shortly afterwards, has been contained since 1997 by a tenuous peace agreement.

POLITICS

	L. House 2000/2005 U. House 2000/2005		President Imomali Rakhmanov		Presidential regime

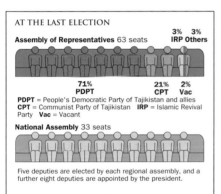

AT THE LAST ELECTION

Assembly of Representatives 63 seats   3% IRP   3% Others

71% **PDPT**   21% **CPT**   2% **Vac**

PDPT = People's Democratic Party of Tajikistan and allies
CPT = Communist Party of Tajikistan   **IRP** = Islamic Revival Party   **Vac** = Vacant

National Assembly 33 seats

Five deputies are elected by each regional assembly, and a further eight deputies are appointed by the president.

The lull in fighting between government forces and Islamist rebels, aided by a 1997 peace accord, has consolidated the regime of former Communists led by President Rakhmanov. In 1998, the Islamist United Tajik Opposition (UTO) joined the government in accordance with the accord, which provided for a National Reconciliation Commission along with parliamentary elections. In the 2000 elections the pro-Rakhmanov PDPT, which headed the poll, claimed some support from former UTO members.

WORLD AFFAIRS

	CIS, OSCE, OIC, EAPC, SCO		1992

Tajikistan remains heavily dependent on Russia for economic and military assistance. A joint operation with Uzbekistan and Kyrgyzstan began in 2000 to combat the Islamic Movement of Uzbekistan, based in northern Tajikistan.

Total Land Area : 143 100 sq. km (55 251 sq. miles)

PEOPLE & SOCIETY

	112 people per sq mile		28% urban 72% rural
	Sunni Muslim 80% Shi'a Muslim 5% Other 15%		Death penalty used

POPULATION
over 500 000 ⊙
over 100 000 ◎
over 50 000 ○
over 10 000 •
under 10 000 ·

LAND HEIGHT
4000m/13 124ft
3000m/9843ft
2000m/6562ft
1000m/3281ft
500m/1640ft
200m/656ft

The main ethnic conflict in Tajikistan is between the Tajiks and Uzbeks, of Persian and Turkic origin respectively. As in neighboring Uzbekistan, however, Russians are discriminated against, and their population has thinned from 400,000 in 1989 to fewer than 200,000. It is estimated that about 20,000 refugees remain in Afghanistan.

ECONOMICS

 143rd $67m
 $280   49.9%

Tajikistan has 14% of known world uranium reserves. Hydroelectric power has considerable potential. Little diversification in agriculture; only 6% of land is arable. Exodus of skilled Russians.

RESOURCES

 14bn kwh   Comb. 2% Hydro 98% Nuclear 0%
 Sheep 1.6m Goats 590,000 Cattle 1m   501 b/d (reserves of 14,640,000 bbl)

Tajikistan has one key resource – uranium – which accounted for 30% of the USSR's total production before 1990. The end of the nuclear arms race has reduced its value, however.

DEFENSE

 $92m   Compulsory
 None   6,000

The Tajik armed forces depend on CIS peacekeeping forces to contain Tajik rebels active in the Gorno Badakhshan region. They are kept at bay by government forces assisted by Russian border guards.

MEDIA

  Censorship   High
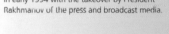 3 daily 21 per 1,000 people   TV: 3/O Radio: 1/0

Communist control over the media was tightened in early 1994 with the takeover by President Rakhmanov of the press and broadcast media.

EDUCATION

 99%   108,200 students
17 years   Primary 95% Secondary 78% Tertiary 20%

School attendance figures are high in Tajikistan. The university at Dushanbe has been weakened by the departure of its Russian academics.

HEALTH

 1 per 476 people   67 years
22 per 1,000 people   20 per 1,000 live births

Tajikistan's health service has always been poor. The infant mortality rate before 1990 was one of the highest in the USSR.

SPENDING

 1 per 1,000 population   7.6%
2.2%   5.2%

More than 80% of Tajik people live below the UN-defined poverty line; the war against the Islamist rebels worsened conditions. The former Communist bureaucrats continue to be the wealthiest group.

AFGHANISTAN

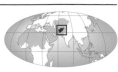

 1919   1919   Aug 19   AFG   +4.5   +93   .af

OFFICIAL NAME Islamic State of Afghanistan   **CAPITAL** Kābul
POPULATION 22.7m   **CURRENCY** Afghani   **OFF. LANG.** Persian & Pashtu

L ANDLOCKED IN CENTRAL ASIA, Afghanistan has borders with Iran, Pakistan, China, Tajikistan, Turkmenistan, and Uzbekistan. Three-quarters of its territory is inaccessible terrain. Agriculture is the main activity, but the country has been torn by armed conflict for decades. In the 1980s Islamic mujahideen factions defeated the communist regime, but rivalries undermined their fragile power-sharing agreement and the hard-line taliban militia swept to power. Islamic dress codes and behavior were vigorously enforced; women had few rights or opportunities. Notorious for harboring extremists, the taliban regime crumbled in the face of the US-led 'war on terrorism' launched in late 2001.

ECONOMICS

 106th $-143m

 $270   56.7%

Continued warfare since 1979 destroyed the economy, which was largely agricultural. Under the taliban production of opium poppies was the most lucrative cash crop.

RESOURCES

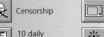 513m kwh   Comb 37% Hydro 63% Nuclear 0%

 Sheep 14.3m Goats 2.2m Cattle 1.5m   No oil No refineries

Natural gas and coal are Afghanistan's most important strategic resources. Restoring the power generation system, which has suffered widespread deterioration and destruction, is a priority.

DEFENSE

$265m   Compulsory

None   No data

There are no formal defense arrangements, although there is a covert arms trade which has expanded with the activity of Islamic militants from abroad. The bulk of these arms originate in eastern Europe.

MEDIA

Censorship   Low

10 daily 6 per 1,000 people   TV: 1/several Radio: several

Most of the mujahideen factions run newspapers and radio stations, which follow the party line and denigrate rivals. Television and the internet are banned, as are VCRs and satellite dishes.

EDUCATION

37.3%   12,800 students

13 years   Primary 49% Secondary 22% Tertiary 2%

The education system is effectively male-only and based on rigid Islamic precepts. Education for girls up to 12 in a few schools in and around Kabul has been officially sanctioned since 1999.

HEALTH

 1 per 7,000 people   46 years

 53 per 1,000 people   147 per 1,000 live births

The health service has collapsed completely and almost all medical professionals have left the country. Infant and maternal mortality rates are among the highest in the world, and life expectancy is very low.

SPENDING

 1 per 1,000 people   14.9%

 2%   1.6%

The vast majority of Afghans live in conditions of extreme poverty. The country does not have the resources to feed its people at present – a situation exacerbated by the severe drought of 2000.

POLITICS

 1988/Uncertain   Uncertain   Uncertain

The political system had virtually collapsed in Afghanistan prior to the taliban takeover. Rival mujahideen factions had been in control since April 1992, when the communist President Najibullah was forced to step down. According to the March 7, 1993 Islamabad peace accord, elections were to be held by the end of the year. They never happened.

Factional fighting escalated with the emergence in early 1995 of a potent new force, the extremist Islamic taliban. Initially the product of Islamic schools in the refugee camps on the Pakistan border, the taliban were mostly ethnic Pashtuns, and their support strongest around Kandahar in the south. Kabul fell to them in 1996, and an opposition alliance headed by the former president, Burhanuddin Rabbani of the Jamiat-i-Islami, failed to reverse the position.

AT THE LAST ELECTION

House of Representatives

Following the downfall of Najibullah's regime in April 1992, both houses were dissolved and an interim mujahideen legislature formed.

Senate

Although a so-called Northern Alliance maintained its resistance, by mid-1998 the taliban had extended their control over most northern regions. A UN-sponsored power-sharing arrangement in 1999 collapsed within months. In September 2001 the prospect of US-led intervention revived the hopes of anti-taliban groups. By November 2001, the taliban were in full retreat. The Northern Alliance, rearmed and reinvigorated, took a series of cities including Kabul. UN-sponsored talks in Germany produced an agreement in early December on a broad-based post-taliban interim government.

WORLD AFFAIRS

ECO, NAM, OIC, IBRD, CP   UN 1946

Afghanistan was a pariah state under the taliban government. The regime defied international opinion, and UN sanctions, by harboring Saudi extremist Osama bin Laden, the head of anti-US terrorist network al-Qaeda. It was also condemned over human rights, particularly the treatment of women, and the destruction of ancient Buddhist statues in Bamian. When a worldwide 'war on terrorism' became the top US priority after the New York and Washington attacks of September 2001, Afghanistan rejected demands that it hand bin Laden over for trial.

It was external material support, including arms from Russia, and intensive bombing by US-led coalition forces, which enabled the Northern Alliance to achieve its dramatic advances in November 2001. The subsequent agreement in Germany on an interim government reflected international concern that it should be broadly based, including supporters of the long-exiled former king and other Pashtun groups.

PEOPLE & SOCIETY

90 people per sq mile	20% urban 80% rural	Sunni Muslim 84% Shi'a Muslim 15% Others 1%	Death penalty used

Ethnic Pashtuns form the largest group in Afghanistan and have been its traditional rulers; the main minorities are Tajiks, Hazaras, Uzbeks, and Turkmen. These ethnic divisions largely determined intra-mujahideen feuding after 1992. The predominantly Pashtun taliban, who took power in 1996, wrested control from a Tajik– Uzbek alliance. Differences between Sunnis and Shi'as became acute under the taliban regime, which was accused of encouraging discrimination against Shi'as.

Some two million of the country's population were killed in the 10-year conflict which followed the invasion by Soviet Union forces in 1979 and in the post-1992 civil war. As many people again were maimed. A further six million people were forced to flee to neighboring Pakistan and Iran; many returned, but the fighting in 2001 created a fresh wave of refugees and left hundreds of thousands more people internally displaced.

Women enjoyed few rights under the rigid Islamic regime of the taliban. They had no access to health care and very little education. They were strictly banned from seeking public employment.

Total Land Area : 652 090 sq. km (251 770 sq. miles)

LAND HEIGHT

3000m/9843ft
2000m/6562ft
1000m/3281ft
500m/1640ft
200m/656ft

POPULATION

over 1 000 000
over 100 000
over 50 000
over 10 000
under 10 000

ECONOMIC FOCUS

EXPORTS

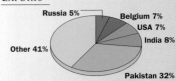

Russia 5%
Belgium 7%
USA 7%
India 8%
Pakistan 32%
Other 41%

IMPORTS

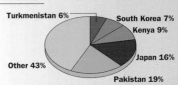

Turkmenistan 6%
South Korea 7%
Kenya 9%
Japan 16%
Pakistan 19%
Other 43%

STRENGTHS

Afghanistan has very few strengths, apart from illicit opium trade. Agriculture is still the largest sector.

WEAKNESSES

Decades of fighting have destroyed the economy; Afghanistan's agriculture and industry are in ruins. Communication links were damaged by the 1998 earthquakes and devastated by bombing in 2001.

PROFILE

The protracted fighting has left Afghanistan one of the poorest and least developed countries in the world. Estimates suggest that $4 billion is needed to rebuild the country and that 80% of its infrastructure has been destroyed. Agricultural activity has fallen back from pre-1979 levels; the Soviets' "scorched earth" policy laid waste large areas, and much of the rural population fled to the cities. Many farmers turned back to growing poppies for opium production, but see little profit from the trade. The taliban belatedly declared the production of opium to be anti-Islamic, and urged farmers to plant other crops instead, under a program funded by the UN, which considers Afghanistan to be the world's largest opium producer.

Mujahideen guerrillas, *members of just one of the many factions vying for power in Afghanistan, prepare to launch a rocket attack.*

PAKISTAN

 1947 1971 March 23 PK +5 +92 .pk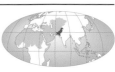

OFFICIAL NAME **Islamic Republic of Pakistan** CAPITAL **Islamabad**
POPULATION **156.5m** CURRENCY **Pakistani rupee** OFF. LANG. **Urdu**

O NCE A PART OF BRITISH INDIA, Pakistan was created in 1947 in response to the demand for an independent and predominantly Muslim Indian state. Initially the new nation included East Pakistan, present-day Bangladesh, which seceded from Pakistan in 1971. In eastern and southern Pakistan, the flood plain of the Indus River is highly fertile and produces cotton, the basis of the large textile industry.

POLITICS

 L. and U. Houses 1997/not known   President Pervez Musharraf   Military-based regime

The military suspended multiparty democracy in 1999. The National Assembly was dissolved in June 2001. The popularity of the October 1999 coup indicated the loss of respect for the country's much-abused democratic institutions. The national security council (NSC) acts as a cabinet under General Pervez Musharraf.

Charges of corruption have entrapped former prime minister Benazir Bhutto and members of the ousted government of Nawaz Sharif, who was himself found guilty of treason in 2000.

Violence in Sindh between Sindhis and Urdu-speaking Mohajirs killed thousands of people in the 1990s. Islamic groups are active, and sectarian violence between Sunnis and minority Shi'as has risen sharply since 1994.

Throughout the 1990s fragile coalitions were forced to rule in cooperation with the president and the army, and are hampered by a large bureaucracy. The military regime which removed Nawaz Sharif in 1999 remains committed to restoring democracy by 2002, but faces growing calls for accelerating the transition from all opposition parties. In June 2001 Musharraf appointed himself president.

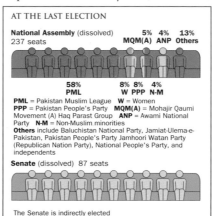

AT THE LAST ELECTION

National Assembly (dissolved) 237 seats

5% MQM(A)   4% ANP   13% Others

58% PML   8% W   8% PPP   4% N-M

PML = Pakistan Muslim League   **W** = Women
PPP = Pakistan People's Party   **MQM(A)** = Mohajir Qaumi Movement (A) Haq Parast Group   **ANP** = Awami National Party   **N-M** = Non-Muslim minorities
Others include Baluchistan National Party, Jamiat-Ulema-e-Pakistan, Pakistan People's Party Jamhoori Watan Party (Republican Nation Party), National People's Party, and independents

Senate (dissolved) 87 seats

The Senate is indirectly elected

WORLD AFFAIRS

 IAEA, SAARC, ECO, NAM, OIC   1947

Although anxious to avoid war with India, Pakistan supports the separatist movement spearheaded by the largely Muslim Kashmiris. Border fighting flared up in mid-1999, briefly threatening full-scale war, and incidents on the border continue. Musharraf traveled to India in July 2001 to meet Indian Prime Minister A. B. Vajpayee, but their talks foundered on the Kashmir issue.

In 1998 Pakistan carried out a series of nuclear tests in response to similar tests by India, provoking international condemnation and the imposition of US sanctions. Pakistan's membership of the Commonwealth was suspended after the 1999 coup.

One of only three countries to recognize the Afghan taliban regime, Pakistan in September 2001 urged the taliban to hand over terrorism suspect Osama bin Laden, and was pressured to back US-led action against the regime despite internal dissent.

ECONOMICS

 45th $-2,187m

 $470   4.1%

One of the world's leading producers of cotton and a major exporter of rice. Corruption at all levels of government undermined economic confidence throughout the 1990s.

RESOURCES

 59.1bn kwh   Comb. 64% Hydro 35% Nuclear 1%

Sheep 24.1m Goats 47.4m Cattle 22m   57,223 b/d (reserves of 209m bbl)

Apart from cotton and rice, Pakistan's major resources are oil, coal, gas, and water. The state hopes that the privatization of the utilities industries will reduce energy imports and shortages.

DEFENSE

 $3,523m   Not compulsory

Undisclosed : Weapons tested in May 1998   612,000

Pakistan has emerged as a significant regional arms trader. It established itself as a nuclear power after conducting a number of successful nuclear tests in May 1998. Defense spending has a high priority.

MEDIA

 Censorship   Medium

264 daily 21 per 1,000 people   TV: 1/1 Radio: 2/1

State-run services dominate the mass media. Journalists who challenge official views are systematically harassed.

EDUCATION

 46.1%   1,053,000 students

Schooling is not compulsory   Primary 65% Secondary 26% Tertiary 3%

Although universal free primary education is a constitutional right, education is not compulsory. Literacy rates in Pakistan are among the lowest in the world. The education system is heavily Islamized.

HEALTH

 1 per 1,667 people   60 years

 34 per 1,000 people   90 per 1,000 live births

Availability of doctors and hospital beds is among the lowest in the world, and there is a shortage of equipment and medicines. Pakistan has a high incidence of heroin addicts.

SPENDING

 5 per 1,000 people   5.7%

 2.7%   0.9%

Members of the bureaucratic and political elite tend to be extremely rich, as are some of the top military. Despite Pakistan's considerable economic potential, much of its population lives below the poverty line.

PEOPLE & SOCIETY

 526 people per sq mile

 36% urban 64% rural

 Sunni Muslim 77% Shi'a Muslim 20% Hindu & Christian 3%

Death penalty used

Punjabis account for 50% of the population, while Sindhis, Pathans, and Baluch are also prominent. Mohajirs – Urdu-speaking immigrants from pre-partition India – predominate in Karachi and Hyderabad. Punjabi political and military dominance of the centralized state has spawned many separatist and autonomy movements. Pathans have frequently threatened to establish a homeland with ethnic kin in Afghanistan. Tensions between the Baluch and Pathan refugees from Afghanistan sporadically erupt into violence, as do those between native Sindhis and immigrant mohajirs.

The gap between rich and poor, as exemplified by the feudal land-owning class, which dominates the ruling elite and their serfs, is considerable. There is an expanding middle class of small-scale merchants and manufacturers.

Recent years have witnessed a marked increase in Islamist militancy, accompanied by growing discrimination against religious minorities. After the 1999 coup, the Musharraf regime trod a fine line in trying to avoid conflict with Islamic militants, both over issues such as the strict application of Islamic *sharia* law and over foreign policy.

The extended family is an enduring institution, and ties between its members are strong, reflected in the dynastic and nepotistic nature of the political system. Although some women hold prominent positions, and Benazir Bhutto has twice been prime minister, relatively few are allowed to work by their religiously conservative menfolk. Pakistan has one of the world's lowest ratios of females to males, implying widespread neglect and some female infanticide. Amnesty International criticized Pakistan in 2000 for its failure to give women's rights sufficient protection.

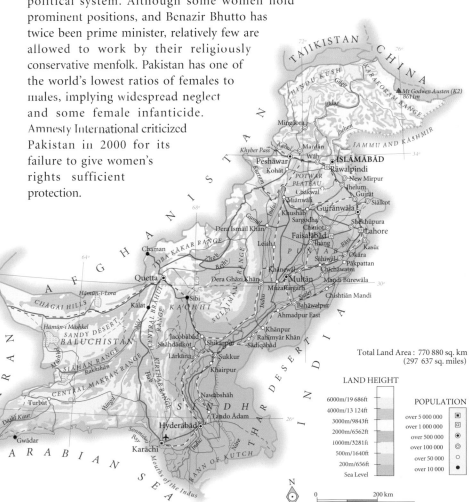

Total Land Area : 770 880 sq. km (297 637 sq. miles)

ECONOMIC FOCUS

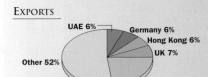

STRENGTHS

Gas, water, coal, oil. Substantial untapped natural resources. Low labor costs. Potentially huge market. One of the world's leading producers of cotton and a major exporter of rice.

WEAKNESSES

Production of cotton and rice vulnerable to weather conditions. History of inefficient and haphazard government economic policies. Weak and overstretched infrastructure.

PROFILE

Pakistan has yet to show progress in tackling its considerable economic problems. Although successive governments have reversed the nationalization policies instituted in the 1970s, private enterprise has been stifled by the rules of a massive bureaucracy. There is some foreign investment in previously state-only sectors such as banking, and water and other utilities. However, corruption at all levels of government undermined economic confidence throughout the 1990s, and it was particularly acute under the administration of Benazir Bhutto. Efforts by the military government to tackle corruption and poverty were praised by the World Bank in 2001. Defense spending remains high.

Paddy fields, with monsoon rains threatening from the Himalayas. Rice is the second most valuable agricultural export after cotton.

COMOROS

| 1975 | 1975 | July 6 | COM | +8 | +269 | .km |

OFFICIAL NAME Federal Islamic Republic of the Comoros **CAPITAL** Moroni
POPULATION 694,000 **CURRENCY** Comoros franc **OFF. LANG.** Arabic & French

THE ARCHIPELAGO REPUBLIC of the Comoros lies off the east African coast, between Mozambique and Madagascar. It consists of three main islands and a number of islets. Most of the population are subsistence farmers. In 1975, the Comoros Islands, except for Mayotte, became independent of France. Since then instability has plagued this poor region, with several coups and counter-coups, and repeated attempts at secession by smaller islands.

POLITICS

 1996/2000 (postponed)   President Assoumani Azzali   Military-based regime

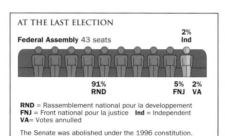

AT THE LAST ELECTION

Federal Assembly 43 seats

2% Ind

91% RND

5% FNJ   2% VA

RND = Rassemblement national pour la developpement
FNJ = Front national pour la justice   **Ind** = Independent
VA = Votes annulled

The Senate was abolished under the 1996 constitution.

The islands' attempts to introduce democracy have been consistently undermined by repeated coups. The island of Anjouan has been at the center of the country's troubles since it unilaterally declared independence in August 1997, with rival militias favoring either cohabitation with Grande Comore or reattachment to France. Renewed violence in April 1999 provided Colonel Assoumani Azzali with the pretext to install himself as president. A "new Comoran entity," with each separate island largely autonomous, was established in late 2000 by the Fomboni declaration. A timetable for a return to democracy was agreed in February 2001.

WORLD AFFAIRS

 OIC, FZ, AL, OAU, COI    1975

France remains the Comoros' main benefactor, although economic ties with South Africa have strengthened in recent years. An OAU assessment team visited strife-torn Anjouan in February 1999, but had to be evacuated after fighting on the island intensified.

Total Land Area : 2230 sq. km (861 sq. miles)

POPULATION
over 10 000
under 10 000

LAND HEIGHT
2000m/6562ft
1000m/3281ft
500m/1640ft
Sea Level

Mitsamiouli
Ntsaouéni   Mbéni
Grande   Koimbani
Comore   Itsandra
(Njazidja)   MORONI
Le Kartala 2361m   Pidjani
Mitsoudjé   Foumbouni
Dembéni

INDIAN OCEAN

MOZAMBIQUE

N

0   20 km
0   20 miles

Mohéli
(Mwali)
Hoani   Fomboni
Ndréméani   Itsamia

Ouani
Moutsamoudou
Sima   Domoni
Anjouan
(Nzwani) Mrémani

CHANNEL

PEOPLE & SOCIETY

 806 people per sq mile   33% urban 67% rural

Sunni Muslim 98% Roman Catholic 1% Other 1%   Death penalty used

The Comoros has absorbed Polynesians, Africans, Indonesians, Persians, and Arabs over time, as well as immigrants from Portugal, Holland, France, and India. Some communities retain their individual character. Ethnic tension is rare, partly owing to the unifying force of Islam, the predominant religion. A more potent divisive factor is regionalism.

ECONOMICS

 183rd $-60m
 $1,200   3%

Vanilla, ylang-ylang, and cloves are the main cash crops. Subsistence level farming. Over 50% of food requirements are imported. Lack of basic infrastructure, especially electricity and transportation.

RESOURCES

 17m kwh   Comb. 88% Hydro 12% Nuclear 0%
 Sheep 20,000 Goats 140,000 Cattle 52,000   Not an oil producer

There are few strategic resources. An HEP plant is under construction on Anjouan, but most fuel for energy is still imported. Fishing remains a neglected source of future growth.

DEFENSE

 $3m (estimate)   Not compulsory
 None   Small number of presidential guard

France and South Africa finance the small presidential guard, the principal security force. Mauritian aid was also sought after clashes on Anjouan.

MEDIA

Censorship   Low
2 weekly No data for circulation   TV: No service Radio: 1/some

France promises to fund the islands' first TV station. Radio is strictly controlled, and there is no single national newspaper.

EDUCATION

 59.6%   348 students
 16 years   Primary 50% Secondary 36% Tertiary 1%

There is a very limited education system beyond secondary level. Schools are equipped to teach only basic literacy, hygiene, and agricultural techniques. Pupil–teacher ratios are high.

HEALTH

 1 per 10,000 people   59 years
 38 per 1,000 people   61 per 1,000 live births

Health care is rudimentary, other than two maternity clinics and 30 recently renovated health centers spread throughout the islands.

SPENDING

 13 per 1,000 people   0%
 3.9%   3.1%

A political and business elite controls most of the wealth. Bridegrooms win social status according to the size of their weddings. Unpaid government workers went on strike in 1998.

MALDIVES

 174th $-60m

 $1,200   3%

OFFICIAL NAME **Republic of Maldives** CAPITAL **Male'**
POPULATION **286,000** CURRENCY **Rufiyaa** OFF. LANG. **Dhivehi**

THE MALDIVES IS an archipelago of 1,190 small coral islands set in the Indian Ocean southwest of India. The islands, none of which rise above 6 feet (1.8 m), are protected by encircling reefs or faros. Only 200 are inhabited. Tourism has grown in recent years, though vacation islands are separate from settled islands. In 1998, President Maumoon Abdul Gayoom, who has survived three coup attempts, was elected for a fifth term in office.

ECONOMICS

Economic reforms since 1989 have eased import restrictions and encouraged foreign investment. Cottage industries employ 25% of workforce; there is little scope for expansion.

POLITICS

  1999/2004   President Maumoon Abdul Gayoom   Non-party democracy

RESOURCES

 66m kwh   Comb. 100% Hydro 0% Nuclear 0%

 Sheep 11,000 Goats 20,000 Cattle 31,000   Not an oil producer

Natural resources include abundant stocks of fish, particularly tuna. Fishing employs over 20% of the working population. Coconut production is important. Oil products and nearly all staple foods are imported.

AT THE LAST ELECTION
Citizens' Assembly 50 seats

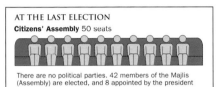

There are no political parties. 42 members of the Majlis (Assembly) are elected, and 8 appointed by the president

Politics in the Maldives is restricted to a small group of influential families. Most were already dominant under the sultanate. Formal parties with ideological objectives are virtually nonexistent, politics being organized around family and clan loyalties.

Former president Ibrahim Nasir abolished the premiership in 1975 and substantially strengthened the presidency. The main figure now is Maumoon Abdul Gayoom, a wealthy businessman who has been president since 1978.

A young Westernized elite has increased the pressure for political reform. Rival candidates may now seek to be parliament's presidential nominee; only one name then goes forward for popular endorsement in a referendum.

DEFENSE

 $41m   Not compulsory

 None   0

The British military presence ended in 1975, when troops were withdrawn from the staging post on Gan, in the Addu atoll. In 1998 the Maldives called on India for military assistance to help suppress a coup attempt.

WORLD AFFAIRS

OIC, SAARC, NAM, WTO, Comm   1965

The Maldives is a long-standing member of the NAM. The government rejects the view that the organization does not have a role to play in the post-Cold War world. The Maldives' international standing was enhanced in 1990, when it hosted the fifth SAARC summit meeting.

MEDIA

 Censorship   Low

 3 daily 19 per 1,000 people   TV: 1/0 Radio: 2/0

There is a marked degree of press censorship. In the past, journalists and satirists have been imprisoned. There are three daily newspapers.

PEOPLE & SOCIETY

  2,466 people per sq mile   26% urban 74% rural

 Sunni Muslim 100%   Death penalty not used

The people live on only 200 of the 1,190 islands. About 25% of the total population live on the island capital of Male'. It is estimated that 12,000 guest workers from Sri Lanka and India work in the Maldives. The country's newfound prosperity has seen the emergence of a commercial elite.

EDUCATION

 96.4%   No data

 Schooling is not compulsory   Primary 100% Secondary 69% Tertiary No data

Primary education has been improved. Secondary education is less developed in the outer islands; the first school outside Male' was opened in 1992.

HEALTH

1 per 1,358 people   66 years

21 per 1,000 people   29 per 1,000 live births

There is a lack of general equipment and facilities throughout the Maldives. Health care is less developed on the outlying islands.

SPENDING

 7 per 1,000 people   9.6%

 6.4%   5.1%

Great disparities of wealth exist between the people who live in the capital, Male', and those who live on the more distant outer islands.

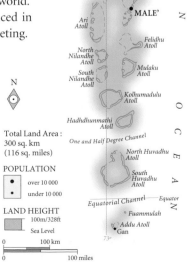

Eight Degree Channel

Ihavandippolhu Atoll
Thiladhunmathi Atoll
Makunudhoo Atoll
North Miladummadulu Atoll
South Miladummadulu Atoll
North Maalhosmadulu Atoll
South Maalhosmadulu Atoll
Faadhippolhu Atoll
Horsburgh Atoll
Rasdu Atoll
Male' Atoll
Ari Atoll
MALE'
Felidhu Atoll
North Nilandhe Atoll
Mulaku Atoll
South Nilandhe Atoll
Kolhumadulu Atoll
Hadhdhunmathi Atoll

INDIAN OCEAN

One and Half Degree Channel

North Huvadhu Atoll
South Huvadhu Atoll

Equatorial Channel — Equator

Fuammulah
Addu Atoll
Gan

Total Land Area : 300 sq. km (116 sq. miles)

POPULATION
• over 10 000
• under 10 000

LAND HEIGHT
100m/328ft
Sea Level
0 — 100 km
0 — 100 miles

BANGLADESH

| 1971 | 1971 | March 26 | BD | +6 | +880 | .bd |

OFFICIAL NAME People's Republic of Bangladesh   **CAPITAL** Dhaka
POPULATION 129m   **CURRENCY** Taka   **OFF. LANG.** Bengali

BANGLADESH LIES AT the north end of the Bay of Bengal and shares borders with India and Burma. Most of the country is composed of fertile alluvial plains; the north and northeast are mountainous, as is the Chittagong region in the southeast. After its secession from Pakistan in 1971, Bangladesh had a troubled history of political instability, with periods of emergency rule. Effective democracy was restored in 1991.

POLITICS

| 1996/2001 | President Shahabuddin Ahmed | Parliamentary democracy |

AT THE LAST ELECTION
Parliament 330 seats

1%
JI

52%
AL

34%
BNP

10%
JD

3%
Others

AL = Awami League   **BNP** = Bangladesh Nationalist Party
JD = Jatiya Dal   **JI** = Jamaat-e-Islami

Elections held in February 1996 were boycotted by opposition parties. 30 seats are reserved for women, of which 27 are held by the Awami League.

Between 1975 and 1990 the military was in power in Bangladesh. The overthrow of President Ershad in 1990 saw a return to multiparty politics; the army remains poised, however, to intervene in the event of a breakdown in law and order. Bangladesh's first woman prime minister, Begum Khaleda Zia, head of the BNP, was elected in 1991. The AL mounted a sustained campaign against her regime, rejecting a February 1996 election as invalid and forcing fresh polls. The AL won the largest number of seats in the rerun election in June 1996. Its leader, Sheikh Hasina Wajed, in 2001 became the first prime minister to complete a full term.

WORLD AFFAIRS

| OIC, SAARC, NAM, WTO, Comm | 1974 |

Good relations with the West, the main source of essential aid, are a priority. Relations with Pakistan have slowly improved since Pakistan's agreement in 1991 to accept the 250,000 pro-Pakistan Bihari Muslims in Bangladeshi refugee camps since 1971. Relations with India are improving.

PEOPLE & SOCIETY

| 565 people per sq mile | 24% urban 76% rural |
| Sunni Muslim 87% Hindu 12% Other 1% | Death penalty used |

Bangladesh is one of the most densely populated countries in the world, despite the fact that three-quarters of the population is rural. As in India, there is considerable Muslim–Hindu tension; in 1992 the destruction of the Ayodhya mosque in northern India triggered violence in Bangladesh.

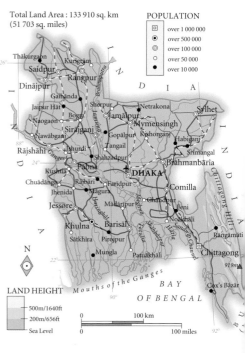

Total Land Area : 133 910 sq. km
(51 703 sq. miles)

POPULATION
over 1 000 000
over 500 000
over 100 000
over 50 000
over 10 000

LAND HEIGHT
500m/1640ft
200m/656ft
Sea Level

0   100 km
0   100 miles

ECONOMICS

| 50th | $-292m |
| $370 | 6.3% |

80% of the world's jute fiber exports come from Bangladesh. Low wages ensure a competitive and expanding textile industry, which provides over three-quarters of manufacturing export earnings.

RESOURCES

| 12.8bn kwh | Comb. 94% Hydro 6% Nuclear 0% |
| Sheep 1.1m Goats 33.5m Cattle 23.4 | No production Reserves of 87,800 bbl |

Bangladesh holds world-class gas reserves, estimated to last as much as 200 years at the present extraction rate. Natural gas from the Bay of Bengal came on stream in 1988.

DEFENSE

| $667m | Not compulsory |
| None | 137,000 |

The military, which dominated politics between 1975 and 1990, still wields considerable influence, despite the restoration of civilian government. Spending on defense is disproportionately high.

MEDIA

| Some censorship | Low |
| 37 daily 9 per 1,000 people | TV: 1/0 Radio: 1/0 |

Press freedom has been gradually eroded under successive civilian governments. The vast majority – over 70% – of TV programs are produced locally by the state-run services.

EDUCATION

| 41.4% | 434,300 students |
| 10 years | Primary 75% Secondary 22% Tertiary 7% |

Education issues in Bangladeshi society have been poorly addressed, although successive governments have promised to improve literacy levels by increasing spending. Exam cheating is a serious problem.

HEALTH

| 1 per 5,000 people | 59 years |
| 28 per 1,000 people | 61 per 1,000 live births |

More resources are needed to boost health care in rural areas. Priority for birth control programs has helped reduce the population growth rate by more than 20% over the last 15 years.

SPENDING

| 1 per 1,000 people | 1.9% |
| 2.2% | 1.7% |

Average incomes in Bangladesh remain very low, but wealth disparities are not quite as marked as in India or Pakistan. State officials tend to be among the better-off sector of society.

1984 | 1984 | Feb 23 | BRU | +8 | +673 | .bn

92nd | $2,085m

$26,286 | 1.0%

Earnings from massive overseas investments, mainly in the US and Europe, now exceed oil and gas revenues. Single-product economy. Failure of diversification programs could lead to problems in the future.

ECONOMICS

OFFICIAL NAME Sultanate of Brunei **CAPITAL** Bandar Seri Begawan
POPULATION 328,000 **CURRENCY** Brunei dollar **OFF. LANG.** Malay

LYING ON THE northwestern coast of the island of Borneo, Brunei is divided in two by a strip of the surrounding Malaysian state of Sarawak. The interior is mostly rain forest. Independent from the UK since 1984, Brunei is ruled by decree of the sultan. It is undergoing increasing Islamicization. Oil and gas reserves have brought one of the world's highest standards of living.

1.7bn kwh | Comb. 100% Hydro 0% Nuclear 0%

Sheep 0 Goats 3,500 Cattle 2,200 | 195,000 b/d (reserves of 1,400m bbl)

Oil and gas are the major resources. Energy policy is now focused on regulating output in order to conserve stocks, since reserves are of limited duration. Almost all food is imported.

RESOURCES

POLITICS

☒ Not applicable | HM Sultan Haji Sir Hassanal Bolkiah Mu'izzaddin Waddaulah | Monarchy

$402m | Not compulsory

None | 5,000

As well as being head of the 5,000-strong armed forces, the sultan has a personal bodyguard of 2,000 UK-trained Gurkhas. The UK and Singapore are close defense allies.

DEFENSE

Since a failed rebellion in 1962, a state of emergency has been in force and the sultan has ruled by decree. Hopes for democracy were dashed when political parties were banned in 1988. In 1990, "Malay Muslim Monarchy" was introduced, promoting Islamic values as the state ideology. This

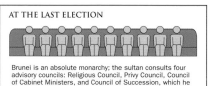

AT THE LAST ELECTION

Brunei is an absolute monarchy; the sultan consults four advisory councils: Religious Council, Privy Council, Council of Cabinet Ministers, and Council of Succession, which he appoints. Political parties have been banned since 1988.

further alienated the large Chinese and expatriate communities. Power is closely tied to the royal family. One of the sultan's brothers holds the foreign affairs portfolio and the sultan himself looks after defense and finance.

Censorship | Medium

3 daily 69 per 1,000 people | TV: 1/0 Radio: 1/0

The state effectively controls all forms of media. Brunei's television service now has a heavy religious content.

MEDIA

WORLD AFFAIRS

OIC, APEC, WTO, ASEAN, Comm | UN 1984

Brunei's claims to part of the Spratly Islands are disputed with China, Taiwan, Vietnam, Malaysia, and the Philippines. Political exiles opposed to the government and based in Malaysia are a main concern. Relations with the UK, the ex-colonial power, are good. Japan is an important economically, taking over 50% of Brunei's total exports.

91.5% | 1,878 students

16 years | Primary 88% Secondary 82% Tertiary 7%

Free schooling is available to the entire population, with the exception of the stateless Chinese, who do not qualify. The University of Brunei Darussalam was opened in 1985.

EDUCATION

PEOPLE & SOCIETY

161 people per sq mile | 72% urban 28% rural

Muslim 66% Buddhist 14% Christian & other 20% | Death penalty not used

1 per 988 people | 76 years

23 per 1,000 people | 9 per 1,000 live births

The national health service is free, although for major surgery many Bruneians tend to travel to Singapore.

HEALTH

Total Land Area : 5270 sq. km (2035 sq. miles)

LAND HEIGHT | POPULATION

- 1500m/4921ft | ○ over 50 000
- 1000m/3281ft | ● over 10 000
- 500m/1640ft | • under 10 000
- 200m/656ft
- Sea Level

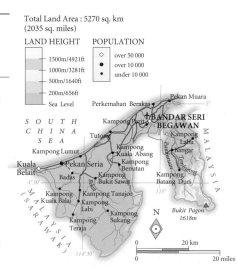

Malays are the beneficiaries of positive discrimination; many in the Chinese community are either stateless or hold British protected person passports. Among indigenous groups, the Murut and Dusuns are favored politically over the Ibans. Women, less restricted than in some Muslim states, are obliged to wear headscarves but not the veil. Many women hold influential posts in the civil service.

497 per 1,000 people | 6.7%

3.1% | 0.8%

The wealthiest people in Brunei are those close to the sultan. A high standard of living keeps discontent to a minimum. Bruneians are major consumers of high-tech equipment and designer labels.

SPENDING

MALAYSIA

ECONOMICS

 42nd

 $12,606m

$3,390

2.7%

Fastest-growing southeast Asian economy until the 1997 financial crisis. Major disk-drive producer. Shortage of skilled labor. Multimedia center is expected to attract major foreign investment.

RESOURCES

57.7bn kwh

Comb. 91%
Hydro 9%
Nuclear 0%

Sheep 162,000
Goats 235,000
Cattle 713,000

805,000 b/d
(reserves of
3,900m bbl)

Thailand has overtaken Malaysia as the world's major rubber producer. Palm oil is now a more important export. Malaysia accounts for nearly half of world timber exports, most of which come from Sarawak.

DEFENSE

$3,158m

Not compulsory

None

96,000

The main defense concerns are Singapore, with its large and highly mechanized army, and, more recently, Indonesia. Also important to Malaysia is the growing Chinese influence in the South China Sea.

MEDIA

 Censorship

 Medium

42 daily
163 per 1,000
people

TV: 3/4
Radio: 3/2

Almost all the newspapers are controlled by UMNO, the dominant political party. Radio and TV are also strictly controlled, and Western commercials are banned. Singaporean TV can be received in the south.

EDUCATION

87.5%

230,000 students

14 years

Primary 100%
Secondary 64%
Tertiary 12%

There is free schooling at government-assisted schools for children between the ages of six and 18. Many students, particularly the Chinese, complete their studies in the UK or the US.

HEALTH

1 per 2,000 people

 72 years

 24 per 1,000 people

 8 per 1,000 live births

There is growing disparity between the modern facilities available in cities and the traditional medicine practiced in rural areas. Acupuncture and herbs continue to be used by the Chinese community.

SPENDING

 170 per 1,000 people

 4%

4.9%

1.4%

The Chinese remain the wealthiest community in Malaysia. However, the UMNO government embarked on a deliberate program of achieving 30% Malay ownership of the corporate sector.

1957	1965	Aug 31	MAL	+8	+60	.my

OFFICIAL NAME **Federation of Malaysia**   CAPITAL **Kuala Lumpur**
POPULATION **22.2m**   CURRENCY **Ringgit**   OFF. LANG. **Bahassa Malaysia**

COMPRISING THE THREE territories of Peninsular Malaysia, Sarawak, and Sabah, Malaysia stretches over 1,240 miles (2,000 km) from the Malay Peninsula to the northeastern end of the island of Borneo. It shares borders with Thailand, Indonesia, and the enclave states of Singapore and Brunei. A central mountain chain divides Peninsular Malaysia, separating fertile western plains from an eastern coastal belt. Sarawak and Sabah have swampy coastal plains rising to mountains on the border with Indonesia. Putrajaya, just south of Kuala Lumpur, is a high-tech new development intended as the future capital.

POLITICS

L. House 1999/2004 U. House varying	Sultan Salehuddin Abdul Aziz	Parliamentary democracy

AT THE LAST ELECTION

House of Representatives 193 seats

5% 2%
DAP PBS

76%
BN

14%
PAS

3%
PKN

BN = National Front (dominated by the United Malays National Organization – **UMNO**)   **PAS** = Pan-Malaysian Islamic Party   **DAP** = Democratic Action Party   **PKN** = National Justice Party (Keadilan)   **PBS** = United Sabah Party

The DAP, the PAS and the PKN form the Alternative Front.

Senate 69 seats

The Senate comprises 26 members indirectly elected by the State Legislative Assemblies, and 43 appointed by the head of state

Supreme power rests in theory with the monarch, who acts on the advice of parliament. Opposition parties, while legal, are under tight control.

The current administration of Mahathir Mohamed has declared that it no longer wishes to discriminate in favor of Malays, but the Chinese community accuses the government of corruption and uncompetitive practices, declaring that Malays are still favored for the placing of government contracts. It is further alienated by the more restrictive Islamic society.

Malaysia has long been dominated by the United Malays National Organization (UMNO), part of the ruling BN coalition, since Malay independence in 1957. It controls a huge network of patronage. However, the economic crisis of 1997–1998 and recent dissent within the ruling coalition have shaken Mahathir's authority. In 1998 Anwar Ibrahim, deputy prime minister and once Mahathir's chosen successor, was dismissed after

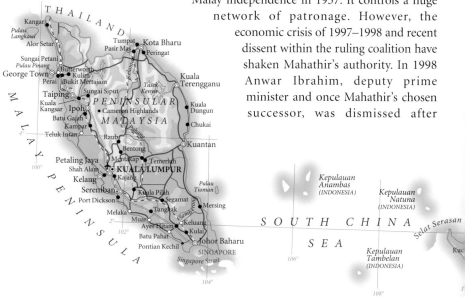

challenging the government's economic policy and calling for political reform. He was found guilty of corruption in April 1999, and sentenced to six years' imprisonment (lengthened to 15 years in 2000 after his conviction for sodomy). The initial verdict sparked riots and gained support for the new opposition PKN headed by Anwar's wife, Wan Azizah. PKN activists have been hounded by the government. In elections in 1999, the BN coalition retained its large majority, but Mahathir's own UMNO lost ground. In an attempt to regain popularity among the Islamic community, the government, although officially secular, appointed officials to oversee the country's 5,000 mosques.

WORLD AFFAIRS

	G15, ASEAN, APEC OIC, Comm		1957

Mahathir sees himself as one of the developing world's leading voices. He maintains a strongly anti-US line in his public speeches and has chastised the West for failing to control currency traders, whom he blames for the Asian economic crisis. Mahathir's pro-Malay policies have caused tensions with Singapore, exacerbated by the latter's dependence on Malaysia for water.

PEOPLE & SOCIETY

175 people per sq mile	57% urban 43% rural	Muslim 53% Buddhist 19% Others 28%	Death penalty used

The key distinction in Malaysian society is between the indigenous Malays, termed the "Bumiputras" (literally, sons of the soil), and the Chinese. The Malays form the largest group, accounting for just under half of the population. However, the Chinese have traditionally controlled most business activity. The New Economic Policy (NEP), introduced in the 1970s, was designed to address this imbalance by offering positive opportunities to the Malays through the education system and by making jobs available to them in both the state and private sectors. There are estimated to be more than one million Indonesian and Filipino immigrants in Malaysia, attracted by its labor shortages and a dearth of employment in their own countries. In addition, nearly 255,000 Vietnamese refugees were offered temporary refuge in Malaysia between 1975 and 1997; most have now been resettled in third countries, but around 6,000 remain. Gender discrimination was only outlawed in 2001. Muslim women are encouraged to take the veil.

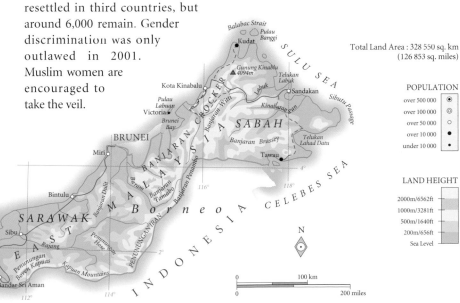

Total Land Area : 328 550 sq. km
(126 853 sq. miles)

POPULATION

over 500 000	◉
over 100 000	◎
over 50 000	○
over 10 000	●
under 10 000	·

LAND HEIGHT

	2000m/6562ft
	1000m/3281ft
	500m/1640ft
	200m/656ft
	Sea Level

ECONOMIC FOCUS

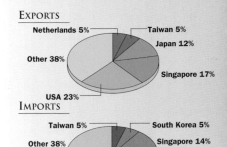

EXPORTS

Netherlands 5% | Taiwan 5%
Japan 12%
Other 38%
Singapore 17%
USA 23%

IMPORTS

Taiwan 5% | South Korea 5%
Other 38% | Singapore 14%
USA 17%
Japan 21%

STRENGTHS

Electronics: major disk-drive producer. Heavy industries such as steel. Palm oil. Latex and rubber; electrical machinery and appliances; chemical products.

WEAKNESSES

High level of debt. Shortage of skilled labor. High interest rates deter private investors. High government budget spending. Competition from NICs.

PROFILE

From 1987, for almost a decade, Malaysia expanded faster than any other southeast Asian nation, at an average yearly rate of 8%, with much of the growth state-directed. However, plans for full industrialization, named "Vision 2020," were revised after the 1997 financial crisis. Nevertheless, growth in the next few years was expected to exceed 7.5%. A project for a Multimedia Super Corridor (MSC), located south of Kuala Lumpur and aimed at attracting world-class companies, is expected to be completed by 2003.

Tea plantations and colonial-style houses and gardens make Cameron Highlands, in Peninsular Malaysia, one of Asia's most popular mountain resorts.

INDONESIA

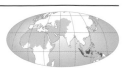

 1949   1976   Aug 17   RI   +7 to +9   +62   .id

OFFICIAL NAME Republic of Indonesia   **CAPITAL** Jakarta
POPULATION 212m   **CURRENCY** Rupiah   **OFF. LANG.** Bahasa Indonesia

THE WORLD'S LARGEST archipelago, Indonesia's islands stretch 3,100 miles (5,000 km) eastward across the Pacific, from the Malay Peninsula to New Guinea. Sumatra, Java, Kalimantan, Irian Jaya, and Sulawesi are mountainous, volcanic, and densely forested. Indonesia, formerly the Dutch East Indies, achieved independence in 1949. Politics was dominated by the military for over three decades, until the fall of the Suharto regime in 1998, when a partial "civilianization" began. In outlying regions, the forcibly suppressed demands for greater autonomy have flared up, bringing renewed violence.

POLITICS

 1999/2004   President Megawati Sukarnoputri   Multiparty republic

AT THE LAST ELECTION
House of Representatives 500 seats

31% PDI–P	24% Gol	12% PPP	10% PKB	7% PAN	7% U	9% Others

PDI–P = Indonesian Democratic Party of Struggle
Gol = Golkar   **PPP** = United Development Party
PKB = National Awaking Party   **U** = Unelected (army) seats
PAN = National Mandate Party

Others include the Crescent Star Party (PBB), the Justice Party (PK), and the Justice and Unity Party (PKP)

General Suharto, autocratic ruler since 1968, was forced to resign in 1998 amid widespread protest over corruption, economic mismanagement, and denial of democratic rights. Abdurrahman Wahid, elected president in 1999, also became embroiled in corruption scandals, and was in turn ousted in 2001.

Under Suharto, the army was dominant. The main political organization was Golkar, an amalgam of various interest groups. After his fall, the mainly Muslim PDI–P, led by

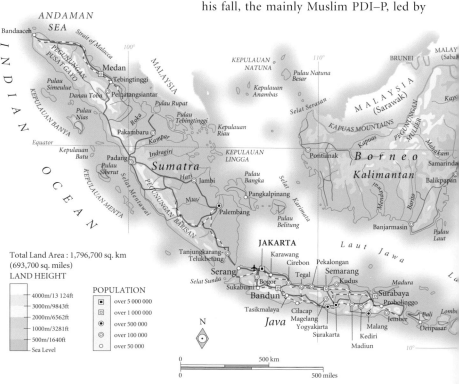

ANDAMAN SEA
Bandaaceh
Strait of Malacca
MALAYSIA
KEPULAUAN NATUNA
Pulau Natuna Besar
BRUNEI
MALAYSIA (Sabah)
MALAY (Saba
PEGUNUNGAN PUSAT GATO
Medan
Tebingtinggi
INDIAN
Pulau Simeulue
Danau Toba
Pematangsiantar
Pulau Rupat
Kepulauan Anambas
MALAYSIA (Sarawak)
KAPUAS MOUNTAINS
PEGUNUNGAN MULLER
KEPULAUAN BANYA
Pulau Nias
Roka
Pulau Tebingtinggi
Kepulauan Riau
Pontianak
Kapuas
Borneo
Kaye
Pakambaru
Kampar
Samarinda
Equator
Kepulauan Batu
Indragiri
KEPULAUAN LINGGA
Kalimantan
Mahakam
Pulau Siberut
Padang
Sumatra
Hari
Jambi
Pulau Bangka
Selat Karimata
Barito
Pulau Laut
KEPULAUAN MENTA
Musi
Pangkalpinang
Balikpapan
OCEAN
PEGUNUNGAN BARISAN
Palembang
Pulau Belitung
Banjarmasin
Tanjungkarang-Telukbetung
JAKARTA
Laut Jawa
Karawang Cirebon Pekalongan
Serang
Selat Sunda
Sukabumi Bogor Tegal
Semarang
Kudus
Madura
Surabaya
Bandun
Tasikmalaya Cilacap Magelang
Java
Yogyakarta
Surakarta
Kediri
Malang
Probolinggo
Jember
Bali
Lombo
Madiun
Denpasar

Total Land Area : 1,796,700 sq. km (693,700 sq. miles)
LAND HEIGHT

4000m/13 124ft
3000m/9843ft
2000m/6562ft
1000m/3281ft
500m/1640ft
Sea Level

POPULATION
over 5 000 000
over 1 000 000
over 500 000
over 100 000
over 50 000

N

0   500 km
0   500 miles

Megawati Sukarnoputri, daughter of the first president, won a majority in elections, but Wahid of the PKB was elected president, and Megawati became vice president. Disenchantment with Wahid pressured him into devolving many of his duties to her in 2000, and increasingly vehement opposition in parliament culminated in his removal in July 2001 and his replacement by Megawati.

WORLD AFFAIRS

 APEC, ASEAN, G15, OPEC, OIC   1950

Indonesia under General Suharto was nonaligned, but its foreign affairs had a pro-Western bias. China remains a major foreign policy concern, despite the restoration of diplomatic ties in 1990. Indonesia and Australia signed a groundbreaking security cooperation agreement in late 1995, and in 1999 Australia led the intervention in East Timor. The post-Suharto government is under pressure from Western governments to improve its human rights record. The scale and nature of the East Timor massacres in 1999 severely damaged its standing.

PEOPLE & SOCIETY

 303 people per sq mile   40% urban 60% rural   Sunni Muslim 87% Christian 9% Others 4%   Death penalty used

The basic Melanesian–Malay ethnic division disguises a diverse society. The national language, Bahasa Indonesia, coexists with at least 250 other languages or dialects. Attempts by the Javanese political elite to suppress local cultures have been vigorously opposed, especially by the East Timorese, the Aceh of northern Sumatra, and the Papuans of Irian Jaya.

Religious and interethnic hostility is increasing. In 1998 there were violent clashes between Muslims and Christians on Ambon island. Similar clashes occurred in Kalimantan in 1999 and 2001 between indigenous Dayaks and ethnic Madurese immigrants, and in the Molucca islands in 2000 between Christians and Muslims.

Discrimination against ethnic Chinese has encouraged vicious attacks on their businesses, as in Jakarta in 1998. Gender equality is enshrined in law, and women are active in public life.

ECONOMIC FOCUS

EXPORTS

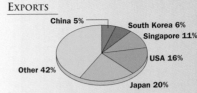

China 5%
South Korea 6%
Singapore 11%
USA 16%
Japan 20%
Other 42%

IMPORTS

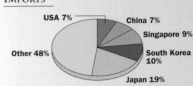

USA 7%
China 7%
Singapore 9%
South Korea 10%
Japan 19%
Other 48%

STRENGTHS

Indonesia has varied resources, especially oil and natural gas. There have been recent signs of a return to high growth.

WEAKNESSES

Oil output is falling, and the country could become a net importer within the next decade. Red tape and bureaucracy hinder growth, as does government corruption. Major debt burden. Collapse of investor confidence.

PROFILE

Under Suharto the economy grew rapidly, fueled largely by oil, until its collapse in 1997–1998. State-owned corporations played a significant role, protected from foreign competition. Non-oil exports, especially manufactures, were diversified, but the debt burden used up a third of export earnings. Promised reform was delayed by conflict between advocates of deregulation and "technologists" who favored industrialization over profit for state concerns. Further reforms have been stymied by the PKB's poor representation in the parliament. Corruption remains rife, embroiling President Wahid himself in 2001.

Rice terraces on Bali, *one of Indonesia's 13,677 islands and its most popular tourist destination. Rice is the staple food crop.*

600–800 CE

EUROPE AND AFRICA

624 Visigoths expel last Byzantine garrisons from southern Iberia
626 Constantinople besieged by Sasanids, Avars, and Slavs

635–42 Conquest of Egypt by Arabs

642 Foundation of Fustat (Egypt) and Great Mosque by Amr ibn al-'As
647 Arab invasion of Tripolitania

663 Byzantine Emperor Constans II invades Italy and sacks Rome
669 Arab conquest of North Africa extended beyond Tripoli to the west
670 Annexation of Tunisia; foundation of Kairouan
680 Arab armies reach Atlantic at Morocco

711 Invasion of Iberian Peninsula by Tariq; conquest of Visigothic kingdom (by 714)
712 Muslim capture of Toledo
714 S and C Spain effectively under Muslim control
718 Christian victory at battle of Covadonga temporarily halts Muslim advance in Iberian Peninsula
732 Arab armies halted at Poitiers, France

755 Revived Umayyad dynasty established at Córdoba by Abd al-Rahman (to 1031)

785 Foundation of Great Mosque at Córdoba; extended in four phases (832-848; 929-961; 961-976; 987)
789 Idrisids establish power in NW Africa (Morocco, to 926)
790 Beginnings of Viking raids on western Europe

SOUTHWEST ASIA

570 Birth of Muhammad in Mecca
595 First marriage of Muhammad
610 Muhammad receives first revelation
611 Arabs invade Mesopotamia
611–626 Sasanid armies capture Jerusalem and overrun Asia Minor
622 Muhammad's emigration with followers to Yathrib (Medina), the Hegira: start of the Islamic era
622 *Qibla* oriented toward Jerusalem
624 Muhammad's rejection of links with Judaism
629 Muhammad's pilgrimage to Mecca
630 Orientation of *qibla* is altered toward Ka'ba in Mecca
632 Death of Muhammad in Medina; succession of Abu Bakr (to 634), beginning of Arab expansion in Arabian peninsula
633–37 Muslims conquer Syria
634 Caliphate of 'Umar (to 644); conquest of Palestine and Syria
635 Arab armies cross Euphrates
636 Byzantine army routed by Muslims on Yarmuk River
637 Arab conquest of Mesopotamia
637 Arabs capture Ctesiphon
637 Arabs defeat Persians at al-Qadisiya; Jerusalem seized
638 Foundation of first mosque in Kufa
641 Arabs capture Nineveh and invade Armenia
642 Muslims invade Persia; Sasanid empire falls
644 Death of 'Umar; 'Uthman appointed caliph
656 Assassination of 'Uthman; 'Ali, son-in-law of Muhammad, attempts to gain control of caliphate (to 661)
660 Mu'awiya proclaimed caliph in Damascus
661 'Ali assassinated; beginning of Umayyad Caliphate (to 750)
670 Reconstruction of mosque in Kufa
683 Anti-caliphate based in Mecca (to 693)
687 Foundation of Dome of the Rock in Jerusalem; completed 692
693 Burning of the Ka'ba; anti-caliph executed
707 Great Mosques of Damascus and Medina built; al-Aqsa Mosque in Jerusalem

744 'Abbasid Caliphate established
750 Umayyad Caliphate is overthrown in Damascus; succeeded by the 'Abbasid dynasty (to 1258)
754 al-Mansur becomes caliph in Baghdad (to 775)
756 Under 'Abbasid Caliphate, new interest in seafaring, focused on Persian Gulf routes
762 'Abbasid capital moved to Mesopotamia; founding of Baghdad
786 Harun al-Rashid becomes caliph; Baghdad becomes center of arts and learning

707 The Great Mosque in Damascus *was built. It is decorated with sumptuous mosaics in the Byzantine style.*

CENTRAL AND EAST ASIA

618 Tang begin to unite China

664 Arab conquest of Kabul
671 Arab armies cross Oxus (Amu Darya)
681 Arabs cross into Transoxania and spend winter
683 Civil war in Khurasan
689 Eastern Turks invade Transoxania
691 Umayyad rule restored in Khurasan

705 Qutayba ibn Muslim marches into Khurasan
711 Eastern Turks conquer western Central Asia
712 Arabs conquer Khwarizm. Eastern Turks take Samarkand
713 Qutayba ibn Muslim reaches Ferghana. First mosque built in Bukhara

725 Restoration of Balkh
729 Muslim rule restored in Bukhara
733 Famine in Khurasan
737 Death of the Khan in Tukharistan
739 Fall of the Western Turkish empire
741 Sogdians restored to their native land
742 Congregational mosque built in Balkh
743 Partisans of 'Ali revolt in Khurasan
745 Foundation of Uighur Empire in C Asia (Chinese Turkestan, to 840)
747 Abu Muslim arrives in Khurasan
748 Chinese destroy Suyab
751 Defeat of Tang Chinese by Arab forces at battle of Talas River; end of Arab advances in C Asia
752 Prince of Ushrusana sends embassy to China
753 Walls and defensive towers constructed at Samarkand

763 Tang China is invaded by Tibetans
766 Qarluqs occupy Suyab

783 Defensive walls constructed near Bukhara
792 Qarluqs expelled from Ferghana
794 Subjugation of Ushrusana. New congregational mosque built in Bukhara

SOUTH AND SOUTHEAST ASIA

687-692 The Dome of the Rock *was built in Jerusalem on orders of Umayyad caliph 'Abd al-Malik.*

711–12 Arab conquest of Sind introduces Islam to South Asia

c.750 Muslim merchants establish Islam in Kerala, SW India

785 The Great Mosque at Córdoba *in southern Spain was founded by Abd al-Rahman.*

800–1000 CE

EUROPE AND AFRICA

800 Start of Aghlabid dynasty in Tunis
c.800 Emergence of trading towns such as Manda and Kilwa on E African coast.
800 Charlemagne crowned Holy Roman Emperor by Pope Leo III in Rome
827 Crete and Sicily attacked by Aghlabids
830 Foundation of Great Mosque at Kairouan
839 Swedes travel through Russia to Constantinople; opening of river trade from Baltic to Black Sea
844 Vikings attack Seville
847 Muslim raiders burn outskirts of Rome
862 Novgorod founded by Rurik the Viking
863 Saints Cyril and Methodius sent as Orthodox Christian missionaries to Moravia
868 Ahmad Ibn Tulun founds the Tulunid dynasty in Egypt (to 905); control spreads to Syria
876 Mosque of Ibn Tulun, Cairo, based on Great Mosque at Samarra
884 Kiev becomes capital of new Russian state
896 Magyars start to settle in Danube basin
899–905 'Abbasid campaign against Egypt
c.900 Arab dhows (sailing ships) begin to ply the coastal routes of East Africa, as far south as Sofala
c.900 First sighting of Greenland by Viking seamen
905 'Abbasids take over Egypt
910 Shi'ite Fatimids expel Aghlabids from Tunis; extend power to Egypt and Syria and claim caliphate (to 1171)
928 Ruler of Córdoba, Abd al-Rahman III, takes title of caliph
936 Córdoba palace complex of Madinat al-Zahra begun

969 Fatimids conquer Egypt, found Cairo
970 Al-Azhar University established in Cairo
972 Zirid dynasty, of Berber origin, rule Tunisia and E Algeria, based at Kairouan (to 1148)
976–1009 Decline of Arab power in Iberia

c.950 Manuscripts of the Qur'an *of this period were all written in the heavy Kufic script.*

992 Ghana captures Berber town of Awdaghost, gaining control of southern portion of trans-Saharan trade route

SOUTHWEST ASIA

809 Death of Harun al-Rashid; start of civil war between al-Amin and al-Ma'mun (ends 813).
813 Reign of al-Ma'mun, development of Arab science
820 Death of al-Shafi

836 Baghdad terrorized by Turkish slave troops; 'Abbasid Caliph al-Mu'tasim builds new capital at Samarra

848 Foundation of Great Mosque at Samarra, with monumental spiral minaret
860 Zaidi Imams rise to power in Yemen; rule intermittently to 1281
862 Qubba al-Sulaybiya mausoleum, Samarra; first monumental Islamic tomb
863 Byzantines annihilate Arab forces to stem Muslim advance in Anatolia
869 Revolt of black slaves in southern Iraq
892 Capital of 'Abbasid Caliphate shifts back from Samarra to Baghdad
894 Shi'ite Qarmatians establish power base in C Arabia

932 Shi'ite Buwayhids (Buyids) establish power base in Persia, Iraq; rule in name of 'Abbasid Caliphate (to 1082)
935 Final text of Qur'an codified
936 Turkic troops in pay of Buwayhids take effective control of 'Abbasid Caliphate
945 Persian Buwayhids conquer Baghdad but allow caliph to reign as figurehead
945 Hamdanids establish power base in Syria and Lebanon (to 1004)
950 Death of philosopher al-Farabi
956 al-Mas'udi's major historical/geographical work *The Meadows of Gold*
970 Fatimids establish control of Damascus
970 Seljuk Turks enter lands of caliphate
976 Byzantine forces threaten to take Jerusalem

CENTRAL AND EAST ASIA

806 Rafi bin Layth revolts in Samarkand

816 Famine in Khurasan
819 Founding of Samanid dynasty in Khurasan and Transoxania (to 1005)
820 The Tughuzghuz take Ushrusana
830 Tahirids proclaim independence at Khurasan

867 Founding of Saffarid dynasty in E Persia (to 1495)
868 *The Diamond Sutra*, world's oldest surviving printed work

907 End of the Tang dynasty in China; Arab disruption of trans-Asian trade
916 Foundation of Khitan Empire

947 Khitans invade northern China, establishing Liao dynasty at Beijing

962 Foundation of Afghan Ghaznavid dynasty
970 Paper money introduced in China

979 Song dynasty unites China

992 Establishment of Qarakhanid dynasty in Transoxania (to 1211)

SOUTH AND SOUTHEAST ASIA

c.800 Arab ships sailing as far as China

830 The Great Mosque at Kairouan *was begun.*
The Tunisian city, founded in 670, was a major Islamic center in N Africa.

977 Founding of Ghaznavid dynasty in India (to 1186)

997 Mahmud of Ghazni extends rule into northwest India

876 The Mosque of Ibn Tulun
in Cairo set the style of north African Islamic architecture.

1000–1200 CE

c.1199 The spectacular Qutb Minar *minaret in Delhi was built by the Ghurid conquerors of northern India.*

EUROPE AND AFRICA

c.1000 Arab merchants begin to set up trading states in Ethiopian Highlands
1015 Hammadids, offshoot of Zirids, rule E Algeria (to 1152)
1025 Death of great Byzantine emperor, Basil II (the Bulgar Slayer)
1031 Beginning of Christian reconquest (*Reconquista*) of Spain
1041 Zirids of Ifriqiyah gain independence
1048 Fatimids lose control of Ifriqiya (Tunisia)
1050 King of Takrur converts to Islam
1054 Final schism between Roman and Orthodox churches
1066 Battle of Hastings; Norman conquest of England
1071 Completion of St. Mark's basilica, focus of public religious life in Venice
1076 Ghana falls to Almoravids
1076 King of Ghana converts to Islam
1085 Christian forces under Alfonso VI of León take Toledo
1086 Almoravids enter Spain
1091 Completion of Norman conquest of Sicily
1094 Christian warlord El Cid takes Valencia
1095 Byzantine empire appeals for aid to pope, who preaches in France to raise support
c.1110 Onset of serious desiccation of Sahel region
1126 Birth of Muslim philosopher Averröes (Ibn Rushd) in Córdoba
1128 Almohad religious revival order starts takeover of Almoravid dominions in N Africa and Iberia (1130–1269)
1132 Palatine Chapel at Palermo; unique blend of Romanesque, Byzantine, and Islamic architectural elements
1136 Independence of Russian state of Novgorod
1137 Union of Aragon and Catalonia
1147 Almohads established in Morocco and southern Spain
1147 Second Crusade; Lisbon taken from Moors, Holy Roman Emperor Conrad defeated by Turks at Dorylaeum
1154 Building of Chartres Cathedral
1169 Shi'ite Fatimid dynasty in Egypt suppressed by Saladin
1171 Founding of Ayyubid sultanate in Egypt (to 1260)
1172 Great Mosque at Seville, intended to be the largest in the world, and the Giralda, a great square minaret
1174 Saladin becomes Ayyubid sultan of Egypt and Syria (to 1193)
1184 Completion of citadel at Cairo
1189 Start of Third Crusade
1189 Succession of Richard I the Lionheart

1194 Emperor Henry VI crowned King of Sicily
1196 Marinids take control of Morocco (to 1485)

SOUTHWEST ASIA

1005 al-Sufi's *Geography*; (now in St. Petersburg) probably oldest extant illustrated Arabic manuscript
1009 Destruction of the Church of the Holy Sepulchre in Jerusalem
1055 Seljuks capture Baghdad, ruling in the name of the 'Abbasid caliph
1069 Seljuks take Konya (Iconium)
1071 Seljuks under Alp Arslan defeat Byzantines at Manzikert
1077 Seljuk province established in Anatolia with capital first at Nicaea and then Konya; dynasty comes to be known as the Seljuks of Rum (to 1307)
1078 Seljuks take Damascus
1079 Seljuks take Jerusalem
1084 Fall of Antioch to Seljuks

1092 'Abbasid vizier Nizam al-Mulk murdered by Ismaili Assassin
1094 Seljuk dynasty of Syria founded with capital at Aleppo
1096 First Crusade
1098 Crusaders take Antioch
1099 Jerusalem captured by crusaders; Godfrey of Bouillon elected King of Jerusalem
c.1118 Crusading order of Knights Templar founded in Jerusalem
1124 Crusaders capture Tyre
1127 Zangid dynasty of Seljuk governors control Syria and Mesopotamia to 1222; initiate Muslim counteroffensive against crusaders
c.1130 Hospital of St. John of Jerusalem (the Hospitallers) becomes military order
1144 Edessa conquered by Zangi, governor of Mosul
1145 The Friday Mosque at Isfahan
1148 Crusaders abandon siege of Damascus
1151 Last Christian stronghold in County of Edessa falls to Nur al-Din
1163 Iplici Mosque at Konya, probably the first to have a campanile (tower) minaret
1174 Saladin takes Damascus
1183 Saladin takes Aleppo
1187 Saladin defeats crusader armies at Hattin; takes Jerusalem and Acre
1188 Saladin completes conquest of Latin kingdoms in Levant; Christians reduced to coastal enclaves
1188 The Mosque at Rabat, like Seville, intended to be the largest in the world
1190 Frederick I (Barbarossa) drowned in Anatolia on way to Holy Land
1191–2 Third Crusade; Richard I of England recovers some of territory taken by Saladin, including Jaffa and Acre; fails to take Jerusalem
1192 Richard I of England makes treaty with Saladin
1193 Death of Saladin
1197 Order of Teutonic Knights established in the Holy Land

CENTRAL AND EAST ASIA

1020 Firdowsi's *Shahnama* – Book of Kings, Persia's national epic
1038 Beginning of Seljuk dynasty, the first major Turkish Muslim empire (to 1194)
c.1040 Seljuk Turks conquer Afghanistan and E Persia
c.1045 Movable type printing invented in China
1077 Seljuk governors in Oxus region establish separate state of Khwarizm Shah (to 1231)

1090 Shi'a Ismailis (of Alamut, Assassins) emerge as major force in N Persia (to 1256)

1123 *Rubaiyat* (quatrains) of Omar Khayyam; also his *Algebra*, for which he is more celebrated in his homeland, Persia

1188 Nizami's *Layla and Majnun*, a Persian recasting of perennially popular pre-Islamic love story in verse

SOUTH AND SOUTHEAST ASIA

c.1025 Conquest of Punjab by Ghaznavids
1030 Tower of Victory built by Mahmud of Ghazni, Muslim conqueror of N India

1126 Averröes, *the influential Muslim philosopher is born in Córdoba.*

1186 Raids by Muhammad al Ghur herald decline of Ghaznavid dynasty, and of Buddhism, in N India

1191–93 Afghan Ghurids defeat Rajputs and seize Delhi and much of N India

1172 The Giralda, *the bell tower of Seville's cathedral, was originally the minaret of the Great Mosque.*

1200–1450 CE

1250–54 Louis IX of France
*embarked on his first crusade,
but was captured and ransomed.
In 1270 he died on crusade
outside the walls of Tunis.*

EUROPE AND AFRICA

1200 Emergence of Hausa city-states, which come to dominate sub-Saharan trade.
1200 Rise of Mali in West Africa
1204 Fourth Crusade never reaches Holy Land; crusaders sack Constantinople; Venetian gains in Adriatic and Peloponnese
1208 Crusade against Cathars, or Albigensians, in southern France
1212 Battle of Las Navas de Tolosa; decisive defeat of Almohads by Christians in Iberia
1226 Creation of the Golden Horde, Mongol state in S Russia (to 1502)
1228 Start of collapse of Almohad Empire in North Africa
1228 Hafsid dynasty established at Tunis (to 1574)
1230 Establishment of Nasrid kingdom of Granada, Muslim stronghold in S Spain (to 1492)
1230 Establishment of the Mali Empire
1236 Christian reconquest of Córdoba
1241 Mongols invade Poland and Hungary
1248 Christian reconquest of Seville
1250–54 First of Louis IX's crusades; invasion of Egypt ends in defeat at Mansura; Louis captured and ransomed
c.1250 Building of stone mosques in Swahili city-states
1250 Mali Empire at its greatest extent
1261 Michael Palaeologus recaptures Constantinople and restores Byzantine Empire
1269 Marinids inflict final defeat on Almohads in Morocco
1270 Death of Louis IX outside walls of Tunis
1273 Foundation of Alhambra Palace at Granada
1282 French driven from Sicily, which passes to Aragon
1306–10 Hospitallers conquer Rhodes, which becomes their base
1312 Knights Templar Order accused of heresy and suppressed by Pope
1324 Pilgrimage to Mecca by Mansa Musa of Mali
1325 Ibn Battuta's first pilgrimage to Mecca
1331 Ibn Battuta's voyage to the Swahili cities of East Africa
1347 Marinids take Tunis
1348–51 Black Death reaches Europe and N Africa
1352 Ibn Battuta's travels to the Mali Empire
1354 First Ottoman conquests in SE Europe at Gallipoli; Ottomans advance into Europe
1366 Capture of Edirne (Adrianople) by Ottomans
1378 Beginning of Great Schism in Catholic church (to 1417)
1381 Peasants' Revolt in England
1389 Battle of Kosovo; Ottomans gain control of Balkans
1393 Ottoman conquest of Bulgaria
1396 Bayezid defeats crusader army at Nicopolis
1415 Portuguese capture Ceuta in Morocco
1430 Sultans of Kilwa begin grand building program
1442 al-Maqrizi writes detailed topographical survey of Egypt

SOUTHWEST ASIA

1204 Maimonides' *The Guide to the Perplexed*
1206 Citadel of Damascus completed
1225 Holy Roman Emperor Frederick II inherits Kingdom of Jerusalem
1229 Frederick negotiates agreement which wins back control over Jerusalem
1229 Rasulids control Yemen (to 1454)
1237 Huand Khatun Mosque, mausoleum, madrasa, and baths at Kayseri, C Turkey, major complex endowed by Seljuk noblewoman
1250 Mamluks, military caste from Caucasus, take over Syria, Egypt, and Hejaz (to 1517)
1256–57 Assassins' stronghold at Alamut falls to Hülegü
1258 Sack of Baghdad and fall of 'Abbasid Caliphate; Hülegü founds Il-Khanate
1260 Hülegü invades Syria; Mongols suffer first major defeat at 'Ayn Jalut
1268 Mamluks capture Antioch from crusaders

1281 Succession of Osman I, beginning of Ottoman dynasty (to 1924) and first phase of expansion
c.1302 Last Christian territory in Levant falls to Mamluks
1314 Rashid al-Din's *Jami 'al-tawarikh*, Persian history of Mongol conquest
1326 Ottomans capture Byzantine city of Bursa and make it their capital
1336 Birth of Timur
1345 Ottomans annex Emirate of Karasi; empire reaches Dardanelles
1347 Black Death reaches Baghdad and Constantinople
1370 Beginning of Timur's conquests; Timurid successors rule his empire to 1506
1372 *Kitab hayyat al-hayyawan* by al-Damiri, encyclopaedic collection of tales, traditions, and scientific observations concerning animals
1378 Foundation of Ak Koyunlu, state based on Turkoman tribesmen in E Anatolia, Azerbaijan, Zagros mountains (to 1508)
c.1380 Foundation of Janissary corps by Ottomans
1380 Timur launches series of attacks on Persia
1384 Herat rebels; Timur suppresses ruling dynasty
1387 Isfahan rebels; in reprisal, Timur kills 70,000 people, building towers with their skulls
1388–91 Timur wages war against Mongol Khanate of the Golden Horde
1389 Accession of Bayezid I

1393 Sack of Baghdad by Timur
1400 Sack of Aleppo and Damascus by Timur
1401 Sack of Baghdad by Timur
1402 Ottomans defeated by Timur at Ankara
1405 Death of Timur
1406 Ibn Khaldun's *Muqaddima*, the first attempt in any language to elucidate the laws governing the rise and fall of civilizations

CENTRAL AND EAST ASIA

1206 Mongols united by Temujin, proclaimed Genghis Khan. The Great Yasa, law code of the Mongols promulgated by Genghis Khan. Mongols begin conquest of Central Asia
1211 Mongols begin conquest of northern (Jin) China
1219 Mongol invasion of Khwarizm Empire
1227 Death of Genghis Khan
1229 Ögödei elected Great Khan
1231 Mongols reconquer resurgent Empire of the Khwarizm Shah
1233 Mongols take Jin capital, Kaifeng
1235 Walled city built at Karakorum as fixed Mongol capital
1237 Start of Mongol conquest of Russia
1253–55 William of Rubruck crosses Asia to Karakorum
1256 Il-Khanate established in Persia; successor state to Mongols (to 1353). Hülegü crosses Oxus
1258 Sa'di's *Gulistan*, major popular classic of Persian literature
1259 Great Khan Möngke dies
1264 Kublai defeats rival for title of Great Khan, ending civil war.
1265 Death of Hülegü
1271–95 Marco Polo travels throughout Asia, returning by ship through Persian Gulf
1274 First Mongol attempt to invade Japan defeated
1275 Marco Polo reaches Kublai Khan's summer palace at Shangdu (Xanadu)
1279 Foundation of Yuan dynasty; Yuan take over Southern Song
1281 Second failed Mongol invasion of Japan
1292 Marco Polo given task of escorting Mongol princess to Hormuz
1294 Death of Kublai Khan
1295 Conversion of the Il-Khan Ghazan to Islam
1320 Outbreak of plague in Yunnan province
1320–30 Mongol armies help spread plague throughout China
1330 Plague reaches northeastern China
1335 Rebellions against Mongol rule in China
1335 Demotte's *Shahnama*, fine example of Persian illuminated manuscript
1346 Plague reaches coast of Black Sea
1368 Establishment of the Ming dynasty
1379 Timur marches on Urgench
1395 Sack of New Sarai, capital of Golden Horde
1405 Beginning of Ming admiral Zheng He's seven voyages to Indian Ocean (to 1433)
1405 The Rigistan, Samarkand, built by Timur and one of the glories of his capital
1424 End of Ming campaign against Mongols
c.1433 Construction of ocean-going junks banned by Ming
1439 Poggio Bracciolini records Asian journeys of Niccolo Conti
1449 Mongols defeat Chinese and capture the emperor
1443 Great Library at Herat, Persia founded

SOUTH AND SOUTHEAST ASIA

c.1200 Muslim Sufi saint, Mu'in al-Din Chishti, founds first Sufi order in Indian subcontinent
1206 Breakaway Mamluk (Slave) dynasty, under Aibak, establishes Delhi Sultanate

1258 First Mongol expedition to Annam

c.1280 Mongol invasions of SE Asia destroy Pagan and eclipse Dai Viet
1283 Expeditions against Annam and Champa
1287 Mongol expedition to Pagan
1288 Kublai Khan abandons attempt to subdue Annam and Champa

1293 Failed Mongol invasion of Java
1295 Conversion of Sultan of Achin (Sumatra) to Islam, which spreads over much of the East Indies

1320 Muhammad ibn Tughluq succeeds to Sultanate of Delhi

1334–41 Ibn Battuta serves as *qadi* (judge) in Delhi
1336 Rebellion against Tughluqs marks beginning of Vijayanagara Empire

1345–46 Ibn Battuta visits Southeast Asia and China

1345 Hasan Gangu, governor of Tughluq Deccani domains, revolts and founds Bahmani kingdom
1398 Timur's invasion of India; sack of Delhi leads to fall of Tughluq dynasty

1445 Conversion of Malacca (Malaya) to Islam

1206-1227 Genghis Khan *led the Mongols in a spectacular series of conquests. Here he is depicted in battle, preceded by Jebe, one of his generals.*

1281 Osman I *founded the Ottoman dynasty, which would rule Turkey and a vast empire until the end of World War I.*

1450–1700 CE

EUROPE AND AFRICA

1453 Constantinople falls to Ottoman sultan Mehmed II
1459 Annexation of Serbia by Ottomans
1464 Beginning of Songhay expansion under Sunni Ali
1469 Marriage of Ferdinand of Aragon and Isabella of Castile; union of Castile and Aragon (1479)
1480 Muscovy throws off Mongol yoke
1484 Ottoman Turks capture Akkerman at mouth of Dniester
1492 Columbus, in search of Asia, reaches Caribbean
1492 Muslim Granada falls to Spain
1494 Treaty of Tordesillas divides western hemisphere between Spain and Portugal
1502 First slaves taken to the New World
1505 First Portuguese trading posts in East Africa
1511 Sa'dian dynasty comes to power in Morocco (to 1659)
1517 Ottomans conquer Mamluks in Egypt
1519 Charles V elected Holy Roman Emperor
1519–22 Magellan begins and del Cano completes first global circumnavigation
1521 Sulayman takes Belgrade
1521 Siege of Rhodes under Knights of St. John by Ottomans
1526 Battle of Mohács; Ottoman invasion of Hungary
1529 Ahmad Grañ leads jihad against Ethiopia
1529 Unsuccessful Turkish siege of Vienna
1538 Holy League against the Turks formed
1540 Portuguese come to the aid of Ethiopia against Ahmad Grañ
1543 Death of Ahmad Grañ, shot by a Portuguese musketeer
1546 Songhay destroys Mali Empire
1547 Negotiated peace acknowledges Ottoman control of most of Hungary
1562 After inconclusive skirmishes, Ottomans gain Transylvania
1565 Ottoman siege of Malta fails
1571 Ottomans take Cyprus from Venetians; at battle of Lepanto Ottoman navy defeated by united Christian fleet off Greek coast
1578 Moroccans crush invading Portuguese
1580 Union of Spanish and Portuguese crowns
1588 English defeat Spanish Armada
1591 Moroccan invaders destroy Songhay Empire
1618 Thirty Years' War in Europe (to 1648)
c.1660 Collapse of Mali Empire
1664 Turkish advance on Vienna turned back at battle of St. Gotthard
1682 Peter the Great becomes czar of Russia
1683 Siege of Vienna ends in Ottoman defeat
1698 Arabs from Oman capture Mombasa
1699 Peace of Karlowitz confirms Austrian conquests from Ottomans

SOUTHWEST ASIA

1461 Ottomans take Christian city of Trebizond

1502 Italian Lodovico di Varthema visits Arabia disguised as an Arab
1512 Accession of Ottoman ruler Selim I
1514 Selim defeats Safavids at Çaldiran
1516–17 Ottomans conquer Syria, Egypt, the Hejaz, and Yemen
1517 Selim I orders construction of Ottoman fleet at Suez; Portuguese attack on Jedda repulsed
1520 Sulayman the Magnificent becomes Ottoman sultan (to 1566)

1525 Ottomans defeat Portuguese fleet in Red Sea
1528 Safavids take Baghdad from Kurdish usurper
1534 Sulayman retakes Baghdad from Safavids
1538 Ottomans subjugate Yemen and Aden and occupy port of Basra on Persian Gulf

1546 Ottomans retake Basra after revolt
1551–52 Ottomans fail to oust Portuguese from Hormuz

1566 Sulayman succeeded by Selim II

1588 Abbas I (the Great) becomes Safavid shah
1592 Zaidi Imams regain control of Yemen, and rule until 1962
1598 Isfahan becomes imperial Safavid capital
1603–19 Safavid war with Ottomans; in first year Abbas recaptures Tabriz
1604 Abbas conquers Erivan, Shirvan, and Kars
1672 Greatest extent of Ottoman Empire

1526 Sulayman the Magnificent leads his troops against the Hungarians at the battle of Mohács.

CENTRAL AND EAST ASIA

SOUTH AND SOUTHEAST ASIA

c.1450 Islam spreads over much of East Indies

1487–89 Portuguese Pero de Covilhã sails through Red Sea to India

1653 The Taj Mahal, *the mausoleum of Shah Jahan's wife was completed Agra. It is one of the greatest examples of Islamic architecture in the world.*

1499 Rise to power of Safavids in Persia
1500 Shaybanid dynasty, of Mongol descent, assumes control of Transoxania (to 1598)
1501 Accession of Shah Ismail I; beginning of Safavid dynasty in Persia (to 1732)

1498 Vasco da Gama rounds Cape of Good Hope and reaches India

1502 First published map to show correct general shape of India, by Alberto Cantino
1507 Portuguese victory over Ottoman and Arab fleet at Diu
1509–16 Portuguese voyages to Moluccas, Malacca, and Macao
1510 Portuguese conquest of Goa; Goa made capital of all Portuguese possessions in Asia
1511–12 Portuguese establish base in Malacca and reach Moluccas
1517 First Portuguese trading mission to China
1526 Babur conquers Delhi and founds Mughal Empire

1534–35 Safavid war with Ottomans, who capture Tabriz and Baghdad

1538 Failure of Ottoman blockade of Portuguese at Diu

1553–55 Safavid war with Ottomans

1557 Foundation of Portuguese colony at Macao

1556 Akbar becomes Mughal emperor (to 1605); Reign marked by territorial expansion and cordial Hindu-Muslim relations

1578–90 Safavid war with Ottomans

1581–82 Yermak begins Russian conquest of Siberia

1598 Anthony and Robert Sherley travel to Persia, where they meet Shah Abbas
1603 Foundation of Tokugawa Shogunate in Japan
1627 Herbert's travels in Persia
1636 Manchus establish Qing imperial rule at Mukden
1644 Qing forces enter Beijing

1600 Founding of British East India Company

1627 Shah Jahan becomes Mughal emperor
c.1647 Completion of *Atlas of India* by Sadiq Isfahani
1653 Completion of Taj Mahal
1658 Aurangzeb becomes Mughal emperor: empire reaches maximum extent during his reign (to 1701)
c.1660 Gujaratis make earliest known Indian nautical charts

1683 This Turkish banner *was captured by the Christian forces after the unsuccessful Ottoman siege of Vienna.*

1689 Treaty of Nerchinsk agrees Russian and Chinese spheres of influence in east Asia

1700–1900 CE

EUROPE AND AFRICA

1701 Start of Asante's rise to prominence
1705 Foundation of Husaynid dynasty in Tunis, which rules until 1957
1716–18 Further Austrian victories, including capture of Belgrade from Ottomans
1729 Portuguese leave East Africa following attacks from Oman
1730 Revival of empire of Bornu in central Africa
c.1730 Emergence of Fulbe confederation of Futa Jallon
1757 Muhammad III becomes Sultan of Morocco
1768 War between Russia and the Ottomans
1776 Abd al-Kadir leads Muslims in jihad along the Senegal River
1798 Occupation of Egypt by Napoleon Bonaparte; defeat of Egyptians at battle of the Pyramids. Battle of the Nile; British fleet defeats French
1804 Fulani leader, Uthman dan Fodio declares jihad and conquers Hausa city-states
1804 Muhammad Ali becomes Viceroy of Egypt
1804 Napoleon proclaimed Emperor of France
1807 Hausa kings replaced by Fulani emirs
1816 Inspired by Uthman dan Fodio, Amadu Lobbo launches jihad in Masina
1820 Egyptians invade Sudan
1820 Uthman dan Fodio establishes Sokoto Fulani Kingdom
1821–33 Greek War of Independence from Ottomans
1830 French invasion of Algeria; Algiers occupied
1840 Ottoman Empire under threat from Egypt; saved by British and Austrian intervention
1852 'Umar Tal conquers the Senegal valley
1853 Russians defeat Turkish navy at Sinop
1854–56 Crimean War; French and British support Ottoman Turks against Russia
1861 'Umar Tal's forces conquer Segu
1861 Abolition of serfdom in Russia
1863 Al-Hajj 'Umar Tal clashes with French in Senegal Valley and creates a Muslim empire; invades Timbuktu
1864 'Umar Tal is killed attemping to suppress Fulani rebellion
1869 Opening of Suez Canal
1877–78 Russia, Serbia, and Montenegro at war with Turkey
1878 Treaty of San Stefano negotiated by Russia and Turkey
1878 Berlin Congress: independence of Serbia, Montenegro, and Romania from Ottomans
1881 Tunisia occupied by French
1882 Revolt in Egypt; occupation by British
1882 Beginning of major Jewish emigration from Russian Empire
1884 Berlin Conference on Africa; Samory Touré proclaims his Islamic theocracy in West Africa.
1885 Bulgaria granted Eastern Rumelia
1887 Bulgaria independent of Ottoman empire

1893 French conquer Dahomey

SOUTHWEST ASIA

c.1750 Emergence of Wahhabi reform movement in Arabia

1774 Ottoman decline follows Treaty of Küçük Kaynarca

1806 Wahhabis take Mecca
1812 Burckhardt discovers Petra, ancient capital of Nabataea
1812 Egyptian forces retake Mecca and Medina
1814 Burckhardt visits Mecca
1818 Sadleir is first European to make east-west crossing of Arabian peninsula
1818 Wahhabi movement suppressed by Egyptian forces
1839–61 Sultan Abdul Majid I makes series of liberal Tanzimat decrees
1843 Fortunes of Sa'ud family restored by Faisal

1853 Richard Burton visits Mecca and Medina in Arab disguise

1876–78 Doughty's Arabian journeys

c.1880 Birth of 'Abdal-'Aziz ibn Sa'ud in Kuwait

1887 Riyadh taken by Rashidis, who dominate Nejd
1888 Publication of Doughty's classic *Travels in Arabia Deserta*

1798 At the battle of the Pyramids *the Egyptian army was defeated by the French under Napoleon.*

CENTRAL AND EAST ASIA

1722–36 Subjugation of Afghans by Persia
1730–34 Suppression of Khazaks by Russia

1736 Nadir Shah becomes Shah of Persia
1747 Foundation of Afghanistan by
Ahmad Khan Abdali
1751 Tibet, Dzungaria, Turkestan, and the Tarim
Basin overrun by Qing Chinese
1758–59 Qing campaigns against Kalmyks
1786 Start of Qajar dynasty in Persia

1839–42 Afghans under Dost Muhammad defeat
British in First Afghan War
1840–42 Opium War; British attacks force
trading concessions from China
1850s Widespread Muslim rebellions against
Qing rule in China
1855–73 Jihad of Yunnan Muslims; ends 1873

1863–73 Northwest uprising in Uighur domains
of Qing empire; largest Muslim jihad in E Asia
1864 Establishment of Russian control in
Kalmykia (Semipalatinsk)

1868–70 Suppression of Muslim states of
Bukhara and Samarkand by Russia

1878–79 Second Afghan War; British attempt to
invade Afghanistan, which is coming under
Russian influence

SOUTH AND SOUTHEAST ASIA

c.1700 Probable commencement of Mughal
military mapping
1707 Death of Aurangzeb heralds decline of
Mughal power in India
c.1720 Marathas start to expand over
most of India
1724 Independent rule over Deccan by Nizam
of Hyderabad hastens disintegration of empire
1728 Marathas defeat Nizam of Hyderabad
and gain supremacy over Deccan with
subsequent territorial expansion
1739 Sack of Delhi by Persians and Afghans
under Nadir Shah
1744–63 Anglo-French (Carnatic) wars; eclipse
of French power in S Asia
1749 Mysore starts to become major power in
southern India
1757 Expansion of Gurkha (Nepali) domains
over much of Himalayas
1757 Battle of Plassey; British victory over
combined French and Mughal force establishes
British power in Bengal
1761 Defeat by Afghans temporarily ends
Maratha hegemony over northern India
1761 British destroy French power in India
following seizure of Pondicherry
1767 Appointment of James Rennell as first
Surveyor-General of Bengal; beginning of
Survey of India
1775 First Anglo-Maratha war (to 1782)
1782 Treaty ending first Anglo-Maratha war
results in territorial losses for Marathas
1788 Occupation of Delhi; Maratha territorial
apogee, Mughal rulers become puppets
of Marathas
1799 Conquest of Mysore ends challenge to
British power in southern India
1803 Second Anglo-Maratha war leads to
British acquisition of Delhi
1815 Victory in Anglo-Gurkha war extends
British possessions into the Himalayas
1818 Third Anglo-Maratha war ends in
Maratha defeat
1819 Stamford Raffles, of the British East India
company, founds Singapore
1849 British annex Punjab after two Sikh wars
1857 Last Mughal emperor, the Maratha
puppet Bahadur Shah II, dethroned and exiled
by British
1857–59 Revolt ("Mutiny") attempts to oust
British from India. May 30, 1857: Lucknow
mutiny. Jun 27, 1857: massacre of British
evacuees at Cawnpore
1858 (Mar 22) British retake Lucknow after
20-day siege
1859 Timor divided between Netherlands
and Portugal
1873 Dutch attack on Achin sultanate in Sumatra
1876 Queen Victoria declared Empress of India,
and a viceroy appointed as her representative
1885 Foundation of Indian National Congress

1722 The Golden Mosque *with
three gilt domes was built in
Delhi in 1722. On March 22,
1739, Nadir Shah stood on its
roof to watch the massacre of
the city's citizens.*

1804-1849 Muhammad Ali
*ruled Egypt as an independent
country, although it was still part
of the Ottoman empire. This is
the mosque he had built in Cairo.*

1900–1950 CE

EUROPE AND AFRICA

1904 French create federation of French West Africa

1908 Bulgaria declares full independence
1908 Bosnia-Herzegovina annexed by Austro-Hungarian Empire
1911 Libya occupied by Italy
1912 Serbia, Bulgaria, Greece, and Montenegro form Balkan League; First Balkan War
1912–13 Balkan Wars; Ottomans lose most of their remaining European lands
1914 Assassination of Archduke Franz Ferdinand in Sarajevo precipitates start of World War I (to 1918)
1914 (Oct) Turkey closes Dardanelles
1915 Gallipoli landings. Establishment of Salonican front

1917 US declares war on Central Powers; Bolshevik revolution in Russia

1918 End of World War I

1919 Treaty of Versailles creates a new European order

1920 (Aug) Treaty of Sèvres
1920 Inauguration of League of Nations

1922 USSR (Union of Soviet Socialist Republics) is formed

1929 Wall Street Crash

1939 (Sep) Invasion of Poland by Germany and Soviet Union; outbreak of World War II
1941 Germans and Italians advance into Egypt
1942 British defeat Germans at El Alamein
1942 Plans for Final Solution agreed at Wansee
1945 (May) Germany surrenders
1945 Yalta Conference; origins of Cold War

1949 Formation of NATO

SOUTHWEST ASIA

c.1900 Baku oil fields in Azerbaijan producing half the world's oil
1902 Ibn Sa'ud reclaims his patrimony by capturing Riyadh
1905 Jewish National Fund established to buy land in Palestine

1908 Ottoman sultan deposed in Young Turk Revolution

1914 Ottomans declare jihad; ally with Germany and Austria (Central Powers) against Allies
1915 About one million Armenians massacred or deported by Turks
1915 (Feb) First Turkish attempt to capture Suez
1916 (Feb) Russians take Erzurum
1916 (Apr) British surrender to Turks at Kut al Amara in Mesopotamia
1916–18 Arab Revolt; Saudi tribes supported by British rise against Turks
1917 Balfour Declaration commits Britain to creation of Jewish state in Palestine. British take Baghdad. British take Jerusalem
1918 Battle of Megiddo. Collapse of Ottoman empire; Turkish surrender
1919 Greek forces land at Smyrna. Kemal Pasha breaks away from authority of Istanbul government.
1920 Armenia cedes half its territory to Turkey
1921 Turkish Nationalist government established in Ankara
1922 Turks recapture Smyrna
1923 Foundation of modern Turkey by Kemal Atatürk
1923 (Jul) Treaty of Lausanne recognizes Turkish sovereignty over Smyrna and eastern Thrace

1926 Ibn Sa'ud crowns himself King of the Hejaz and Sultan of Nejd
1927 Oil discovered in Iraq

1932 Kingdom of Saudi Arabia proclaimed
1933 US company, Standard Oil of California, granted concession in Saudi Arabia
1936 Arab revolt in Palestine against Jewish immigration
1938 Commercial quantities of oil discovered in Saudi Arabia

1944 Standard Oil reformed as ARAMCO (Arabian American Oil Company)
1945 Foundation of Arab League

1947 UN partition of Palestine
1948 Foundation of state of Israel leads to war; invading Arab armies repulsed in Israel; some 725,000 Arabs flee Palestine

1908 Abdul Hamid II, *having failed to modernize the Ottoman empire, was deposed by the Young Turks.*

CENTRAL AND EAST ASIA

1909 Anglo-Persian Oil Company (later BP) founded in Iran
1911 Qing dynasty overthrown by Sun Yat Sen's nationalists and Republic of China declared

1925 Reza Shah deposes last Qajar shah and is proclaimed ruler of Iran. He introduces Western-style reforms

1941 Abdication of Reza Shah; his son, Muhammad Reza Shah Pahlavi, succeeds him

1945 Atomic bombs at Hiroshima and Nagasaki force Japanese surrender
1945 (Aug) USSR declares war on Japan
1945 (Aug) Atom bomb dropped on Hiroshima
1945 (Sep) Japanese surrender
1945 Stalin begins transfer of ethnic-minority peoples to labor camps in Siberia

1946–49 Chinese Civil War between Nationalists and Communists

SOUTH AND SOUTHEAST ASIA

1904 Partition of Bengal: nationalist agitation in India
1906 Foundation of All-India Muslim League

1918 Indian contribution to World War I earns it membership in League of Nations
1919 Amritsar massacre leads to surge in Indian nationalism
1920 Mahatma Gandhi gains control of Indian National Congress
1920 Start of civil disobedience campaigns by Gandhi in support of independence struggle

1926–27 Rebellion against Dutch rule in Java and Sumatra

1942 Indonesia, Indochina, Malaya, the Philippines, New Guinea, and Singapore seized by Japan
1942 (Feb) Surrender of British forces to Japan in Singapore
1942 (Mar) Dutch surrender East Indies to Japan

1945 India becomes UN charter member
1945 Sukarno and Ho Chi Minh declare independence for Indonesia and Vietnam respectively

1947 India and Pakistan gain independence
1947 New independent dominions of India (Hindu) and Pakistan (Muslim) are born
1947 Start of Indo–Pakistani War fought over Jammu and Kashmir; UN ceasefire line agreed in 1949

1949 Indonesia gains independence from the Dutch

1916–18 Emir Faisal, *seen here with his bodyguard, united the Arabs and together with Colonel T.E. Lawrence led a successful revolt against the Turks. After the war, Faisal became king of Iraq under the British mandate.*

1948 The UK blockaded *the seas around Israel to prevent ships carrying Jewish refugees from landing. The 700 Jews aboard the ship swam safely to shore at Haifa, using a lifeline.*

1951–2001 CE

EUROPE AND AFRICA

1954 Algerian uprising against French rule

1960 Fifteen African countries gain independence

1963 Foundation of Organization of African Unity (OAU)

1974 Revised Yugoslav constitution grants Kosovo autonomy

1981 President Sadat of Egypt assassinated by Islamic fundamentalists
1983 Islamic law imposed in Sudan
1986 US bombs Libya in retaliation for terrorist attacks
1987 Famine in Ethiopia
1989 Fundamentalists seize power in Sudan
1989–90 Collapse of Communism in Europe
1991 Islamic Salvation Front poised to win Algerian general election; army cancels second round of voting
1991 Start of civil war in Yugoslavia
1991 Unsuccessful coup attempt in USSR; disintegration of Soviet Union
1991 Croatia, Slovenia, and Bosnia declare independence from Yugoslavia
1992 Civil war in Georgia, Bosnia-Herzegovina
1994 Russian troops invade Chechnya
1995 Peace agreement (Dayton Accord) ends the Bosnian war; UN troops remain
1998 US bombs Sudan and Afganistan in retaliation for al-Qaida bombing of US institutions in Kenya and Tanzania
1998 Slobodan Milosevic sends troops into areas controlled by Kosovo Liberation Army (KLA)
1999 Kosovo Peace talks collapse; NATO begins bombing campaign
2000 Milosevic forced to step down
2001 Milosevic arrested to face charges of war crimes in Bosnia and Kosovo

SOUTHWEST ASIA

1956 Suez crisis; Israel, France, and Britain invade Egypt; fail to block Egypt's nationalization of Suez Canal
1958 Oil strikes in United Arab Emirates

1961 Foundation of Organization of the Petroleum Exporting Countries (OPEC)

1967 Egypt closes Gulf of Aqaba to Israel; Israel defeats Egypt and other Arab nations in Six Day War; Israel takes Sinai, Gaza, Golan Heights, West Bank, and Jerusalem

1973 Arab states fail to defeat Israel in Yom Kippur War
1973 OPEC restricts flow of oil to world markets; raises price of crude oil by 200%; oil crisis causes inflation and economic slowdown
1977 Start of Middle East peace process
1978 Camp David summit between Egypt, Israel, and US
1979 Egypt and Israel sign peace treaty based on Camp David accords
1980 Start of Iran–Iraq War
1981 52 American embassy staff held hostage in Tehran since 1979 are freed
1982 Israel invades Lebanon

1988 End of Iran–Iraq War

1990 (Aug 2) Iraq invades Kuwait; UN demands Iraq's immediate withdrawal
1990 (Aug 7) US troops sent to Gulf
1990 (Nov 29) UN resolution authorizes members to use "all necessary means" against Iraq
1991 (Jan) UN deadline for Iraqi withdrawal passes; Operation Desert Storm begins with bombing of Iraqi troops and installations
1991 (Feb 24) Allied land offensive in Iraq
1991 (Feb 28) Ceasefire in war in Iraq
1993 Oslo Accords between Israel and PLO based on principle of "Land for Peace"
1993 Islamic countries issue Cairo Declaration to curb fundamentalism
1995 Israeli-PLO agreement extends Palestinian self-rule within the West Bank
2000 Ariel Sharon's visit to Dome of the Rock inflames Israeli-Palestinian violence
2001 Sharon becomes Israeli premier; violence continues

1969 Yasser Arafat *becomes Chairman of the PLO. He has campaigned for the creation of a Palestiniian state and the recognition of Palestinian rights ever since.*

CENTRAL AND EAST ASIA

1955 Afghan government supports movement for separation of Pakhtunistan from Pakistan

1962 Land reform in Iran reduces power and influence of religious establishment

1973 Rebellion in Afghanistan

1979 Islamic revolution in Iran; deposition of shah; proclamation of Islamic republic
1979 Deposition of monarchy in Afghanistan; Soviet invasion and civil war

1989 Crushing of pro-democracy demonstrators in Beijing
1989 Soviet troops withdraw from Afghanistan
1990–91 Collapse of USSR; creation of Central Asian republics; Islamic revival throughout region

1995 Taliban militia reignites Afghan civil war
1996 Taliban forces capture Kabul

2001 Saudi millionaire Osama bin Laden identified as mastermind behind al-Qaida attacks on New York and Washington on September 11; US demands his extradition from Afghanistan
2001 US-led coalition declares "war on terrorism"; coalition forces attack and overthrow Taliban regime in Afghanistan in response to al-Qaida terrorist attacks

SOUTH AND SOUTHEAST ASIA

1952 First Indian general election won by Congress Party
1954 Sukarno abrogates union with Dutch and declares unitary state of Indonesia
1956 Pakistan constituted as Islamic Republic
1957 Malaya granted independence from Britain, despite ongoing Communist insurrection
1958 Abortive secessionist uprisings in Baluchistan, Pakistan

1963 Federation of Malaysia incorporates Singapore, Sarawak, and Sabah, along with Malaya
1965 Second inconclusive Indo–Pakistani war over Jammu and Kashmir
1965 Failed Marxist coup and military countercoup in Indonesia ends Sukarno regime

1971 Secession of E Pakistan leads to creation of Bangladesh. Third Indo-Pakistani war as India intervenes

1975 Indonesia annexes East Timor

1989– Revival of violent insurrection against Indian rule in Jammu and Kashmir

1998 Economic crisis in Indonesia leads to overthrow of government
1999 Referendum in East Timor produces overwhelming vote for independence
2001 Attack on Indian parliament by Muslim terrorists leads to increased tension between India and Pakistan over Kashmir

1967 Israeli trucks transport
Egyptian prisoners from the battlefield in the Six Day War. Israel defeated the combined forces of Syria, Jordan, and Egypt.

1989 Ayatollah Khomeini,
Iran's leader and symbol of the Iranian revolution is escorted to his grave amid scenes of uncontrollable grief.

ISRAEL AND THE PALESTINIANS

THE CONFLICT BETWEEN ISRAEL and the Palestinians – the Arab population of the pre-1948 British mandated territory of Palestine – is crucial in Middle East politics. In 1947 the UN approved a plan to partition Palestine, to create separate Jewish and Arab states. This was accepted by the Jewish side but not the Arabs. When the British Mandate ended in May 1948, Arab states invaded Palestine but were pushed back well beyond the UN partition lines by Israeli forces. Nearly a million Palestinians became refugees. The 1949 armistices left only East Jerusalem, the West Bank, and the Egyptian-administered coastal Gaza Strip not in Israeli hands. Jordan declared East Jerusalem and the West Bank to be part of its territory, only renouncing this claim formally in 1988.

In the 1967 Six-Day War Israel took East Jerusalem, the West Bank, and Gaza. Jewish settlers began moving in, regarding these occupied territories as part of the biblical-era Land of Israel. The Palestine Liberation Organization (PLO) led by Yasser Arafat claimed to be the Palestinians' "sole legitimate representative". It did not recognize Israel's right to exist until 1988, while Israel refused to "negotiate with terrorists". In 1993 the PLO concluded a historic "land for peace" deal with Israel, the "Oslo Accords." The two sides formally recognized one another, and Arafat and Israeli Prime Minister Rabin signed a Declaration of Principles in Washington D.C. A five-year timetable for "permanent status" negotiations would tackle the future of Jewish settlements in the

West Bank and Gaza and the Palestinian demand for East Jerusalem as their capital. Palestinians were to get interim self-rule, initially in Gaza and Jericho (achieved in 1994), and gradually in the whole West Bank. This meant Palestinian police taking over responsibility for security from the Israeli military, who had been struggling since 1987 to end an insurrection led by the radical Islamic organization Hamas. The Palestinian National Authority (PNA) was established on Palestinian territory, based in Gaza. Arafat – its chairman – made a triumphal return in July 1994 and in 1996 won a mandate as president of the 88-member Palestinian Legislative Council.

The "Oslo B" accord extended PNA rule from Gaza and Jericho to six more West Bank towns in 1995. Mutual mistrust and violence, however, threatened to derail the peace process before it reached the stage of "final status" talks, and Arafat risked losing credibility among radical Palestinians. After Israel's 1999 elections, a Labour-led government under Ehud Barak established with the PNA an ambitious timetable for a permanent agreement. US diplomacy helped keep this plan alive until the eleventh hour, but heavy-handed Israeli retaliation to violent incidents in September–October 2000 provoked Palestinian rage and a return to the tactics of *intifada* (uprising). In a bitter climate of atrocity, retaliation, and counter-strike, Israeli policy hardened under a new government headed by Ariel Sharon, who was elected prime minister in 2001.

INDEX

ACKNOWLEDGMENTS

All translations from the Qur'an used in this book are from *The Koran Interpreted* by Arthur J. Arberry (OUP 1964)

The publisher would like to thank the following for their kind permission to reproduce their photographs: (Abbreviations key: t=top, b=bottom, r=right, l=left, c=centre, a=above)

Agence France Presse: 20bl, 40cl.
AKG London: 182clb; Biblioteque Nationale, Paris 66tl.
Max Alexander: 176cl.
Ancient Art & Architecture Collection/Ronald Sheridan: 50bl, 52bl, 71tr, 83tr, 92tl.
The Art Archive: HarperCollins Publishers 41; Museo Correr Venice/Dagli Orti 70bl; Real Biblioteca de lo Escorial/Dagli Orti 60clb; Topkapi Museum Istanbul/Dagli Orti 68cla; Victoria and Albert Museum London/Eileen Tweedy 66clb; Victoria and Albert Museum London/Sally Chappell 73.
Ashmolean Museum, Oxford/Geoff Dann: 27crb.
Bodleian Library: Ms Marsh 144 p. 167 95tr; Ms Pococke 375 fol.3v-4r 97crb.
Bridgeman Art Library, London/New York: Biblioteque Nationale, Paris, France 63crb, 65crb; Bibliotheque Nationale de Cartes et Plans, Paris, France 94cl; Chateau de Compiegne, Oisne 106cla; British Library, London 39tr, 64tl, 96bl; Cordoba, Andalucia, Spain 175tr; Institute of Oriental Studies, St. Petersburg, Russia 97tr; Jean-Loup Charmet 78tl, 104cla; Lauros-Giraudon 180cl; Louvre, Paris, France 60tl; Ma'daba, Jordan 49tr; Musee Conde, Chantilly, France 24tl; National Museum of India, New Delhi 74tl; Palacio del Senado, Madrid, Spain 61tr; Private collections 31bc, 76clb, 90clb, 177tr; School of Oriental & African Studies Library, University of London 37br; Topkapi Palace Museum, Istanbul Turkey 71cr, 95br, 178clb; University Library, Istanbul, Turkey 99.

British Library, London: Lawrence Pardes 29bc; 89br,172clb; Alan Hills 102tl; Janet Peckham 18bl.
Corbis: 3tr; Angelo Hornak 36tl; Arte & Immagini srl 91cr; Charles & Josette Lenars 6; Chris Hellier 92clb; Ed Kashi 100; Nik Wheeler 4; Paul Amasy 84cl; Roger Wood 72cl; Tiziana and Gianni Baldizzone 19tr.
Alistair Duncan: 21cr.
Mary Evans Picture Library: 77cra.
Werner Forman Archive: 85br, 93cr, 173cra, 173crb; Spink & Son, London 46.
Gables Collection: 179tr.
Sonia Halliday Photographs: 106clb; Biblioteca Nacional, Madrid 49bc; Biblioteque Nationale, Paris 16tl; Topkapi Palace Museum, Istanbul, Turkey 177crb.
Robert Harding Picture Library: 83crb.
Heeresgeschitliches Museum, Vienna: 179crb.
Hulton Archive: 183crb, 185tr; Keystone 79crb; Three Lions 107tr.
Imperial War Museum: 183tr.
Dinesh Khanna: 75cr, 174tl.
Neil Lukas: 175br.
Paul Lunde: 16bc, 32tl, 42clb, 88tl, 105cr, 171cl.
Christine Osborne: 13fp, 28tl, 31tr, 34tr, 87, 109; Camerapix 17br; Chris Barton 62tr; Julian Wurker 82cl; Patrick Syder 45cr, 55tr, 85br.
Popperfoto: Reuters 3bl, 43tr.
Ram Rahman: 74clb, 181tr.
Rex Features: 107crb, 184clb.
Peter Sanders: 14, 22cl, 26, 29cra, 35br, 38clb, 80, 171tr, 171crb.
Tony Souter: 45tr.
Jon Spaull: 56tl, 57, 59cr, 181crb.
Frank Spooner Pictures: Gamma 108tl, 185crb.
Linda Whitwam: 25br, 39br, 61crb.
Francesca York: 30cl, 33br, 44cal, 86clb.
All other images © Dorling Kindersley.

For further information see: www.dkimages.com